DALITHAN

K.K. Kochu

Translated by Radhika P. Menon

SPEAKING TIGER

SPEAKING TIGER BOOKS LLP
125A, Ground Floor, Shahpur Jat, near Asiad Village,
New Delhi 110049

First published in Malayalam by DC Books in 2019
First published in English by Speaking Tiger Books in 2024

ISBN: 978-93-5447-852-9
eISBN: 978-93-5447-819-2

10 9 8 7 6 5 4 3 2 1

Typeset in Adobe Garamond Pro by SÜRYA, New Delhi
Printed at: Rahul Print O Pack, Z-57, Okhla Phase-2, New Delhi-110020

K.K. Kochu was born on 2 February 1949 at Kallara in Kottayam district in Kerala. He attended the Kallara NSS High School and Maharaja's College, Ernakulam. Even as a student he was involved in political activism, and was jailed for 16 days. An aspiring writer from a very young age, Kochu was awarded the second prize in a play-writing contest for college students, conducted by the *Mathrubhumi* weekly in 1971. He went into hiding for six months following the Emergency. Subsequently, he played a major role in the creation of organizations like the Communist Youth Forum, the Peoples' Workers' Union, the Human Rights' Committee and so on. In 1986, Kochu became a member of the central committee of the SEEDIAN, and the editor of its weekly. He joined the KSRTC in 1977 and worked there until his retirement as Senior Assistant in 2001. Since 1990, he has been active in struggles for protecting the rights of Dalits and Adivasis, human rights and the environment.

Besides innumerable articles on literature, films, politics, gender and subaltern studies, Kochu has authored several books in Malayalam—*Kalaapavum Samskaaravaum*, *Buddhanilekulla Dooram*, *Ambedkar: Jeevithavum Dauthyavum*, *Idathupaksham Illaatha Kaalam*, *Dalit Nerkaazhchakal*, *Kerala Charitravum Samooha Roopikaranavum*, *Deshiyathakkoru Charitrapadhom* and so on. He is a recipient of the Arali Award, the Vaikom Chandrasekharan Nair Award and the Kerala Sahitya Akademi Award for Overall Contributions.

Radhika P. Menon has translated several works from Malayalam to English. The most notable ones are K. Madhavan's *On the Banks of the Tejaswini* (NBT), Devaki Nilayangode's *Antharjanam* (OUP), S.K. Pottekkatt's *Tales of Athiranippadam* (Orient BlackSwan) and *In the Land of the Kappiris* (CUP), Moyarath Sankaran's *Autobiography of a Freedom Fighter and Martyr* (Chinta), M.K. Sanoo's *Dr Palpu: The Champion of Justice* (Open Door Media), Joseph Muliyil's *Sukumari* (Folio), Sebastian Joseph's *Naxal Varghese: Take-Off and Tailspin* (Dream Bookbindery) and Dr Sosamma Iype's *The Vechur Cow: A New Lease of Life* (Vechur Conservation Trust). Her translations of N.N. Pillai's autobiography (*Yours Truly*) and Appukuttan Vallikunnu's *The Unknown EMS* are forthcoming. She won the ICWT (International Center for Writing and Translation Award) of the University of California, Irvine in 2011 for *Tales of Athiranippadam*, along with Sreedevi K. Nair.

K.K. Kochu was born on 2 February 1949 at Kallara in Kottayam district [illegible] Kerala. He studied at the Kallara NSS High School and Maharaja's College. [illegible] political activism [illegible] a very young age, Kochu [illegible] a study centre for college students [illegible] weekly in 1972. He wrote [illegible] following the Emergency [illegible] He played an important role [illegible] the Communist Youth [illegible] Kerala [illegible] Republican Party [illegible] of the SEEDIAN [illegible] KSRTC in 1977 and [illegible] Assistant in 1986. Since 2001, he [illegible] the rights of Dalits and Adivasis [illegible]

Kochu [illegible]

[illegible] has [illegible] several books in Malayalam [illegible] He is a recipient of the [illegible] Kerala Sahitya Akademi Award for Overall Contributions.

Radhika P. Menon has translated [illegible] works from Malayalam to English [illegible] by Sethu [illegible] (Niyogi Books, 2020) [illegible] Kerala Sahitya Akademi Award for translation [illegible]

Contents

Kinship Terms

Amma	:	mother
Ammavan	:	uncle
Ammayi	:	aunt
Chaachan	:	father
Chechi	:	elder sister
Ichaayan	:	elder brother
Valyaachan	:	father's elder brother
Valyachan	:	grandfather
Valyamma	:	grandmother

Chasing the 'Purest Ray Serene'

Translator's Note

The tradition of Dalit life-writing, both biographies and autobiographies, in Malayalam is not a very rich or long one. Research work in the field of ethnographic history, done in recent times, has unearthed several slave narratives of the Pulayas and the Parayas embedded in missionary records of early twentieth century. But they are fragmentary and, at best, rudimentary discourses because they do not have the characteristics of voluntarily undertaken works of self-expression. Rather, they are either merely responses to certain pointed questions regarding basic information about their identity (name, mother's name, master's name, caste, place of origin, where they were sold and so on) or strings of narratives recorded and woven by missionaries from their subjects' oral accounts. Therefore, as documents that do not provide detailed stories of their personal or social lives, they can hardly be accommodated under the label of life-writing.

Viewed from this perspective, it becomes quickly obvious that the number of Malayalam Dalit autobiographies is fewer than what we can count on our fingers. Kallen Pokkudan's *Kandal Kadukalkkidayilude Ente Jeevitham* (My Life Amidst Mangrove Forests), published in 2002 and its revised version *Ente Jeevitham* (My Life), written in collaboration with his son Sreejith

Paithalen, published in 2010; C.K. Janu's *Janu: C.K. Januvinte Atmakatha* (Janu: C.K. Janu's Autobiography), published in 2003; Seleena Prakkanam's *Chengara Samaravum Ente Jeevithavum* (The Chengara Struggle and My Life), published in 2013; K.K. Kochu's *Dalithan* (Dalit), published in 2019; and M. Kunhaman's *Ethiru* (Oppose), published in 2020 constitute what can be described as a canon-in-the-making.

Among these, Pokkudan's work focuses exclusively on his interventions in the environmental problems in the state, especially his work to arrest the decline of mangrove forests along the coastline of Kerala. C.K. Janu's autobiography is the result of a collaborative effort, as it was narrated to a fellow activist named Bhaskaran, and talks about her attempts to restore the right to ownership of land to the Adivasis. Seleena Prakkanam's work has a similarly narrow ambit. It revolves around her struggle to wrest the lands unlawfully held by a plantation company, and redistribute them to the indigenous people. M. Kunhaman's memoir talks about how he faced and opposed seemingly insurmountable odds and deeply entrenched prejudices to make it to the top of the academic world. It also contains a cerebral analysis of the prevalence of caste prejudice—both subtle and gross—even in the present day.

But none of them give a close-up view or a sustained narrative about the texture of raw life they experienced because of the overt and covert hegemonic practices of the savarnas, the upper castes. In one way or another, they fail to engage the reader's deep and emotional involvement in the life of humiliation and deprivation suffered at various levels and on a daily basis; or to draw the reader's attention to the casual acts of cruelty committed on the underdogs by the mainstream society; or to sharpen the reader's sensitivity to the creation of certain spaces that make way for newer forms of marginalization and ghettoization.

It is in this context that K.K. Kochu's *Dalithan* becomes relevant. It stands head and shoulders above the works previously mentioned for the sheer range of trajectories it covers. One, experiential. *Dalithan* takes the reader through all the sensory experiences of Kochu, and immerses him/her completely into the life of the subaltern. Two, socio-cultural. It gives detailed accounts of Kochu's interventions as an activist, fighting injustice and discrimination, challenging structures of cultural dominance, and working towards the creation of a community identity. Three, literary-intellectual. It deconstructs several entrenched beliefs, institutionalized practices and grand narratives (including language and literature) that perpetuate savarna hegemony, and tries to retrieve history from marginalized sources and forgotten corners of society in order to underscore the fact that Dalit initiatives and discourses have from time immemorial been swept under the carpet of mainstream historiography. Four, ideological. The book points out how Dalits themselves have to critically evaluate the beliefs and values propagated by leaders like Mahatma Ayyankali, Narayana Guru, Poykayil Appachan, Pampady John Joseph, Periyar Ramaswamy, Dr B.R. Ambedkar and others—instead of blindly idolizing or worshipping them—in order to bring about qualitative improvement in their lives. Five, political. It underscores the need for Dalits to form a broad-spectrum alliance with the other similarly abused communities, like women, Muslims and so on, for their voices to be heard and rights re-established. Considering all these factors, it can be justifiably argued that *Dalithan* is the first vital, full-blooded and comprehensive Dalit autobiography in Malayalam.

In fact, Kochu's desire to write the autobiography came as much from a realization that the marginal voices have always been smothered and silenced throughout history, as from an intention to speak not for himself alone but for an entire community. As he says in *Dalithan*:

> The inspiration behind [the composition of this autobiography] was a sliver from Brecht's poem titled 'A Worker Reads History': 'Young Alexander conquered India. / He alone? / Caesar beat the Gauls. / Was there not even a cook in his army?' In my analysis of the story 'In the Flood' ['Vellapokkathil', a highly-celebrated short story by the famous Malayalam novelist Thakazhi Sivasankara Pillai], the reason for sidelining Chennan Parayan and making the dog a Dalit was no different. This autobiography is an elaborate version of that textualization. Mega-narratives are full of kings, castles and battles; there are no servants, no people who are trampled upon, no animals who slump in sheer exhaustion after pulling the vehicles. These people who are ignored and rendered invisible too are creators of history. Microcosms, that are ostracized, too, need to get space alongside the macrocosm.

But if this were all to K.K. Kochu's *Dalithan*, there would be no special reason to celebrate its publication or even to recommend its translation. The work would merely be seen to underscore the yawning chasm between two worlds and suggest that it is virtually unbridgeable. However, its claim to greatness lies in a refusal to succumb to this all-too-familiar (or tired?) portrait of dichotomy, and its readiness to nurture a sanguine hope of transcending differences. This is where *Dalithan* (in its revised version) becomes philosophical in tone. Kochu ends his narrative in the hope that intellectuals will arise from among the Dalits so that in leading their community towards 'freedom' they can lead others, too, towards the same goal. That is because, ultimately, no human is an island, each is part of the main land, and the bond of inter-dependence and complementarity is what will help the human race firm up its position in Nature. At this point, *Dalithan* comes closest to what Nelson Mandela says in *Long Walk to Freedom*:

> A man who takes away another man's freedom is a prisoner of hatred, he is locked behind the bars of prejudice and narrow-

mindedness. I am not truly free if I am taking away someone else's freedom, just as surely as I am not free when my freedom is taken from me. The oppressed and the oppressor alike are robbed of their humanity.

Translating *Dalithan*

There is an interesting phrase in the diamond industry that is used to assess as well as advertise the clarity grade of this precious stone—'eye-clean'. Although diamond experts break down this standard into more and subtler categories, generally speaking, the value of a diamond is calculated in terms of the absence of imperfections or flaws in it. Or, to put it positively, in terms of its cleanliness or ability to allow light to pass through without even a slight blemish blocking its path. In more poetic terms, a perfect diamond allows the 'purest ray serene' to shine forth.

It is my personal opinion that every translator should use 'eye-clean' as a thumb rule to ensure the diamond of the translated text is as free of the blemish of her egoistic intervention as is humanly possible. While a perfect, 'eye-clean' translation is only an ideal, and perhaps rarer than a flawless diamond, its value as a reference point cannot ever be over-emphasized.

Maintaining such a culture of discipline is, however, extremely hard to execute. The first and possibly most obvious reason is the challenge posed by the need to remain constantly vigilant. The translator has to select her words and phrases carefully, making sure they do not tilt towards either accentuating or diluting the importance of the content. The second is the difficulty inherent in being aware of one's own nature and the extent to which it is different from the author's. This self-awareness has to lead the translator to understand the predominant tone of the work and replicate it without dramatizing or subduing the original voice even to the smallest degree. In other words, the translator's personality has to be kept on a tight leash so that no trait of hers permeates the translated version. That her readers will never be able to detect any shift in thrust or tone from the original only adds to the translator's responsibility.

The translation of K.K. Kochu's Malayalam *Dalithan* to the English *Dalit* demanded a high level of such unremitting self-audit. The primary reason was the vast difference in the personalities of the author and the translator. Despite his keenness of vision and sharp intellect, Kochu is self-restrained, not given to strong emotional reactions or judgements. Consequently, his language and his style move on an even keel, avoiding all extremes. So, the greatest challenge lay in selecting a style that was equivalent to the visible layer of ash that occasionally moves a little to reveal the embers within.

No chapter strained my translator-heart as much as the twenty-second one in *Dalit*. Titled 'The Colour of Death', it triggered in me (as I hope it will in all the readers) all the colours of emotion that form the stormy spectrum of tragedy—righteous indignation, impotent anger, rage, pity, frustration, claustrophobia, helplessness, heartburn, despair and hopelessness—all roiling one over the other as though caught in a centrifuge. But none of these had any place in Kochu's deadpan narration. To be loyal to his tone of philosophical apathy, I had to make sure no unnecessary adjective got tossed in and no verb more dramatic, colourful or connotative than the one Kochu used was chosen. The live embers of the raw emotions that the tragic situation might have triggered in Kochu's heart are covered over by an ashy tone of dispassion. That had to be respected, and my language rendered as 'eye-clean' as possible, without streaks, spots, clouds or knots of my emotions compromising its transparency.

An example may be in order at this point. A set of three sentences right in the middle of the chapter—in which

Kochu learns of the death of his elder brother—proved to be extraordinarily tricky. In English, it has been rendered as follows:

> What gripped me then was an unimaginable sense of dread. I was sure it wasn't his condition that had deteriorated. He had probably died.

The original in Malayalam, even without the use of so many pronouns, conveys the meaning without any ambiguity. But an absolutely loyal translation would have demanded something as mangled as the following:

> Unimaginable sense of dread was experienced. The condition would not have deteriorated. Rather, death would have taken place, I was sure.

Determined to avoid this cumbersome style, I straightened out the sentences, by inserting the appropriate pronouns. The translator's mild intervention did not have the effect of converting the self-effacing author into an egotist.

But almost immediately, I came across a sentence more self-introspective, marked by a similar absence of possessive pronouns: 'Did I think frequently that death was preferable to the present condition of life?' From the immediate context, it was safe to assume that the 'death' and 'the present condition of life' referred to the brother's state. Therefore, rendering it as 'Did I think frequently that *his* death was preferable to the present condition of *his* life?' could not be blamed. But I knew it could be applied, with the same compelling logic, to Kochu's predicament too. (In the earlier paragraph, he mentions the purposeless life he had been leading then—when, being jobless, he has no salary, lives off the charity shown by inmates in the Pre Matric Hostel, has severed relations with his family, and is generally listless.) This time, however, I had to take a conscious decision not to insert either 'his death' or 'my death' for the sake of disambiguation. Instead, I let the equivocal sentence stand just as it did in Malayalam so that my interpretative translation did not come between the author and his English readers.

I can only hope my respect for the author and commitment to the readers have made my surveillance uniformly strict so as to allow the 'purest ray serene' to shine forth through the translated text.

Radhika P. Menon
April 2024

DALITHAN

1. My Initiation

I belong to the Pulaya caste, considered one of the Dalit categories in Kerala. Today, this caste is not only a community but also a unit of a vast group of people known all over India as Dalits. Such a situation has come about as a result of a long period of social, communitarian, political, ideological and agitational activities of various Dalit groups. I came into being because I was able to be a part of these spheres of knowledge and activism, and this autobiography owes its birth to that emergence.

A great majority of Dalits in Kerala are either followers of the Communist party or believe in their cause. I was no exception. Doubts that cropped up when I began to lose faith in communism were what initiated an enquiry into my communitarian identity. But neither books nor studies that could help me understand myself were available then. To overcome this limitation, I sought to explore by talking to my Chaachan's elder brother, Thaithara Chothi. Valyaachan was nearly 85 years old then. I started by asking him about the geography of the place and the people that lived here back when he was ten.

Valyaachan was the manager of a Namboodiri household called Neythassery Mana at Madhuraveli village. The family owned more than 1,000 acres of land, in the form of garden plots and paddy fields, in the neighbourhood and other places. This was what Valyaachan had to say about how the family came into these huge land holdings:

Many years back, the land was unpopulated and barren. There

were only a few houses, the residents of which possessed no land ownership documents. The land served merely as a habitat. Land surveyors appointed by the British government in Travancore used to visit the place from time to time. They were hosted by the Namboodiris of Neythassery Mana. In return, the surveyors gave title deeds of vast stretches of land to the Namboodiris exclusively, without measuring the plots or marking their boundaries. The Pulaya and the Ezhava[1] families that resided in these lands were retained. The Nairs who were dependent on the Namboodiris also brought Pulaya and Ezhava families from places like Vadayar and Cherthala. Next, other people including Christians began to be evicted from there. The first step to achieve this goal was to supply Pulayas and Ezhavas with generous quantities of alcohol. Inebriated groups, armed with lighted country torches, set out at night not only to torture people who resided in various areas, but to burn their thatched houses as well.

It seems this was how all the land came into the hands of Neythassery Mana.

When the entire country was reeling under famine (this must have been the time of the First World War), the coffers of Neythassery Mana overflowed. Forests were cleared for paddy cultivation, and vast fields came into being. Those areas, rich in alluvium and decomposed leaves deposited over several centuries, yielded extraordinarily bounteous harvests. But the reason for the prosperity was the hard labour of the Pulayas and the Ezhavas. When the grains they received as wages did not suffice to appease their hunger, the Pulayas and the Ezhavas ate whatever they could gather from the canals—fish, taro, Chinese senna and water lily bulbs. After harvest, as the fields lay fallow, the Namboodiris, who filled their treasure chests by making the simple folk toil from early morning to late night, focused on coconut and arecanut plantations in their garden plots, and thus converted waste grounds into agricultural lands.

According to traditional historical records, social structures in Kerala formed around a temple. E.M.S. Namboodiripad, the Marxist ideologue and indisputable leader of the Communist party, wrote thus about the impact of the feudal system that came to define the rural economy: 'The biggest advantage of the feudal system was that it paved the way for a massive economic revolution. What the transference of ownership of land—from the hands of those who felled forests, in order to use agricultural land, into those who had to make both ends meet by taking those lands on lease—meant was the laying of the foundation of a new awareness about the right to property.'

The social structure at Madhuraveli, however, defied such inferences. What existed there was not a Namboodiri society but a Namboodiri family that had private ownership of a temple. Neither were relations of production influenced nor working classes installed to serve the needs of the temple. That was because the temple permitted entry only to the members of the Mana.

The Namboodiris of Neythassery Mana were not torturers, as feudal lords are typically portrayed to be. Their world was confined to their family and the temple they owned. Yet they were revered figures. To everyone in the village, cutting across caste and religion, the eldest Namboodiris were *Valiyathambran* (senior lord), and the younger members, *Cheriyathambran* (junior lord). The womenfolk were either *Valiyambratti* (senior lady) or *Cheriyambratti* (junior lady). The latter were seldom seen in public, and when they stirred out, it was to pay visits to the temple. On such occasions, they held cadjan parasols, and draped themselves in white robes from head to toe. Everyone else had to maintain a specific distance, and take care not to approach their line of vision.

The Valiyathambran of Neythassery Mana was a fair-skinned, short old man with an enormous potbelly. He spent the evenings in an outhouse at some distance from the main building where the entire family lived. Only Valyaachan could speak to him at length. Their conversation invariably took place when the workers, after having finished their day's labour, waited at the gatehouse for the day's wages. Valyaachan, with his *thorthu*—a small cotton towel, usually thrown over the shoulder—removed from his shoulder and tucked under his armpit, would hold a hand over his mouth and stand in the front yard, at some distance. As the Valiyathambran talked, Valyaachan merely uttered *raan* ('as you wish') or *adiyan* (literally, 'slave')[2] from time to time, rarely ever speaking much more in reply. The men and women, exhausted after a long day, had to continue waiting as the monologue would extend late into the night. On certain days, it would be their children who stood waiting for the day's wages, given in the form of grains. These were brought out by the Nair managers when the conversation between Valiyathambran and Valyaachan came to a close, measured and distributed. This was the usual practice. Then the workers took their familiar paths back home. I wrote a story titled 'Karkidakam' on the theme of this long wait. It was published in the SEEDIAN[3] weekly, and on reading it P.P. Thomas, a resident of Pathanamthitta, was inspired to become a SEEDIAN activist. He told me so himself.

Valyaachan was a prosperous man. He owned nearly 150 acres of upland and paddy fields. He was illiterate but respected by all. Despite being well-off, he was obsequious towards the Namboodiris. Institutionalized and traditional belief was the reason behind this servility.

The Namboodiris of Neythassery Mana were not Vedic scholars, or authorities on epics or well versed in the *Shrutis* and *Smirtis*.[4] They did not even have a respectable level of modern education. Yet in the eyes of the public, they had a divine aura. This had nothing to do with their ownership of property. They were not respected for their status as managers of the temple either. No one could get a glimpse of the idol of the goddess within the Namboodiris' temple, which was surrounded by high walls. Nor did the local people imagine that the pujas and rituals conducted there were performed for their welfare. But everyone feared the Brahmin's curse. No one attempted to steal the grains, coconuts or arecanuts that belonged to the mana. In short, not only the Namboodiris but their wealth too had absolute protection.

---

2. The Story of the Land

Like Gabriel Garcia Marquez's Macondo, my native village of Madhuraveli of ancient times was unpopulated and desolate. Thick jungles covered, and numerous islets dotted, the western regions that were part of Upper Kuttanad. According to the heroic tale narrated in *Edanadan Paattu* ('Edanadan Song'),[5] compiled by Dr K.R. Sajitha from its oral renditions, Madhuraveli lies in a straight line from Ezhumanthuruthu in the west and Ezhupunna near Cherthala. Both these areas were heavily wooded. The description in the song goes like this:

> Ezhupunna woods, Ezhumanthuruthu (island),
> Stretching to the south, Ezhumanthuruthu,
> Stretching to the south, Ezhupunna woods,
> Woods so thick, no rat snake can wriggle into,
> Woods so high, no sparrow can fly above.

The regions close to Madhuraveli—Kappikkadu and Kalambukkadu—bear names that carry memories of those forests.[6] Besides Ezhumanthuruthu, the place names Katturuthu and

Thuruthumma suggest islands situated within forests. According to the Edanadan song, it took several days to destroy the forests of Ezhumanthuruthu. The work was done by the Pulayas.

> We should make ridges on all four sides,
> O listen, Chathan Pulaya,
> We should make ridges tomorrow.
> Call the Pulaya men of Chennanganad,
> Four or twelve of them.

Pulaya women too joined in the effort.

> Now, what is to be done, Chathan Pulaya?
> Women should be brought over.
> All the women of Chennanganad,
> You must bring them over.

As time passed, by the sweat of the Pulaya brow, all forest lands became paddy fields. The islands in between drew human settlements and were used for coconut farming.

During my childhood, the western areas had already changed into vast *kari* lands of peaty soil, flooded with saline water. What grew in profusion in this black soil was a plant called bulrush (Schoenoplectus articulates). Their roots went into the clayey soil, and then raised their crests above the stagnant water. These were sliced by the local residents, dragged along the channels that criss-crossed the fields, brought to dry land and used as fodder. Buffaloes were let loose on these to graze and herded back to their sheds in the evenings.

Even today, the remains of the forests—decomposed logs of wood—can be found buried deep in the fields. Earlier, people would dig them out, dry them and use them as firewood. Coconut trees stood on the embankments that surrounded the fields. There would be canals on all the sides of a field. They held water that was so clear you could see the bed, and were full of water lilies and ferns, swimming fish, water snakes and frogs. On the sides, Portia, Mastwood and Suicide trees as well as screw pine shrubs grew in profusion. These canals, over which small and big boats glided by, drained into the Vembanad lake in the west. And it was through these same canals that stalks of grain harvested from the western paddy fields were brought in boats to the threshing floors.

During the rainy season, the fields overflowed and became a sea. The canals and embankments merged into it. Whenever this happened, it was possible to move around easily in boats, over the fields and canals. As the rains stopped and the waters subsided, the first phase of paddy cultivation began with the firming up of the outer ridges. Black clayey soil, that was scooped from the fields and brought in boats, as well as coconut leaves and arecanut logs were used for this purpose. Thereafter temporary thatched huts were rigged on embankments to house engines, powered by kerosene. For days on end, these engines were operated continuously until all the water in the fields was spat into the canals. As the fields became dry, people from various places converged on them to catch fish. Eagles, crows and storks too came in droves. While the men tilled the land, the women readied it for sowing. Besides the Pulayas, the Ezhavas, poor Christians and, only very occasionally, Nairs did the farming work, sowing either mature seeds or planting young saplings. Green leaves and cow dung provided the manure. This was the pattern of paddy cultivation practised in the western parts of Madhuraveli.

The eastern areas began where Upper Kuttanad ended. A few regions were level ground. These may have been the first places that were inhabited. There were many mango, jack and tamarind trees here, besides coconut and arecanut palms. Beyond the plains stood laterite hills, similar to the Western Ghats. On the slopes of the hills grew thickets, small trees and thorny bushes. Besides, there were many wild trees and bamboo clumps that covered the hills. Like the western parts, this area did not have the problem of water-logging. And allowed for tapioca, banana and ginger cultivation.

The people of Madhuraveli had actually come from different lands, far and near, and they came at various periods of time. While a few families took possession of land either on purchase or on lease, from the government or the feudal lords, certain others simply grabbed it. As the population was sparse, and land easily available, competition for ownership was hardly fierce. While the monopoly over paddy cultivation remained in the hands of the Neythassery Mana and a few other families, it was the prospect of cultivating cash crops that led more people to reside there. Another reason was that the fields where paddy was cultivated were not habitable, primarily because of a scarcity of drinking water. In the eastern parts, though, water was plentiful in all the wells.

There were no good transport services to Madhuraveli, which was six kilometres from Kaduthuruthi, the nearby town. The uneven mud tracks were fringed by shrubs and thickets. These areas, that remained dark even during daytime, were full of rabbits, foxes, mongooses and civets. Houses were few and far between. It was generally believed that the deserted places were the haunts of ghosts and ghouls. And many had elaborate stories to tell about them.

According to the poem *Unnuneeli Sandesham*,[7] written in the 14th century CE, a messenger sets out from Ettumanoor, travels through Kothanalloor and reaches Kaduthuruthi. There is no reference to Kuruppanthura whatsoever although it is situated between the two places. Kuruppanthura became a major commercial centre only with the construction of the Kuruppanthura–Kuravilangad road.

Kaduthuruthi has been recorded in history as a well-known commercial centre. This region was the headquarters of the Vadakkumkoor kings before it was annexed by force to Travancore when it was seized by Marthanda Varma. Although written records about this royal line are scanty, Kaduthuruthi became famous through *Unnuneeli Sandesham*. The location of the Mundakkal *tharavad*, or ancestral house, where Unnuneeli lived has not been ascertained so far. Yet the references to the Thaliyil temple and other places made by the messenger indicate clearly that the Mundakkal tharavad was situated somewhere near the temple.

It is believed that the local names of Kaduthuruthi were Kadantheri and Vadamathira. It was referred to in Sanskrit as Skandapuram. During the time of the *Sandesham*, Kaduthuruthi was a lakeside region adjacent to the sea. Evidence of this was identified when historians discovered the presence of sea shells, oysters and remains of catamarans while the Kottayam–Ernakulam railway line was laid. The regions west of Kaduthuruthi are paddy fields, full of black clayey soil. It was linked to the uplands via a big canal. The messenger reveals that dried ginger and cardamom were taken in boats through this canal to be loaded into ships. In short, the past of Madhuraveli was like that of any other village in Kerala.

---

3. The Pulayas

The villages of Kerala are rich in legends and oral narratives. If Kottarathil Sankunni (1855–1937),[8] who compiled the legends of Kerala in *Aithihyamaala*, could empathize with the lives of the depressed classes, Untaan the Pulaya youth would have found a place in it. According to local belief, Untaan lived nearly a hundred years back. He stayed at Mathirapally island, west of Mundar that linked Kappikkadu (which stood to the south of Madhuraveli) to Upper Kuttanad. That region encompassed revenue forests that a man from Kodungalloor named Mohammed Haji had taken on lease from the Thirumala Devaswom. During that time, the region had huge trees, marshy lands and small canals. Untaan lived alone in a hut below a wild jack tree in this wilderness. His usual habit was to sleep during the day, and rob people at night, like Kayamkulam Kochunni, the Robin Hood-like hero of Kayamkulam in Travancore.

Untaan was not a native of Mundar. He hailed from Ullala near Vaikom where he had worked as a slave in a Nair household. Following differences with that family, he left the place and took up residence at Mathirapally. According to popular accounts, he was a dark-skinned and extraordinarily tall man who always wore white clothes. As he had gained renown in athletic prowess, and had no one to equal him in physical strength and courage, he was described as a braveheart. During nighttime, he took out his boat that was concealed in a canal close to his house, rowed it, stole grains, coconuts, tapioca, bunches of banana and so on, and took them to the poor Pulaya houses. He helped and gave protection to women who went into the forest to gather firewood and those who went to catch fish.

Here's one of the most popular stories about Untaan:

Once a poor Pulaya family, that did not have money to buy new clothes for the daughter's wedding, sought his help. He took a huge, stuffed bag to a textile shop at Cherthala. There he selected all the clothes that were required, and the shopkeeper gave them to him, imagining the bag he had brought to be full of coins—paper currency had yet not come into being. Untaan left the shop, promising to return soon with the clothes. When he did not come back for a long time, the shopkeeper opened the bag Untaan had left behind. It was full of sea shells! Outwitting the shopkeeper, Untaan helped a poor family conduct their daughter's wedding.

As far as the Pulayas of Kallara, Kappikkadu, Madhuraveli and Ayamkudi were concerned, Untaan was not merely a heroic figure. He was a protector too. Syrian Christians nursed a very strong feeling of vendetta against him, though. They knew that it would require more than a couple of men to bring down Untaan, who enjoyed the support of all Pulayas. So an organized effort was made, and that attack marked the piteous end of Untaan.

The Vattamattam family at Kappikkadu treated the Pulayas like slaves. When their two-acre fields were ready for harvest, Untaan and his helpers stole the entire crop within a single night, and distributed the grains among the poor Pulayas of Ullala. This was what triggered the joint effort to kill him. A Pulaya turned spy, and located Untaan's place of stay. He went there and asked for a tender coconut. As soon as he got permission, he climbed a tall coconut tree, and on reaching its crest, waved a white cloth. The Christians who thus identified Untaan's house, went there when he was asleep, bound his arms and feet with a thorthu, flung him into the boat and beat him up mercilessly with stout wild jack sticks. Then they took him in the boat and handed him over to a group of Christians in Kalambukkadu. They dragged him to a spot near an abandoned well, and hacked him to pieces which they threw into a pond.

On receiving complaints from the Pulayas, revenue officials and the police arrived. They stayed in the house of a prominent Nair, at Kallara. The case of murder was wiped out without a trace by the Nairs and Christians in collusion with the police.

Untaan's story was later made into a short film titled *Vishamullukal* ('Poison Thorns') and released by the Public

Relations Department of the Government of Kerala as part of an awareness-building programme against anti-social activities. And yet, Untaan emerged as a trailblazing icon among activists in Dalit organizations.

Madhuraveli and neighbouring areas have a rich past of the Dalit community's organizational activities. As all the families in the region except one, which belonged to the Velan caste, were Pulayas, the initial organizational activities centred around the Pulayas. But since none of them were recorded, all that exist are oral accounts that are unclear and undependable. Old-time workers who could have confirmed the facts have passed on. Another reason for this lack is the emergence of political parties. Both the Congress and Communist parties claim to be keeping the torch of the Renaissance[9] burning. But as micro-history has been rejected and macro history institutionalized, the experiences of the community have all but vanished.

During my childhood, members of the savarna castes used to say: 'Did Ayyankali[10] *Amman*[11] come? Did he give something? He would have!' The sarcasm notwithstanding, what this statement indicates is the importance of the Ayyankali movement in the oral tradition. But the past has left behind another historical fact. In the bylaw of the All Travancore Pulaya Maha Sabha that was registered as per the Travancore Companies Act in May 1942, of the 58 names that get mentioned—including Ayyankali, T.T. Keshavan Shastri and others—the fifth signatory is T.K. Kutty of Chelamala House, Madhuraveli, Kaduthuruthi, who lived in my village, far away from Thiruvananthapuram. However, the more recognizable movement was Cheramar Sangham of Pampady John Joseph of the early 20th century.[12]

Although he was a native of Kanakkari near Kottayam, he stayed in Thiruvananthapuram for a long time. In the eyes of his village folk, though, John Joseph remained Kanakkari Paappan.

He forged a link between Dalits and Dalit Christians. In fact, there were no differences between the two in his movement. Moreover, many Pulayas even got converted to Christianity. There used to be a thatched hall in the plains of Upooruthikunnu where those who underwent proselytization could assemble. On some days, the prayers sung by women there till late in the night would flow past the hill slopes and reach the villages. Pulayas who did not convert to Christianity also attended such prayer meetings. What is noteworthy is that in those days, there was no differentiation between Dalits and Dalit Christians as is evident today. Ceremonies associated with weddings and obsequies were conducted jointly by all. Chaachan's second wife was Maria, a Dalit Christian. A son and a daughter of Valyaachan's married Dalit Christians. Such weddings took place everywhere in the region, including in the Thaithara household.

It was Kollamkode Varghese who brought the Madhuraveli branch of Cheramar Sangham into being. Although there is little definite information available regarding their organizational activities, the members of the association did compose and stage a play titled *Cheramar Charitam* ('The History of the Cheramar'). Pampady John Joseph's historical account formed its plot. In his view, during the Sangham period, Kerala was part of Tamizhakam,[13] and ruled by Pulaya kings. Pulayas were the successors of the Chera kings who along with the Cholas and the Pandyas belonged to a single clan. On the basis of this belief, he even sent an application to the Travancore government and succeeded in changing the term 'Pulayas' to 'Cheramar'. Further, he argued that in order to re-establish the royal tradition, attempts should be made to consolidate the clan and not the caste. That was why the drama became the story of the Chera, the Chola and the Pandya kings.

The cast in the play consisted of 30 men, who would don

the roles of women too. The venues were invariably the fields, lying fallow after harvest, or the outskirts of the village. There was neither a proper stage nor a microphone. Yet many people including women and children would assemble at night to see the play, which lasted eight hours. Thaipparambil Kuttappan, who enacted the role of one of the characters, remembered a song in it:

> My darling children!
> How can I leave you and go away?
> Ayyo!
> The Lord will appease your hunger.
> Call Him always, my children.
> Three children I bore, for thirty months,
> And delivered into this earth, O God!

Though he couldn't recall the full plot, he remembered that such scenes would make the spectators cry. The play was staged not only in Madhuraveli and neighbouring places but in various parts of Vaikom taluk.

Possibly due to these initial steps in community organization, even before the land reforms of the 1960s and '70s were implemented, most of the Pulayas in the area were landowners. That was why when a Harijan colony was established in Madhuraveli, very few Pulaya families in the neighbourhood sought refuge there. Members of the Thaithara family owned most of the landed property. Moreover, many Pulayas had acquired primary education even without the help of Christian missionaries. Chaachan had studied up to the seventh standard, a creditable educational qualification in those days.

4. Not a Word in Sight

Chaachan was born in the Thaithara house, which was some distance from the Neythassery Mana but clearly visible from its western gatehouse. His name was Kunjan. The small garden plot of the house—like the *pulayathara* (literally, 'the land of the Pulaya') described in Paul Chirakkarode's novel[14]—was a tiny corner of the Namboodiris' paddy fields that had been levelled using black clayey soil. It was fringed by paddy fields on three sides and a canal on the fourth. The two or three old coconut palms in that area were evidence of the long years of human habitation there. During the rains, when the area got flooded, mudfish, Asian stinging catfish, snapper and others fish swam about everywhere. If anyone in the family had to reach dry land he or she had to walk over the slippery ridges. Even during summer months, the ridges were the only paths, though not as slippery.

Chaachan's father was named Unnimailan, and his mother was Azhaki. Chaachan and his siblings—Azhakan, Ulakan, Theyyathan and Chothi—were very proud of their father. The fact that Chaachan called himself Unnimailan Kunjan makes me feel that the forefather had played a key role in the creation of the Thaithara family. I never got any detailed accounts of him from Amma. But Chaachan's mother, my Valyamma, gave me a very elaborate picture.

Valyamma was a very skilled reaper. She believed that all her children, upon maturity, ought to fend for themselves. Therefore she did not render them any further help. A portion of the grains that she received, either as wages or as *patham*, a share of the harvested crop, was spent at the liquor shop on her daily quota of toddy. The rest she stocked in wicker baskets and left with certain Christian households for safekeeping. During the month of *Karkidakam* (July–August), when famine and starvation performed their death dance, Valyamma, like Kunjenaachan in the novel *Ara Nazhika Neram* by Parappurath,[15] went to all her children's houses. If she noticed a hearth fire not burning, she blamed the family, chastised the members, and eventually sent a portion of her nest egg of grains to appease their hunger.

Valyamma had a brother who was born partially blind. Dark-skinned and uncommonly tall, he was peaceable by nature, and remained a bachelor throughout his life. He was skilled not only at household chores but also at threshing grains during harvest season, catching fish and hewing firewood. He was the pillar of support to the Thaithara family. Called Pottakkannan Achan (blind father) by all, he hanged himself for some inexplicable reason. It was a devastating blow to Amma and the entire family.

Unnimailan had two wives. By the first, he had three children—Kunjan, Ulakan and Kunjayi. They stayed at the Chembakassery, Thaipparambu and Nediyakala households respectively. By the second, he had Chaachan, Azhakan, Ulakan, Theyyathan and Chothi. They belonged to the Thaithara household. Like in olden times, all the members of these households remained branches of the same parent tree. The reason for this could have been the social acceptance of the casual sexual/family links of those times, and the self-sufficiency people acquired through sheer hard work.

Nearly all the Pulaya families in Madhuraveli had been uprooted from other places. These families no longer had any relatives in the places they left so long ago. And yet, the illams[16] their lives were entwined with in such faraway places as Idappally, Varanad and Trippaikudam, and some temple or another there, found a place in their collective memory. The Thaithara family that was attached to the Nedungad illam[17] now had the job of plucking tender coconuts for the Namboodiris. They were also the custodians of the *pathi*, sacred ground, where the stone idols of the forefathers had been installed. Black magic rituals were held there annually. The chickens brought by each household were ceremonially killed, and the blood offered to the ancestors.

Where did the members of the Thaithara family come from? At what point of time? Not even oral versions available. Poykayil Appachan[18] sang thus about the vanished past of the Dalits:

> I don't see a single word
> About my race.
> I do see pictures of many races.
> The story of mine
> To record, in ancient times,
> Alas! There were
> None on earth!

As information, transmitted through word of mouth from the previous generations has disappeared from the memories of the living, it should be assumed that life in other lands must have been a remotely distant one.

What could be the reason for this break in memory? The answer is to be sought in the possibilities of history. Like other clans, my forefathers' or ancestors' clans too might have led a tribal life. They must've been nomads, wandering about in search of natural resources as hunter-gatherers, before they settled down to life within an agricultural economy. Such small groups may not have cultivated mutual dependence through ties of blood. And so, when they sought out places of residence near farming areas, their blood relations might have become irrelevant. Another reason could be the dislocation caused by slavery and oppression. The Travancore government itself had slaves, with the exclusive ownership of more than 15,000 Pulaya slaves as late as 1847. The proclamation abolishing slavery came into effect in Travancore on 24 June 1855. T.H.P. Chentharassery[19] writes this about slave trade:

> The practice was to auction slaves at the open market. Some would buy them wholesale in order to sell them at retail prices. The slaves with diseases were bought at cheap rates, cured through treatment, and sold at a profit. Blood relationship was ignored in this business. Children were wrenched away from parents, wives from husbands, and brothers from sisters in the most brutal fashion. Those who were separated thus most probably never met one another ever again. There were markets in places like Kottayam, Alappuzha, Kayamkulam, Attingal, Chirayinkeezh, Pettah and Kovalam for the sale and purchase of slaves, who were seen as equivalent to animals.

Yiramyavu (b. 1896) was the last slave in British India to be sold. He was sold directly, not through the slave market. The second of seven children born to Nadappalliyil Umman and Maria of Manganam in Kottayam, Yiramyavu was sold when he was 12 years old by his own father to one Paulose, a supervisor at the Cheenthalar estate. For a long time, he was subjected to the most brutal torture at Cheenthalar estate and later at Mundapla plantation. He somehow made an adventurous escape and returned to his native village to be reunited with his relatives. Unlike Yiramyavu, the ancestors of the Thaithara family cast off their native village and their relatives from their memory. But the experiences of slavery, through which the past can be re-read, have been captured in Poykayil Appachan's songs.

Poykayil Appachan's experiences of slavery are not history. They are part of a myth retrieved from the community consciousness of the Dalits. I link this myth to my awareness of life as a tear-soaked experience of generations. Through it, I recapture the times when a community, that includes myself, suffered the pangs of separation. I do it in order to re-establish blood relationship, as if it were intact and suffered no scars.

There is no clear evidence as to where the ancestors of the Thaithara family came from. A certain group believes they came along with the Namboodiris of Neythassery Mana from Palakkad. There is no incontrovertible proof for it. But there are some clues. The original temple of the family is located at Varanad near Cherthala. But they have no relatives there. Most have not even seen that place. Yet *Edanadan Paattu*, compiled by K.R. Sajitha, carries a reference to Varanad. The story takes place against a Kuttanad setting. If the Ezhupunna which it mentions is close to Varanad, then Ezhuvanthuruthu is today's Ezhumanthuruthu situated to the west of my village. Edanadan, who travels by boat as a suicide attacker, with the aim of taking revenge on the Menons who killed Kaimal, his father, says:

> To the Bhagavathy temple of Varanad
> I should row my boat
> I should.
> And
> As I approach the temple entrance
> As I stand at the temple entrance
> I should say, 'I'm Edanadan.
> I will give food offerings, do puja.
> Call the deity,
> And give votive offerings.'

In the song, Edanadan starts from Thrinayankudam in a boat, travels through Ezhumanthuruthu, reaches a chapel, and kills the Menons of Muttuchira in order to take revenge. Regardless of what the story is, if we take into consideration the time the chapel was constructed, what becomes clear is that Pulaya families, including the Thaithara household, had a distinct social existence as far back as 70 to 80 years. This is what the family's connection with the Varanad temple suggests.

Whenever the elderly members of the Thaithara family died, they were installed in the Varanad temple. The ritual was performed when Chaachan passed on too. As part of it, Thaipparambil Kochu, my younger brother Mani, sister Shanta, wife Usha and younger brother Baburaj's wife Jancy went to the Varanad temple, offered a silver statuette and made offerings of *kadumpayasam*, a thick rice-and-jaggery pudding. This ritual reinforced the belief that a member, separated from the goddess, has been returned to Her presence. What this suggests is that the Thaithara family, in the course of their tribal life, must have at some remote point in time migrated from Varanad. Or, they may have been bought at a slave market. But we can't be sure.

5. Sleep-soaked Dinners

My birth took place at Amma's house near Thalayolapparambu on 2 February 1949. Amma's name was Kunjipennu. The house named Kuzhiyamthadam was situated to the west of Puthenthode, which was one-and-a-half kilometres south of the small town of Thalayolapparambu. Most of the people who lived in that region were Pulayas. There were a few Ezhavas too. All the Pulayas and a small minority of the Ezhavas were landless *kudikidappukar*, or hut dwellers. The Nair and Christian landlords—though they did not have extensive holdings—resided in places close to the town.

On two sides of the Kuzhiyamthadam house were canals full of algae and water lilies. The third side had an embankment full of screwpine, Mastwood and Portia trees. On the fourth were gravelly paddy fields. During summer, the water in the canals and the fields turned salty and sour. Water drawn from any hole dug in the garden plot had the same taste. As a result, we had to walk some distance along the ridges to collect water from a pond that belonged to a house named Njaravelil. That pond was nature's bounty. The gravel on the pond bed were spiky and uneven. But it was a marvel to look at. Vessels were dipped into the pond to collect water. It was the refuge of many families. When the water in it dried, everyone had to go farther, to a well near Vazhiyambalam, a kilometre away.

During the rains, water rose in the garden plots and the fields, crept up the front and back yards, and nudged the open veranda. It would be bitterly cold inside the house. Even after the waters receded, the front and back yards were covered in mire. One had to wade through knee-deep water in the paddy fields to reach upland.

Amma's house was constructed on land that had been levelled using the black clayey soil common to these parts. Woven coconut leaves were used to make the four walls of the house but there was a room in the middle made of palm leaves. We had no furniture like cots, tables or chairs. Earthen vessels were used for everything, even to serve food in. Such deprivation was not exclusive to Amma's house. It was the same in every Pulaya household.

My Valyachan's name was Karuppan, and Valyamma's Ponnava. Amma's brother was named Vava. Initially, Valyachan was a slave at a Nair household in Pothiyil, east of Thalayolapparambu. He quarrelled with that family for some reason and ran away from there, taking his wife along. At Thalayolapparambu, he became a slave at another Nair household named Kaniyampadikkal. By the time I was born, Valyachan was long dead but Valyamma lived to a ripe old age.

It was when she became pregnant with me at Madhuraveli

that Amma went to Kuzhiyamthadam. The cause of this relocation was a fight with Chaachan, following his second wedding. She went to her home, taking Chechi—Pennamma—along with her and leaving her elder son, Kunjukunju, with Chaachan. Amma had a special place for me in her affections, one based on a superstition. My Chechi's zodiac was Pooraadam. The astrologer who prepared her horoscope said that it indicated *Ammakkaal*, that is, she would be the cause of Amma's death if she crawled and touched Amma's feet. It seems my zodiac, Aayilyam, saved her from untimely death! Amma would repeat this story endlessly.

Amma's ancestral temple was at Keezhoor. She was deeply devoted to Bhagavathy, the deity of that temple. The deity occupied her subconscious mind while Amma was on her deathbed. As she slipped from and into consciousness, Amma would see Bhagavathy, dressed in finery and covered in ornaments from head to toe, sitting close by, asking her to join her immediately. She wished to be united with her at the Keezhoor temple after her death.

My Ammavan's wife was also named Pennamma. She was from Vadakkethuruthu, close to Chembu. By the time Amma went back to her house, Ammavan already had three children. As his feudal lord, who belonged to the Kaniyampadikkal house, did not have large land holdings, Ammavan worked on the fields and garden plots of other landlords as well. He also caught fish, from the fields during the rains and at other times from the canals, and took his catch to the market and sold it. His expertise at fishing earned him the moniker *Varaal Vava* (Mudfish Vava). Dark, tall and mild-mannered, Ammavan neither smoked nor drank alcohol. He never wore a shirt. Even when he travelled long distances, he wore only an undershirt and a thorthu over it. He studied only up to the third standard.

Crops like tapioca, banana or ginger were not cultivated in

the place where Ammavan lived. Paddy was the most important crop here. Coconut farming was done on a small scale only because the place was always water-logged and the islands in between were very small. But since the land-holding Nair and Christian families occupied small garden plots, coconut farming wasn't too widespread either. Backwardness in the farming sector affected Dalit lives the most. With the opportunity for work on the fields limited, and for a short period each year, fishing, for some residents, was not a subsidiary occupation but the main one.

In such circumstances, women bore the brunt of life's burdens. Besides helping in the paddy fields if they could, they cut grass, bundles of which they would take to the market for selling. Men did this very rarely. A few women would take small boats on rent and cut grass all day long. After a light breakfast they did this hard labour without food or water for the rest of the day. Exposed to the sun as they went about their work, their bodies turned black and sunburnt. Amma and Ammayi never trudged long distances. Early in the evening, they went to the water-logged fields and the sides of canals to cut as much grass as they could. They returned home with their bundles, took a bath, and changed into a fresh set of *mundu*[20] and blouse before heading for the market. Long lines of women proceeding to the market in the evenings with their headloads of grass used to be a common sight. I once wrote an article entitled 'Grass Sellers of Thalayolapparambu' in my column titled 'How do we live?' in the SEEDIAN magazine.

Another occupation of the womenfolk was weaving mats. Like in spinning coir, in weaving mats, Ezhava women were also involved. Women wove not only different types of baskets but also *puttil*,[21] small containers for holding paan, purses that could be accommodated in the waist flap of their mundus, and so on. Amma was an expert at weaving mats. The work was labour-intensive. Leaves of screwpine were cut from shrubs growing on the sides of ridges and canals, their thorns removed, all the leaves arranged in a tight circle, and left to dry. Later, water was sprinkled to make them pliable before they were woven into mats. Amma made mats of different sizes—for lying on, for drying grains, for threshing and so on. These were sold either in the market on Sundays or in the premises of temples, churches and mosques during festivals. The money she made in this manner was used to buy clothes, vessels and other things.

The market and the Puthenthode canal were an indispensable part of the daily life not only of the Pulayas but all the people of Thalayolapparambu. The market was established by Velu Thampi Dalawa (1765–1809),[22] the prime minister of Travancore from 1802 to 1809. The merchants belonged to the Nair, Christian and Muslim communities. Provisions, textile items and vessels were sold in two buildings that had tiled roofs. The road leading to the market was lined on both sides by small structures that housed tea shops and other stores. These shop owners were the ones who procured grains. Business was run by women too. While the provisions shops sold rice, salt, kerosene, chilly, coconut oil and similar things, in the evenings, other items like coconut pieces, tamarind, dried fish, amaranthus, colocasia, elephant yam and mango too would be available at prices ranging from a quarter ana to one ana. The advantage of such businesses was that each family could manage to live on the smallest income.

The lives of women who sold grass, including that of Amma, were utterly miserable. They had to forgo their lunch in order to reach the market by evening, and wait beside their grass bundles for buyers, cattle-raisers in the neighbourhood. The sale took place only after intense bargaining. Sometimes the women had to wait till late in the night, and at other times, be content with the meagre price offered. The bundles of grass that could not be sold had to be carried back home.

Even a good price was a mere pittance, but it was all they had to buy foodstuff for the night. If tapioca was brought home to be cooked for the next day's breakfast, children, totally famished by then, would eat a good chunk of it raw. Another item was jackfruit, cut into small pieces. Each child would get only one or two bulbs of the fruit, either raw or ripe. During the harvest season, rice grains were boiled, dry-heated on a pan, de-husked and then cooked to make gruel. As a result, food was invariably served late, by which time the small children would generally be fast asleep. They had to be woken up in order to be fed. The rice was typically eaten along with fish curry, red in colour, spiced with chilly and Malabar tamarind crushed on a stone mortar. There were no other ingredients. On days when fish was not available, either Chinese senna, uprooted from the ridges close to the canal, or dried fish was crushed along with chilly to make *chammanti*,[23] and that served as a side dish. Never once did we have more than one curry.

Then there was the problem of water and firewood. Utensils were cleaned with water from the Puthenthode canal. We bathed in the canal too. But as I said earlier, for potable water, we had to depend on the pond at the Njaraveli compound or Vazhiyambalam. As we did not have many vessels or pots, it was not possible to store enough quantities of water at any given time. Firewood was scarcer than water. What we used were dry spathes of screwpine, dry twigs and branches of Portia and Mastwood trees or the dry stems of fallen coconut leaves. Ammayi used woven coconut leaves that formed the walls of her house, and sometimes even half-dry leaves.

Puthenthode canal, like the market, played an important role in keeping alive the people of that area. It sliced the Thalayolapparambu town in half, flowed southwards, before changing course towards the west to become a waterway leading to Ezhumanthuruthu and Kuttanad. While products were transported from the eastern parts to the market either as headloads or on bullock carts, those from the western side took the Puthenthode canal. As a result, there was a continuous flow of boats, both big and small, over it. These would make frequent stops at houses to purchase cow dung, ash and other things. Earthen vessels and even women's ornaments were sold in this manner along the Puthenthode canal. In short, like the market, the canal was an inevitable part of people's lives.

Wetland agriculture was introduced in Kuttanad as a way to overcome the famine brought about by the First World War, and later as part of a paddy cultivation promotional drive. In the poem 'Kudumba Puranam' ('Family Lore'), Ayyappa Paniker[24] looks back with nostalgia on those times. Paddy cultivation began with the levelling of 500 acres of wetlands of Thalayolapparambu. It must have been due to the influence of former Congress leader and Madras Governor A.J. John that numerous people took paddy fields on lease. That place would later come to be known as the Alamkeri block. The filling of this lake area, which was infested with crocodiles and full of ferns and algae, was done by workers including my Ammavan, and farmers who joined them.

By the time the Land Reforms Act came into force, and lands got transferred permanently into the hands of those who had held them on lease until then, my Ammavan had been a watchman of these land holdings for 42 long years. Besides doing the work of firming up the outer ridges, organizing men and women workers, maintaining contact with farmers and so on, he used to help on the fields owned by Kaniyampadikkal family. When he retired from his job after such a long innings, the land holding committee gave him a parting gift of Rs 4,000. Besides, on the intervention of the farmers, his younger daughter, Lalitha, who had passed the JDC (Junior Diploma in Co-operation) examination was offered a job at the Thalayolapparambu Farmers' Co-operative Bank.

Ammavan had six children in all. He never made efforts to improve his financial condition or arrange for his children's higher education. Despite that, one of his sons, Sukumaran, became an officer in the Kerala state government service. Although Ammavan had acquired only basic education, up to the third standard as I mention earlier, he was of great help to a lot of people. After the Land Reforms Act was implemented, he fought a legal battle and acquired 12 cents of land he had taken on lease from the Kaniyampadikkal family. (A cent is equivalent to one-hundredth of an acre, 435.6 square feet.) Besides, he helped numerous hut dwellers in their litigation against the landowning Kallampparambu family. The person who gave him professional advice on all such issues was the father of Dr Jancy James, the vice chancellor of Mahatma Gandhi University.

It was my Valyamma's stock of experiences and store of stories that have helped me remember what I do about my childhood. Although I couldn't fully comprehend them as a child, repeated narrations helped engrave them in my mind. She was the last link to that period of our history. The mundu she wore at the waist never went beyond her knees. Nor did she cover her breasts. She usually went about in the house and the immediate vicinity in this manner. But, succumbing to pressure from others, she threw a thorthu over her breasts whenever she went out on social visits or for other purposes to more distant places. Her earlobes, with large holes in them, hung long and loose above her shoulders. Her wedding was conducted when she was nine years old and she naturally remembered very little about her native village and its surrounding environs. As she did not bear children for a long time, Valyachan married a second time, after seeking her permission. It was after two children were born of that union that Valyamma gave birth to Amma and Ammavan.

Just as Kurumbiamma's mind in M. Mukundan's novel *Mayyazhipuzhayude Theerangalil*[25] is full of thoughts of the French era, Valyamma's mind was occupied by Kuttanad. In the remote past, Kuttanad symbolized survival for the Pulayas. Most of the stories she narrated were about the experiences she had during the harvest season. As soon as the season began, three or four families took a boat on rent and rowed jointly to Kuttanad. They carried kitchen utensils and household items with them—vessels for making gruel, mats, baskets and so on. It took them one day and one night to reach Kuttanad. There they pitched sheds either on the coconut farm close to the fields, where the ears of corn stood ripe for harvest, or on the embankments that were overgrown with wild plants and thickets. The boat was required for the entire season because the families had to travel long distances to collect water, and for procuring items of daily use. Men and women worked in sync to harvest the fields that stretched as far as the eyes could see. The harvested stalks of corn were carried in bundles on the head and taken to threshing floors in the coconut farms or on the embankments. On the way, the women picked up *kalaperukku*, grains that fell down during harvesting, or sometimes caught fish from the smaller canals.

The stalks were threshed during the night. Men and women did it under the light of chimney lamps suspended from coir ropes attached between the pillars of the threshing floor. Later, they collected whatever grains they were given as patham in baskets and kept them safe in the sheds. A portion of these grains, collected either as kalaperukku or patham, was sold in order to purchase salt, chilly, paan and other items. It also bought toddy for the men folk, and occasionally, for women too. Valyamma's knowledge of the world came from the conversations she had with the women from other places, on days when there was no harvesting or threshing.

The stock of grains received during two months of harvesting was what saw the family through the monsoon months—Idavam (May–June), Mithunam (June–July) and Karkidakam (July–August)—of privation. The interaction with people from different places, and the grains that helped her family survive the lean months were what made Kuttanad dearer to Valyamma than her native village.

Valyamma's stories unspooled themselves in the evenings when Amma, Ammavan and Ammayi left for the market. Night would have slowly begun to creep in by then. It used to be dark, though sometimes there would be a kerosene lamp burning. The three children of Ammavan, my Chechi and I sat or stretched ourselves out on the mat unfurled at one end of the open veranda of the house. Some soon fell asleep. Valyamma's stories at these times were invariably about ghosts and ghouls. And the setting of those stories was always Kuttanad. A few of the ghouls in her stories were evil. Sometimes a lone traveller passing through a graveyard at noon would meet with an untimely death, hacked by ghouls, in her accounts. Blood would congeal below the skin on the chest of the deceased, she said, and leave bluish marks there. Certain other ghouls would cause all kinds of distress short of murder.

One story Valyamma often repeated was about her cousin who was waylaid by a ghoul on his way back in a boat from Kuttanad with grains. When the boat crossed the lake and reached a huge river, a voice told him that the landing ghat was elsewhere. When the man rowed to that place, the same voice told him the ghat was on the other side. The ghoul misdirected the man all through the night.

The most frightening person in Valyamma's stories was a character named Marutha. Women who died in childbed became Marutha. Such an untimely death was seen as the result of some curse. Consequently, no obsequies were performed. The dead body was covered in woven coconut leaves or mats and buried at night. Men, fortified by toddy, did the deed. It was believed that Maruthas drank the blood of the newborns and thus killed them. Young mothers in places where such untimely deaths had created Maruthas lived in mortal fear. The innocent ant-eater, which was seen in the countryside only rarely, was thought to be the Marutha.

It seems Valyamma had also seen flaming torches moving over fields and garden plots submerged in water. On some nights a white bull with a tinkling bell tied to its neck walked along the fields on the western side of the house.

Amma was no less adept at narrating similar stories. While most of those she recounted were Valyamma's Kuttanad tales, some were her own. C. Ayyappan's fictional world[26] has proven that such tales of the marginalized classes could be made symbols of their social identity.

Ammayi was also a story-teller. Among the stories she narrated, the most significant one was about a unique type of revenge. The plot went thus:

A fair-skinned and handsome Pulaya youth participated in the wedding feast held in a Nair household. Although he was not recognized in the beginning, his unusual manner of eating attracted attention. The Nairs not only created a row but also beat him up. The Pulaya youth ran and hid himself inside a haystack not far away. Those who had pursued him with sticks and stones ordered him to come out. When he refused for a long time, they set fire to the haystack and burnt him alive. But the story does not end here. The murdered youth became a ghost, went to the houses of all the Nairs who had committed the crime, and spread madness and fatal diseases there. All the Nair families perished. This story had been passed down for so many generations it had almost become a legend.

However, what Amma also recounted were slivers of first-hand experience of history, dimly lit and vague though they may have been. It was during her early youth that she heard a speech by Mahatma Ayyankali. In those days, prior to the Vaikom Satyagraha,[27] Ayyankali was a familiar figure in different parts of the Vaikom taluk, which included Thalayolapparambu. Besides, there was organized social activity too among the Pulayas. And thus, even before the Vaikom Satyagraha took place, it was decided at a Pulaya Maha Sammelanam convened at Ullala that the untouchables would use the road around the Vaikom temple they were not allowed to take. It must have been against this background that Ayyankali addressed the Pulayas of Thalayolapparambu. According to Amma's account, the meeting took place in a pavilion on the harvested fields on the western side of our house. Many Pulayas of the land—men, women and children—assembled to listen. Although Amma was not clear about the contents of the speech, what captured her attention was the advice he imparted. One of the most important instructions he gave was that women should wrap their mundu in such a way as to cover their knees, and also wear a bodice and blouse. Further, he advised his audience to take a regular bath, send their children to school and educate them. Men, he said, should keep away from alcohol.

One should surmise that such organizational activities played a key role in transforming the lives of the Pulayas. Amma's life was no exception. The most visible aspect of this change could be seen in attire. She made her daughters wear petticoats and panties made of coarse cloth, and her sons wear shorts with suspenders. The awareness she gained was brought to bear on other matters in her life too.

I also came to learn from Amma about a clash between the Ezhavas and Muslims at the Thalayolapparambu market. There were complaints that the Muslim traders misbehaved with people, including women, who went to them to sell goods, by quoting ridiculously low rates, threatening them and sometimes even engaging in scuffles. This led to intense hatred for Muslims as a whole, not just the traders, and soon a clash broke out. When a procession carrying a picture of Sree Narayana Guru[28] was being taken out, many people threw stones at it. A young man was hit on his forehead. The Ezhavas scattered, after leaving him on the veranda of a school, going in various directions. By evening, crowds of people from adjacent areas had assembled, and they began to attack the Muslims, and even torch their shops. Many were burnt to death inside their store houses. Widespread arson followed but care was taken to ensure that Anapparambu, the house of A.P. John, was left untouched. Although no one could gauge the number of casualties or the extent of the damage caused, it took a cavalry unit from Thiruvananthapuram to re-establish law and order there. Following this clash, the Muslims left for different lands.

Later, as I enquired further, I learnt that Vaikom Muhammed Basheer's[29] family never came under attack. They lived at Palamkadavu, two kilometres from Thalayolapparambu, and had amicable relations with the Ezhavas. Amma, however, who recounted the incident, had no idea who he was.

In my childhood, there used to be a talkie house at Thalayolapparambu. It had a thatched roof. After the first show, everyone except Valyamma and Ammavan went there, with flaming torches in their hands, to see the film. I remember seeing a film called *Manthravadi* ('Magician') at that talkie house, although that was not the first film I watched there.

Chaachan took Chechi from Amma's house to admit her in school. Since I did not accompany him, I was left behind with Amma. My Ammavan admitted me to the first standard in a government school nearby, entering my name as Gopalakrishnan. But then Chaachan and Amma decided to live together, and so, Amma and I too returned to Madhuraveli.

6. Life at that Time

Even before my birth, the Thaithara family had split into various branches and spread to different parts of Madhuraveli. Chothi constructed a house at Puthenpura, Theyyathan at Kunnumpuram, Ulakan at Pattarakala, and Chaachan at Kazhuthoottu. Azhakan, who lived at Thaithara, and Chaachan were hut dwellers. But all the members of the family had their own plots of land. Chaachan had three or four acres of upland at two different places and two acres of kari land to his name.

Kazhuthoottu parambu was a large coconut farm that belonged to Neythassery Mana. Earlier, a Christian family lived there. The Ezhavas and the Pulayas had evicted them on the orders of the Neythassery Mana. There were huge mango trees on the southern and eastern ends of the plot. And on the northern side was a long boundary wall. On the other side of it was the mud track leading to the Kaduthuruthi road. On the western side were embankments and coconut farms that nudged the border of Upper Kuttanad. If the canals were full of water lilies and algae, the embankments were full of Malabar melastome flowers.

Bricks made of clay were used to lay the floor, and the mud walls of the single-room house were topped with a thatched roof. Woven coconut leaves were pitched all around the house, which stood facing the east. It was always dark inside. The door was made of wood. There used to be a huge chest full of grains in this living area. The kitchen with its mud walls and thatched door was on the northern side. It led to an open veranda that surrounded the house on three sides. On the eastern veranda was placed a coir cot that was used by Chaachan. In other words, even so many years back, ours was not a Pulaya hut but a fairly decent house.

It was Amma who admitted me as Kochu in an *asan kalari*.[30] It was housed in one of the two-room shops owned by Chanakkal Kuruvilla on the roadside. The master was a native of Kappikkadu. I used to go there wearing shorts with suspenders. I learned the alphabet here by using a stylus on palm leaves. Chechi, who studied in the Madhuraveli Lower Primary School, wore a blouse and skirt. She chaperoned me to the kalari. On the way, as we climbed up and down the Uppuruthikkunnu hill, we plucked and ate Spanish flag berries, jungle geranium fruits and jackal jujube berries that grew copiously on plants that covered the slopes. Maybe because she played the role of a protector, Chechi always had a warm place in my heart.

Neither the Namboodiris of Neythassery Mana nor their Nair dependents interfered in the farming activities. The entire responsibility rested on Valyaachan's shoulders. The relationship between the Namboodiris and Valyaachan was an extraordinary one. The latter was honest and trustworthy. The senior Namboodiri not only entrusted him with the supervision of farming activities but also consulted him on domestic matters. Valyaachan was given his morning and afternoon meals at the mana. The same food that the members of the mana ate was served to him in a reasonably large *uruli* (a flat-bottomed vessel, usually made of bronze). Usually, he took a portion for himself in a banana leaf, and gave the rest to any of his co-workers, never considering the caste of that person or checking whether he was related by blood.

In the work of supervising the farming activities, Chaachan was Valyaachan's second-in-command. He worked on his own fields as well, raising tapioca, banana, ginger and so on. He employed a couple of workers too, and the produce was taken in boats to Alappuzha for sale.

Chaachan had a good relationship with all, regardless of caste or religion. Amma was like him in this regard. Chaachan never hesitated to help others—in cash or in any other way. And Amma was a good cook. Their congenial nature made our house a refuge for many. All this so endeared Chaachan to the members of the savarna caste that instead of calling him 'Kunjan Pulayan', they called him Kunjaachan. And the Pulayas addressed him as 'Appachi' and Amma as 'Kunjaami'.

The house on the eastern side belonged to Kochuparambil Narayanan, an Ezhava. He was a hut dweller. We used to draw water from a well in his plot. Narayanan's mother not only came to our house every day but also sometimes ate with us. Hers was the first death I ever saw. It is among the several scattered glimpses of those days I still carry in my mind.

The dead body was draped in a white cloth and laid on the floor of the veranda plastered with cow dung. She was cremated at dusk. Relatives and neighbours came over and helped cut down a mango tree which stood on the southern side of the plot to prepare the funeral pyre. We could see it burning from our house. That night I was so terrified I covered myself with a mat. I thought the smell of the burning corpse would float through the air, and her ghost would come to our house with it. Did I know that death meant not only exit from one world but entry into an invisible realm too?

The object that my young mind found most fascinating was the gramophone. It was my first window into the world of arts. Our neighbour on the southern side, Thottipparambil Narayanan's household owned nearly three-quarters of an acre of land. Yet their main source of income was the manual labour they did for Neythassery Mana. The youngest son of Narayanan's house studied with me at the asan kalari. Narayanan's wife was a plump, fair-skinned woman from Cherthala. She never went out for work. Owing to caste pride, she did not allow us into the house beyond the veranda. Their eldest son had brought a gramophone from Cherthala. As soon as a record was placed on it and the key turned, theatre songs flowed out. The gramophone was kept on the veranda in the evenings, and when records were played, many, including myself, converged there to listen. We were drawn by a kind of curiosity, laced with amazement. As I heard those songs repeatedly, I realized there were worlds beyond that of ghouls and ghosts.

Edavam, Mithunam and Karkidakam were monsoon months. There was no work to do on the fields or the garden plots. Those were the months when the land roiled in misery. Whatever grains were earned during the harvesting months of Makaram (January–February) and Kumbham (February–March) served to feed us only through the next two, Meenam (March–April) and Medam (April–May). But since work on the coconut farms was available then, we could keep the wolf from the door. What followed thereafter, until the end of Karkidakam was a period of intense privation. It affected not only the Pulayas but everyone in the land. Many procured palms from the eastern regions. These were available at cheap rates. They could be cut into small pieces, powdered and boiled to make gruel. Wheat that was bought from ration shops replaced rice. Dried-and-preserved tapioca was another edible item.

Chaachan never saved for a rainy day. He did not keep aside anything for use in the future. Amma would hoard a small portion of grains she received as patham, and give them to certain Christian families for safe-keeping. During lean months, she collected them, roasted and powdered them in a mortar before boiling the stuff to make gruel. Although we never had enough to enjoy a hearty meal, we just about escaped going completely hungry at this time of the year.

The new moon day of Karkidakam was the day for obsequies, to remember the dead ancestors and make offerings to them. At night, rice and meat would be served on banana leaves. Beaten and puffed rice were served on the smaller leaves and toddy was kept with it all in earthen pots. The belief was that the dead ancestors would come and partake of the feast. Later, Amma served all the food to us.

We would cover ourselves with mats at night to keep the cold at bay, and go to sleep cursing the rain. But as the next day dawned, the sky would appear clear. By then, not only the fields of Upper Kuttanad but those close to the uplands too would be submerged in flood waters, and appear red in colour. Water continued to flow in streams through the garden plots. Fish like the Asian stinging catfish, mudfish, snapper and carp tumbled about in them. Shoals of small fish, known as striped panchax, would also swim through the canals in the uplands. People from neighbouring areas and even the eastern regions came with nets and fishing lines to catch them. Fishing was a festival in the month of Karkidakam. That miserable month was memorable for another reason. To Christians, the unremitting rain was a reminder of St Thomas's arrival in Kerala.[31]

Everyone mostly remained indoors as it poured outside. As the month ended, and Chingam (August–September) began, the days were spent in arranging floral carpets and going to the temple. Chechi loved this time of the year.

---

7. Pathithullal

When I was old enough, Amma admitted me in the first standard at the Infant Jesus Lower Primary School at Madhuraveli, where Chechi too studied. I used to go to school along with her. It was run by the Latin Catholic Church and had classes up to the sixth standard. The school building was a long hall, partitioned into classrooms with wooden boards. All the teachers, except one, were nuns. The first standard teacher was Varkey sir who was from Adyitapuram. Tall and slim, he wore a jubba-like shirt with half sleeves and always carried a long cane in his hand. I cannot remember anything else.

Although Chechi's name was Pennamma, Chaachan, Amma, Ichaayan and others called her 'Ummanna'. Chaachan loved her dearly. It would always be her name he hollered from afar, signalling his return, as he came home in the evening, invariably drunk. Chechi was doted on at home, quite unlike the girls in other ordinary households such as ours who faced neglect and discrimination. She was fair-skinned and always wore good clothes. She had gold studs in her ears. Amma was very particular that her children should be neat and tidy. Ichaayan exercised considerable influence over all of us, including Chechi. As a result, we learned to lead a disciplined life right from childhood. Back when we were in school, Chechi also received training in dance under a master at Kaduthuruthi. Her aesthetic sense and religious devotion influenced me a great deal during my childhood. I believe it helped me view my future differently, and think beyond leading an isolated existence.

Chechi maintained a flower garden in front of our house. Most of the flowers were Mexican marigolds and four o' clock plants. She tended them with care that seemed almost maternal, never permitting us to pick even a single one. Whenever Chechi and Mani, my younger brother, fought, Mani took revenge by plucking the four o' clock flowers. For Chechi, this crime would be an unbearable one. If she ever cried, it was mostly for her flowers. It was with her as the model human being in my eyes that I once presented a paper titled 'Dalit Community Formation: Problems and Perspectives' on the grooming of Dalit girls at a state conference of the Dalit Students' Movement.

Chechi was devout. No religious or caste differences were recognized among her friends, with whom she went, every Sunday, to the Adityapuram temple. I too would tag along. Those trips were really enjoyable. We trekked together like a group of pilgrims, walking along the mud tracks lined with thickets and wild plants on both sides, climbing up and down the hill on the way. The temple doors closed before nine in the morning. I had to remove my shirt and leave it on the veranda of the temple before stepping inside. We prayed to the Sun God first and dropped the customary small-value coin of one-quarter anna in the collection box. The Sun God was a granite idol drenched in oil. Next, we circumambulated the temple, and stopped at a stone mandapam to pray to another idol that was exposed to both sun and rain. Then, as we reached the door of the sanctum sanctorum, the high priest, a Namboodiri, threw nuggets of red sandal paste into the palms of the outstretched arms of devotees. It was smeared on the forehead, chest and forearms. To me, the temple visit was not merely a source of joy but a matter of great pride as well.

The Adityapuram temple was privately owned by the Marangattu Mana of Kappikkadu. I don't know when it was thrown open to the depressed classes. It must have been after the Vaikom Satyagraha, and the Temple Entry Proclamation.[32] For a long time, the temple did not attract many devotees. Even the annual *kaavadiyattam*[33] was a mere ritual. So, the temple had a paltry income. When the mana lost its land holdings, thanks to the Land Reforms Act and the agricultural labourers' struggles, the temple became its sole source of revenue. The meagre amount it brought pushed the family into acute poverty.

Later, when a Namboodiri took over as the high priest of this temple for a short while, after his retirement from the Regional Engineering College, Kozhikode, the situation changed drastically. Since he had a vast network of friends, including some from the Malayalam film industry, the temple began to attract many devotees. He influenced the media, and popularized a legend about the temple that was essentially a figment of his imagination. His story, linking the temple to the Puranas, went something like this:

When Lord Shiva refused to marry Goddess Parvathy, the goddess went into a long spell of meditation. But the Lord's heart did not melt. The distraught goddess decided to take her own life. At this point, the Sun God intervened to dissuade her from the act, and advised Lord Shiva to marry her. Pleased with the Sun God, Goddess Parvathy installed him at Adityapuram.

In order to lend credibility to this legend, which does not find mention anywhere in the Puranas, it was widely advertised that if a young girl participated in *bhajana irikkal*[34] for a week, she would be blessed with a good marital alliance.

Today, the Adityapuram temple is famous throughout Kerala. Besides, the flow of cash offerings has increased tremendously. The income has considerably improved the financial status of Marangattu Mana.

There were plenty of bael trees all around the temple. Chechi and her friends plucked bael flowers, and on the way back, jungle geranium and Malabar melastome flowers as well as fruits from the plants that grew on the slopes of hill we had to climb. Devotion was not the only incentive for our trek to the temple.

Chechi became particularly high-spirited during the Onam[35] season. She would make a mud platform in the front yard, plaster it with cow dung, and create floral designs on it. In the evenings, as soon as she returned from school, she headed for the hill slopes, plucked different types of flowers, brought them home in a wicker basket, and sprinkled water over them to keep them fresh for the next morning when, after her bath, she would devote herself to laying them out. This would go on for ten days—from Atham to Thiruvonam, the first and last day of Onam—without a break. On Thiruvonam day, she wore new clothes, and took part in the Onam games.

Two days before Onam, all the workers of Neythassery Mana were given two *paras*[36] of paddy grains, oil and some money. And so, all kinds of curries and *payasam*[37] could be prepared to celebrate Onam.

But the community and the house had not bid goodbye to the old world. The Pulayas did not have the same gods and goddesses or rituals and traditions as the caste Hindus. As worshippers of ancestors, their place of worship was the *pathi*. In the seven-cent piece of land gifted by the Neythassery Mana, there was a raised platform made of clay and stones, and the stones placed on top of it were our ancestors. The main ritual that took place here every year was the *pathithullal*. As there were neither daily pujas nor the custom of lighting a traditional lamp there, the pathi and its surroundings were invariably overgrown with creepers and wild plants, which were cleared days before the pathithullal each year. On the evening of the ritual, a huge leafy branch of the blackboard tree was fixed in front of the stones. The function began at night with the sorcerer named Moolethara Azhakan taking the lead. All the adult men, including the sorcerer, would be drunk by then. Each man broke a twig from the blackboard tree branch, held it in his hands and went into a sort of trance, shaking (*thullal*) quite like a patient of epilepsy. During this time, the sorcerer uttered mantras, and drummed loudly on the rim of a bell metal plate with a nut-cracker knife. As the night progressed, he first took a chicken presented by a devotee, bit into its neck and drank its blood. Then he cut the necks of the rest of the chickens and poured their blood as libation on the stones.

Women participated in a different role in the pathithullal ritual. They came from various places and formed groups according to the illams they were associated with. Each group prepared a hearth, placed a new earthen pot over it, and made payasam using rice and jaggery. Reminiscent of the *pongala* offered in modern times, this ritual was called *kalam karikkal*. The pathithullal came to an end when the night-long thullal and kalam karikkal got over. The belief was that, honoured with such functions, the dead ancestors would bless the community with good fortune and prosperity. Whatever be the fact, it cannot be denied that pathithullal not only offered an opportunity for people associated with an illam to come together, interact with one another and renew their communitarian bonding ever year but also transformed them into a distinct group with their own unique rituals and traditions.

~

The old and the modern systems converged in the time of treatment of illnesses. Amma had immense knowledge of folk medicine. If anyone had fever, she crushed touch-me-not leaves, mixed them in gruel and gave the potion to the patient. She made other medicines—using the leaves of Malabar nut; crushing leaves of the velvet leaf plant, extracting its juice and sun-drying it till it came to a viscous consistency—in order to give them to children, and so on. In case of jaundice, our neighbour Narayanan's father gave me a herbal medicine which was administered along with some sugar. Besides all these were the concoctions and tablets bought from an Ayurvedic physician of Njarakattu at Kallara; there were no allopathic or homoeo treatments. The main form of treatment was of course black magic, and the most sought-after sorcerer, Moolethara Azhakan, who served not only our village but the neighbouring regions as well.

Amma's belief in black magic was unshakeable. If anyone fell ill, Moolethara Azhakan was promptly called. He spun and tossed a conch shell into a winnowing pan full of paddy grains. Then he picked up a few grains and sorted them in groups of odd and even numbers. On the basis of that, he predicted which ghoul had taken possession of the patient's body. If the ghoul was not of a troublesome sort, he exorcised it by beating on the rim of a bell metal plate with a knife, while uttering some mantras. Then he shivered and shook. Occasionally, he added turmeric powder into a basin with a limestone paste solution to make it blood-red in colour. On certain other occasions, he put a burning wick in a tiny earthen pot and placed it on the patient's stomach. I used to be fascinated watching all this as a child.

If these minor remedies failed to effect a cure, a more elaborate session—lasting a whole night—was arranged. Moolethara Azhakan was entrusted with that ritual too. He came to the house in the evening, prepared a square-shaped platform using the pith of the banana plant, and fixed coconut leaflets upright on all four sides. Then, jungle geranium flowers were sprinkled on the floor all around the platform. Beaten rice and puffed rice were placed on banana leaves next to an earthen pot containing toddy. All the ceremonies were similar to those performed to exorcise a spirit from the patient's body, the idea being to confine the illness to the platform. The next morning, the platform, the jungle geranium flowers, the beaten and puffed rice were all thrown into a lake. It was only when even this remedy failed that a physician's help was sought.

In my childhood, I did not hear about gods like Lord Rama or Lord Krishna. Nor did I know about the *Ramayana* or the *Mahabharata*. All the stories that Amma recounted were about ghouls. Although we went to the Adityapuram temple on Sundays, I did not know that I was worshipping a Hindu god. One day, Chechi bought a booklet titled *Harinamakeerthanam* from the Adityapuram temple. It began like this: *Rama Rama pahimam / Rama padam cherane / Mukunda Rama pahimam.*[38] In the evenings, Chechi and I sat in front of a kerosene lamp, brought our palms together in a namaste, and sang this prayer. This was how religious devotion seeped into me, without my own knowledge. Even then, I did not recognize that I was a Hindu.

8. The Dining Table Called Nature

I was a timid child during my years of education at the lower primary school. This was not because I suffered neglect or ill health. It was just that I was an introvert. So, there are no friends, either boys or girls, that I remember from those days. I was closest to Narayanan, whose family was the only blacksmith household in the entire village. They too were hut dwellers of Neythassery Mana. Sometime during my first years at high school, the family relocated to Neeleshwaram in Kasaragod district.

Maybe because I never had enough to eat at Amma's house, at least to my heart's content, I was extremely greedy. Precisely for that reason, Nature, to my eyes, seemed like a huge dining table. With my younger brother Mani in tow, I raided the garden plot of the Alunkal house, situated to the south of ours, plucked cashew fruits, ate them, and gave the nuts to the family. Besides, I ate wild jack fruits and their roasted seeds as well as mangoes that had fallen at the base of the trees early in the morning. I would gather fallen coconuts from the Neythassery Mana garden plot, and large circular leaves (used for wrapping food items), and supply them to provision shops in return for lumps of jaggery or toffees and the like. But despite my greed, I never stole paddy grains or anything else from the house, to eat or to sell. I was afraid of doing so for the shame I would suffer should anyone come to know of it.

Fishing was an activity I was greatly interested in. I used to spend whole mornings on holidays, and a few evening hours after school, catching fish from the canals and fields. During summer months, when the canals and paddy fields were drained, I would catch fish either by using a basket or searching with my bare hands. Even on days when the catch was sizeable, I never sold it. Selling fish was considered rather demeaning. So excess fish were dried and preserved for future use. Chaachan did not like this habit of mine because all the wandering, often done on an empty stomach, and exposure to sun as well as mire, made the body dark. I would receive a good beating by him every now and then.

Although I could not understand or accept the changes that overtook my village, the market on either side of the Kaduthuruthi–Kallara laterite road fascinated me to no end. It was through the market that I walked, leaving the isolated and desolate area where my house stood, in order to go to school. Much later, when I came to know more about the interactive spaces in the market, it opened itself to a different political reading altogether. My education with regard to the social formations of modern Kerala, and especially the communitarian and political undercurrents of liberation struggles, would then begin to take shape.

The first commercial centre in the market was a toddy shop owned by a Christian family named Kannarathil of Kappikkadu. It was situated a little away from the roadside, a thatched hall covered with planks of wood that were plastered with limestone solution. The hall opened into a room where the toddy brought in by the tappers was stored. There were also desks and benches in the hall where toddy was served in earthen pots and tumblers. As caste differences did not matter in the toddy business, since most of the regulars were Pulayas who were manual labourers, everyone could sit together inside the shop.

The conditions were different before the coming of the toddy shop there. Toddy used to be sold at the toddy tappers' houses. During those days, there was even a saying: 'The *chokan* taps, the *chokothi* sells.' That is, the Ezhava is the toddy-tapper, and the Ezhava woman the seller. Such a norm, where poverty and illiteracy were inextricably intertwined, wreaked havoc on families, reinforcing their educational backwardness and making other social conditions worse. It was why Sree Narayana Guru had exhorted the Ezhavas to neither 'tap, drink or sell toddy'. But his words were ignored. The Ezhava toddy-tappers were reluctant to give up their traditional line of work. Besides, the establishment of toddy shops made them prosperous too.

Other shops sprouted as well—provisions shops, tea shops, barbershops, shops selling knick-knacks and stationery and so on—though the market was mostly empty during daytime. Besides the salesmen in the toddy shops, the other regulars at the market were the traders themselves as well as the beedi workers. There used to be some troublemakers who belonged to certain Christian families. They were small-scale traders or beedi workers who settled differences among households or among siblings of the same household through physical fights, usually in the evenings and within the market premises.

There were two groups of Pulayas in the Madhuraveli and Kappikkadu regions. Members of one worked as manual labourers for Neythassery Mana but they had land holdings of their own and looked after themselves. They educated their children and farmed on their own fields. But most members of the other group were slaves in Nair or Christian households. They were either hut dwellers or lived on leased land, and a few among them also earned through fishing. Much of their income, however, was spent on alcohol. Whenever they got into drunken brawls, the Christian troublemakers of the market beat them up. The general public, including the Pulayas, suffered this in silence. A certain hatred for the Christians began to take hold in my mind too, out of a sense of empathy for the sufferers.

Another person who, besides the Pulayas, was subjected to constant torture was a barber named Kailasan. He was from Kappikkadu. When he was sober, this young man was soft and good-natured. But he was a different person when drunk. He didn't have the physique to start an actual fight, so he would let loose expletives at people. I used to enjoy the 'Bobanum Moliyum' cartoon series and the 'Jokes Corner' in the *Malayala Manorama* weekly that Kailasan had in his barbershop. So I had a soft corner for that man. He eventually sold his house and whatever property he had at Kappikkadu and went with his family to the high ranges, possibly because he could not tolerate the excesses of the goondas in the market any longer.

There is a reason I remember all this. When all the Christians of the region, as well as Valyaachan and a few Ezhavas joined the Congress party, this violent gang in the market became the party members' protective shield. The hatred I felt for that gang was what made the Congress party an enemy in my eyes.

Sometime later the Communist party made its entry. Chaachan was one of the first Communists in the village. Such a transformation was not the result of an ideological awareness gained through study classes. Nor was it because he led any struggle himself. Neither EMS nor AKG[39] was Chaachan's hero. K. Damodaran[40] was the model he looked up to. In the days when doubts swirled in my mind about Marxism, I happened to ask Chaachan about his reasons for becoming a Communist. What I got in reply was a personal anecdote.

Once, nearly 20 men and women, including Chaachan, were working in the fields called Siennakkari owned by Padmanabha Paniker who hailed from Vaikom. It so happened that lunch was brought for the workers when the landlord was away. The men waited long for Paniker to return, but when it got late, one of them served lunch to everyone. Incidentally, Paniker appeared just then. Enraged at the workers' behaviour, he threw their meals, along with the banana leaves on which they were served, into a canal nearby. No one protested. In fact, they continued to work on an empty stomach. This incident sparked an acute hatred in Chaachan, but was also cause for sorrow. It was a desire for revenge that made him a Communist.

Police atrocities became widespread in Vaikom and Ullala in the wake of the Calcutta Thesis, the path of insurrection, which was decided upon at the second congress of the Communist Party of India in 1948. This was the time when the activities of the Communist party became more extensive with leaders like P.S. Sreenivasan, C.K. Vishwanathan and others organizing the toddy tappers. At Kaduthuruthi, party activities were led by K.K. Joseph. With the help of a Dalit Christian named Samuel, Chaachan established contact with the Communists of Vaikom and on their leaders' instructions, became a follower of Joseph.

For a long time, the Communist party did not form committees in the village or conduct struggles through its feeder organizations. Nevertheless, leaders' visits and discussions in the villages succeeded in making politics part of the everyday lives of the people. When the Christians put their weight behind the Congress in the eastern regions, the Ezhavas and the Pulayas in the western parts gravitated towards the Communist party. When the Communist party was suppressed, the western region even became a hideout for leaders on the run. Thekkedathu Gopalan, a dark and stout middle-aged man who was a party activist, sought refuge in our house for some time. He became a toddy shop contractor during the rule of the first Communist government.

Turning Communist did not help improve the personal or social lives of ordinary activists or sympathizers, including Chaachan. They continued to live life as before, drinking, playing cards, indulging in domestic brawls and so on. Occult rituals didn't stop either, even in our house. Most importantly, there were absolutely no conscious efforts to overcome the boundaries of caste, no instances of people forming fellowships, or stepping out of their caste boundaries. Individuals continued to be known by their caste names. Although Valyaachan was a prosperous man in the village, he was widely known as and called Chothi Pulaya. An Ezhava was addressed with the label 'Chokon' appended to his name. To those who belonged to castes below him, the Ezhava was 'Achan'. A Nair, like a Namboodiri, was addressed as 'Thampuran'. A Christian had 'Koyil' or 'Mappila' attached to his name. Such forms of address were not affected by differences in financial status of the person concerned. The old custom of relatives and people of the same caste assembling for ceremonies like weddings and rituals like obsequies continued. Those belonging to one caste did not eat food at the house of another. The Nairs did not permit members of the low castes to draw water from wells in their compounds. If Ezhavas or Pulayas wanted water, they had to place their vessels near the well, having to wait until someone from the house the well belonged to drew water and poured it in them. Members of the low caste had to step aside when a Namboodiri walked along a path. In short, the claims made by the Communist party about how it maintained the spirit of the Renaissance ran contrary to facts.

Party sympathizers, including Chaachan, were drawn less to the ideology or the aims of the party than to the leaders, towards whom they had a somewhat submissive attitude. If these savarna leaders came to their houses and partook of their hospitality, it was a matter of great pride. Party loyalty demanded that there be no political activities other than participation in demonstrations and public meetings and the seeing of plays produced by the Kerala People's Arts Club (KPAC).[41]

It was when the party was still limited to only a few sympathizers that P.U. Yusef, a young homoeopathic doctor from Ullala, came to our village. It was not known whether the party had appointed him. As soon as he set foot in Madhuraveli he sought out Chaachan, who not only arranged for a rented accommodation but also gave him all the assistance required to set up a dispensary. Yusef never organized any party committees or led any struggle. But he commanded the respect of all, with his polite and pleasing manner. Through him, the number of Communist sympathizers increased in the area. But the party could not attract anyone other than Ezhavas and Pulayas.

The ideology and political activities of the Communist party could not dismantle social and caste equations. What is more, the submissiveness of the leadership towards the rich was unconcealed. Ownership of vast landholdings by landlords, including those of the Neythassery Mana who had more than 1,000 acres, continued as before. The party could not put forward demands like reducing the number of hours of work of the slaves, raising their wages, ensuring the fair payment of patham due to the workers, solving the problems of hut dwellers and so on. At the same time, the foremost leaders of the party like E.M.S. Namboodiripad, V.R. Krishna Iyer and others not only paid regular visits to the mana, but also accepted contributions from those landlords. The same leaders also approached Valyaachan, who was a prosperous man but a Congress loyalist. During one such visit, Valyaachan removed a five-sovereign gold chain he wore around his neck, and handed it over to E.M.S. Namboodiripad. While the Communists of the village celebrated these visits as symbols of their leaders' magnanimity of spirit, the benefits were reaped by the Namboodiris of Neythassery Mana and other rich landlords who owned vast agricultural lands.

---

9. Whose Communism?

The Christians were a model worth following in the financial life of our village. Instead of raising food crops in their own lands or on the plots taken on rent, they opted for cash crops. By co-opting children too in the enterprise, they showed their indifference to education. They did farming, but many were also engaged in business. All the shops in the market except the barbershop belonged to them. Besides meat, they collected dried coconut, eggs and betel leaves, and sold them in the market. The stinginess of the Christian families was proverbial. Women held the purse strings. Items of daily use—like rice, salt, chilly, coconut oil and so on—were measured meticulously and used thriftily. If fish curry was prepared, it was made to last for the maximum number of days. Women were given very little to eat. One can learn a lot about their lives in the writings of Ponkunnam Varkey[42] as well as early plays and films like *Thommante Makkal.*

A few prominent Christians even criticized Chaachan for

educating his children, including myself. The reason for this was Chaachan and Amma's refusal to convert three or four acres of land in their possession into a plantation for cash crops, and their dependence on manual labour to eke out a living. Fortunately for his children, Chaachan never bothered about such accusations.

It was in a totally different way that Chaachan the Communist sympathizer influenced me. He opened the doors to knowledge. After he was done with work at Neythassery Mana and his customary drinks at the toddy shop, he returned home at dusk. There was invariably a copy of the newspaper *Deshabandhu*[43] in his hand. After dinner, as he lay on the coir cot on the eastern veranda of the house, Chechi read the paper loudly in the light of a kerosene lamp. This responsibility later fell to me. Thanks to the training I had received at the asan kalari, I could read well.

While landownership and manual labour continued as before, high school students and other people with some basic education began to come together with little regard for caste differences. Ichaayan was a member of this fellowship. He had certain physical characteristics that marked him out from among his peers. He was dark, tall and lean. On the left side of his forehead was a protrusion that was clearly visible. He was very particular about cleanliness and wearing good clothes, and did not allow Chechi, Mani or me to compromise on such things. He was a thorough non-conformist, and so, he often picked up quarrels in school or at the playground. The three of us feared him more than Chaachan.

Ichaayan was a discriminating reader. Besides newspapers, he read books borrowed from the library. He was particularly fond of poetry and knew Changampuzha's *Ramanan*[44] by heart. P. Bhaskaran and Vayalar Rama Varma were particular favourites of his and he would recite the works of all the three poets for us. He also used to write poetry. When I was in high school I found a notebook of his in which he had penned a number of poems. A couple of them even came out in publications though not the mainstream ones. Along with this love for poetry, he cultivated a fascination for plays and *kathaprasangams.*[45] He regularly visited churches and temples to see them. He also greatly admired songs in KPAC dramas and film songs as well. He used to sing bits of these songs later, when he became mentally ill.

But it was T.U. Kunju, Chaachan's elder brother's son, who took the lead in activities related to art and literature organized by the above mentioned fellowship. He would be the lead actor in the plays staged during school anniversary functions. He once put up a sterling performance as a blind man in G. Sankara Pillai's *Sabarmati Dooreyaanu* ('Sabarmati is Far Away').

The land was slowly transforming with the emergence of this new generation. Boys began to wear mundus and shirts. The girls wore blouses and skirts, and when they became adolescents, they switched to the half-sari. Parents scrimped and saved to send their children to school. The spoken language of the Pulayas changed too. Their Malayalam, which earlier had a generous sprinkling of Tamil, became chaste. The language of the older generation came to be looked down upon. Football and volleyball captured the imagination of the youth. Arts and sports clubs sprouted, and the Independence Day began to be celebrated. Most of those who participated in such activities later became active Communist party workers.

It was during the 1957 elections that the trajectories of regional politics became discernible, though in a nebulous fashion, in my mind. The celebrations that accompanied the formation of the first Communist government affected me as well. I had wished for the Communist party to win. In my village, the Congress party, like the Communist party, conducted few activities to speak of. However, in the unremarkable sort of programmes that did take place, were led by the Christians, as well as Valyaachan, and a few Ezhavas who supported them.

The first khaddar-clad men I saw came from Kaduthuruthi and Kottayam. Most of these leaders sought out Valyaachan. As he was generous in extending financial support to the local Congressmen, the toddy shop was as crowded during daytime as in the evening. The propaganda that Communists were atheists soon gained currency. On certain evenings, the Congress party conducted demonstrations that began in the market, radiated out in various directions and concluded at different places. Those who led them, with shouts of 'Mahatma Gandhi ki jai' and 'Congress party ki jai', were the goondas of the market. I obviously looked at these demonstrations with distaste.

The victory of the Congress candidate in the Kaduthuruthi constituency had been a foregone conclusion. The celebratory demonstrations began at the market in the evening of the announcement of the results. The Christian troublemakers formed the vanguard of the procession. One of them had a dog on a leash. As was the custom, the procession began at the eastern part and on reaching the western side approached our house. The Congressmen came into the front yard and asked Chaachan to step out. Amma, Ichaayan, Chechi, Mani and I shook with fear. No one could speak a word. Most of the members of the group had at one time or another been helped by Chaachan and Amma, in cash and in kind. Such things seemed to have little relevance in politics driven by vendetta. Realizing that Chaachan was not at home, the members kept aggressively shouting slogans against the Communist party for a long time. Later stating that they had killed and buried Thaithara Kunjan, they beat the dog to death and buried it in our front yard before leaving. None of us could sleep that night.

Despite my support for it, the first Communist government

did not fill me with enthusiasm. I was too young to recognize a momentous change. The other reason was, of course, the inability of the Communist government to effect any significant change. Untouchability wasn't practised as it was once, and this had preceded the government assuming office. There was now little to prevent Pulayas from getting admission in schools or sitting beside and learning along with children of other castes. All of us had the freedom of movement, freedom to worship and freedom to wear clothes. A range of wicked customs of the past had been wiped out, and new Hindu as well as Christian rituals had come into being. These were not the result of conscious interventions made by the Congress or the Communist parties. They were in fact the forgotten achievements of the Renaissance movement.

Yet it would be a stretch to claim that the distinctions of high and low within the caste structure had been removed. Though there few overt signs of repression, other castes were unwilling to accept the Pulayas as their equals. Though there were fellowships that ignored caste differences, cross-gender friendships did not cross caste boundaries. Some of the first glimpses I got of the lives of partners in inter-caste marriages revealed the ugly face of caste-based violence. This was what happened once: A Pulaya youth from my village went to his mother's house at Thalayolapparambu. When his neighbour, an Ezhava woman, stepped out to go to the market, he requested her to purchase a few beedis for him, and gave her some money. This was the extent of their brief interaction. They were not close and certainly not in love. But the woman's father, who noticed the exchange, subjected her to cruel torture and ordered her out of the house. With no alternative in sight, the Pulaya youth and the Ezhava woman came back to my village and got married. I wrote an article about this incident titled 'The Story of an Inter-Caste Marriage' in my column in the SEEDIAN weekly. This article and a request sent to the District Collector of Kottayam helped them get the allowances due to married inter-caste couples. However, their domestic life in the Harijan Colony at Madhuraveli was rife with differences. But not once could the woman gain re-entry into her father's home. Her husband, who became a manual labourer, subsequently committed suicide.

Our eviction from the Kazhuthoottu plot, which too belonged to Neythassery Mana, is the reason why the Communist regime has become an undying memory in my mind. E.M.S. Namboodiripad, the chief minister of the first Communist government, wrote thus about their work of helping agricultural labourers:

> Farmers and other communities in the villages were the first to enjoy the benefits of the Communist government. They experienced it within a week of the government assuming office. The government promulgated an ordinance on 11 April banning all forms of eviction. Not a single tenant, subtenant or hut dweller can be evicted for any reason, including non-payment of lease amount. Besides, all court proceedings initiated by the landlords against their tenants and subtenants have been stopped. Never before have the poor village folk received such an extensive relief from oppression by the landlords.

Namboodiripad's claim was belied by facts, at least as far as my village was concerned. The thousands of acres of land holdings of the Neythassery Mana, which included garden plots and paddy fields, did not have tenants but nearly 20 hut dwellers. They were Ezhavas and Pulayas who worked as farm hands for the mana. The problem that required redress was that of the hut dwellers.

Our eviction took place during the second year of Communist rule. This was the interval between the Land Reforms Ordinance and the Land Reforms Bill. In other words, the Land Reforms Bill had not been passed in the Legislative Assembly then. During the eviction of hut dwellers that took place, the Neythassery Mana took a very liberal stand. If the hut dwellers had a right to 10 cents of land in the panchayat, as per the rules, each of them received somewhere between 15 and 30 cents. They received it not in the plot where they had pitched their huts but at various spots on the periphery of the extensive lands that the Neythassery Mana owned. We did not get any tenancy rights. That may have been because we had our own land or because Chaachan was a Communist. Since he was not aware of the law that would shortly be enforced, Chaachan had no objections either. The Neythassery Mana also bought two-and-a-half acres of land at Madhuraveli, which was uneven and full of rocky outcrops, and gave it to the government for the establishment of a Harijan colony. With this done, the Neythassery Mana was immune to the Land Reforms Bill.

C. Achutha Menon alleges in his memoirs that through his intervention in the Neythassery Mana's affairs before the implementation of the Land Reforms Act, E.M.S. Namboodiripad had actually subverted the spirit of the land reform. I think the Neythassery Mana incident may not have been an isolated one. Similar incidents would have taken place throughout Kerala.

What is the actual fact of the matter? EMS's wife Arya Antharjanam's house was at Kudamalloor near Kottayam. Her younger sister was married to a member of the Ezhumanthuruthu Mana, to the west of Madhuraveli. The families of Neythassery Mana and Ezhumanthuruthu Mana were related. Was it because of family ties or casteist reasons that EMS and V.R. Krishna Iyer made regular visits to the mana and solicited contributions? Whatever the reason, it is clear that it was on the instructions of these leaders that the eviction and establishment of the Harijan colony took place. That was why neither the Neythassery Mana nor Valyaachan, who had nearly 150 acres of land, had to give away their excess land. Later, even before the proclamation of the end of feudalism took place, they divided their land holdings into small bits and sold them. The place saw a huge increase in the number of small landowners as a result.

---

10. The Hunters and the Hunted

Although constructing and living in a house on one's own plot of land was a happy development, the eviction was not. The reason was the peculiarity of the place of stay. Kazhuthoottu parambu was located at the boundary of Kuttanad. There were canals and fields close to the vast coconut farms there. But the thought that activities like bathing, catching and eating fish were not as accessible upset me. What really hurt, though, was the extinction of the fishes and the birds. (It is a subject that Jayasuryan, my son who has a post-graduate degree in environmental studies, has asked me to write about at some point in future.)

The use of chemical fertilizers and pesticides in the paddy fields began during Communist rule in a bid to solve the problem of food grain shortages. Prior to that, only cow dung and green leaves were used as manure. Neythassery Mana had about 16 buffaloes and bulls in their sheds, which were used in the paddy fields to pull the yoke and were valuable for their dung too. The first pesticide to be used in the extensive fields owned by the mana was Folidol. Soon, many species of aquatic life—mudfish, Asian stinging catfish, pearl spot, snapper, lobster and orange chromide, smaller varieties like green stripe barb, Periyar barb and striped panchax—frogs, Asiatic water snakes and other water snakes that lie submerged in mire like the Malabar swamp eel, came up floating dead on the surface of the water in their thousands. It was distressing to see. Subsequently, the crows, storks and eagles that pecked at and gulped these dead fish down fell dead in coconut farms and fields. The stench hung in the village air for days. Fishing was my favourite pastime, and I could not indulge in it now. But for the many fishermen, it meant the loss of their source of livelihood.

Yet the countryside remained largely peaceful during the Communist regime. Samuel, a Dalit Christian who introduced Chaachan to Communism, used to be a regular visitor to our home. I respected that man. He was dark and tall, wore glasses and was past his middle age. He cared for us children like a father. During the time of the Calcutta Thesis, he continued to be active, in hiding or in the open, along with P.S. Sreenivasan and C.K. Vishwanathan. He had to suffer brutal police torture and was jailed too for some time.

The Liberation Struggle—the period of anti-Communist protest in 1958–59—in our area began at the St Thomas Church at Kallara. The vicar of the church rang the bell several times to draw all the local Christians, and called upon them to participate in the struggle. The crowd was so taken up by his speech, that they closed down the St Thomas High School nearby, gathered the teachers and the students, made them join the struggle, giving shape to a Christopher Army centred around the church. The high schools under Nair Service Society[46] management, notably, did not stop working. As waves of the struggle progressed, it moved east, where Christians lived. The western side, where the Ezhavas and the Pulayas resided, remained calm. Yet the demonstrations that began in the market ended on the western side. I used to view these protests with utmost hatred.

The Liberation Struggle was strong at Kaduthuruthi and Muttachira where the Christian population formed the majority. There was widespread violence on the Pulayas here by the Christopher Army. It did not matter whether they were

Communist sympathizers or not. The Ezhavas were attacked too, but it was the Pulaya community that paid the heaviest price. In those days, the Christians would say, '*Pelene thallaan njaanumundu!*' (I too shall join to beat up the Pulaya!) In other words, even those Christians who were apolitical nursed racial hatred. Forty-two houses in the Kaduthuruthi–Muttachira area were torched. After the struggle ended, AKG accompanied T.K. Ramakrishnan and K.K. Joseph to visit these places.

Years later, when the fiftieth anniversary of the Liberation Struggle was being observed, I wrote an edit-page article in *Mathrubhumi* titled 'The Hunters and the Hunted', in which I pointed out that the struggle rose out of the racial hatred that the top brass of the Church harboured against the Ezhavas and the Pulayas. Although articles by Dr Thomas Isaac and Adv Jayasankar admit to Christian participation in the struggle, they remain silent over the racial vengeance that fuelled it. When I pointed this out to Adv Jayasankar, citing facts, he acknowledged them and in the second edition of his book, *Communist Bharanavum Vimochana Samaravum* ('Communist Rule and the Liberation Struggle'), he wrote: 'Soon after the President's proclamation, participants of the Liberation Struggle went on a rampage in the whole of central Kerala. They destroyed the Communist party offices, tortured their activists, raped women and torched huts.'

As most Communists were either Ezhavas or Pulayas, the violent business was quickly and easily executed. Every dark-skinned person was hounded and beaten up. Even toddy shops and the coconut trees earmarked for toddy tapping were not spared. The shops were razed, and bunches of coconuts cut down. Twelve toddy shops were decimated in this manner in North Parur and surrounding areas. Violent incidents took place in areas like Kalady, Malayattoor, Thodupuzha, Ramapuram, Mundakkayam, Cherthala, Pullad, Thevalakkara, Kizhakkekkalada and Kottarakkara.

Kuzhikkattussery, near Mala, was a stronghold of both Catholics and Communists. On 1 August 1958, church bells pealed to call the faithful to assemble. Armed with short sticks, the gangs beat up toddy tappers. A young man named Velayudhan was killed. Seventeen men were grievously injured.

The *Janayugam* carried an editorial on 8 August with the heading 'This draconian rule must end'. On 10 August, Chathan Master published a statement deploring the attacks on members of the Scheduled Castes. The Sree Narayana Dharma Paripalana Yogam (SNDP)[47] leadership was severely displeased by the attacks mounted by the Liberation Struggle participants on the members of their caste. K.P. Narayanan, general secretary of the SNDP and Congress leader, even informed the KPCC (Kerala Pradesh Congress Committee) president, a member of his own caste, of these developments. All this is to point out that there was little doubt the Liberation Struggle was a series of racial attacks on the Ezhavas and the Dalits.

The experiences during the Renaissance proved that the Ezhavas and the Dalits were capable of resisting such attacks. But what happened during the Liberation Struggle? The Christians organized themselves under the church, and the Nairs, under the leadership of Mannath Padmanabhan. As a result, these communities could be easily converted into mobs. The Ezhavas and the Pulayas within the Communist party met these mobs as individuals, not as groups. Had it be otherwise, the Struggle would not have succeeded. Unfortunately, the communism of E.M.S. Namboodiripad and Dr Thomas Isaac did not permit the Ezhavas and the Pulayas to organize themselves or form a communitarian identity to resist and quell the attack.

---

11. The Steps

When we were evicted from Kazhuthoottu parambu, we moved to our own, called Parayan parambu, put up a shed there, and started living in it. This garden plot too was in Madhuraveli, on the western side of the Kaduthuruthi–Kallara road. From the legends that have been transmitted by old timers, this is what we knew about Parayan parambu:

At some point in the remote past, the Parayas of the village rebelled against the Vadakkumkoor dynasty that had its capital at Kaduthuruthi. The royal army not only suppressed the rebellion but also drove all the Parayas, women and children included, to Parayan parambu, dismembered them and wiped out their line. That was why, the belief goes, there were no Parayas in the land. On this ground, long back, ghosts would scream at night and dance as if possessed!

Whatever may or may not have happened, there was a *kaavu*[48]-like spot, full of trees, creepers and climbers, in the middle of the southern boundary of the plot that stood as their memorial. Full of wild rocks, that area was never cleared.

My high school education began with my joining the seventh standard in the NSS High School at Kallara. It was one-and-a-half kilometres from my house. The school comprised five huge buildings with many classrooms in it. There was a vast playground as well. There were many students—boys and girls—and a lot of teachers. P. Krishna Pillai, who had a close bond of friendship with Mannath Padmanabhan, the NSS Karayogam Secretary, and was locally known as Kallara Mannam, was its manager. He was a regular speaker at public functions in the area, including inaugurations of local clubs and reading rooms. Most of the teachers, and even the peons, were members of the Nair community. A few of them were the manager's relatives.

Although the students belonged to all castes and even to the Christian religion, there was no discrimination on the basis of caste or religion. Without their caste identity being mentioned, students eligible for lump sum grants were called by their names and instructed to bring their guardians to school. Once every week, there was a meeting of the literary club in every class, which gave students opportunities to sing, deliver speeches, present solo acts or participate in other cultural programmes. Only once did I make preparations to deliver a speech. The subject was Kalidasa. I had rehearsed all the points in my mind before stepping onto the stage. But as soon as I saw the crowd, stage fright took over. My arms and legs began to tremble. No words came out, however hard I tried. After a few minutes, all I could utter was, 'Maha…' The collective laughter it provoked among the students was so thunderous that I withdrew. I never made a second attempt.

Small story books, including Greek legends, were given on loan by the school library. It was through them that Hercules, Narcissus, Procrustes and others became part of my imagination. But what held my attention for the longest period of time was a Japanese folk tale:

A boy from the countryside of Japan regularly went to sea in order to fish. The money he made out of selling his catch helped him look after his elderly parents. So he took up fishing as his profession. But one day, despite waiting till the evening, he could not catch any. Just when he was about to wind up in utter disappointment, he caught a small fish that was exceptionally attractive, and had an unusual body. The scales were golden in colour. The boy removed the fish from the hook, and held it in his cupped hands. At that moment, the fish said, 'I am not an ordinary fish. I am a princess, the daughter of the king of this sea. If you free me, I shall grant you all the fortunes of life. You'll remain youthful for a very long period.' Hearing this, the boy released the fish into the sea and returned home.

The next day, when the boy went to the sea shore with his fishing line, the fish called him and invited him into the depths of the ocean, taking the boy to her palace. The lavishly decorated palace was a feast to his eyes. It contained all the pleasures the world could offer. Household items were made of gold, and studded with precious stones. The food tasted divine. As soon as the boy entered the palace, the princess touched him with a finger. Immediately, he was transformed into a handsome youth. Subsequently, they married each other. Even with the passage of many years, the man did not lose his youthful looks.

Aeons passed by. One day, he felt the desire to see his parents and his relatives. When he spoke of his desire to the princess, she was initially reluctant to let go of him. But finally she gave him her consent. As he was about to set out, the princess gave him a tiny box and said, 'You should not open this box.' She then transported him to the sea shore. On reaching his village, the youth could not locate his parents or his relatives. The land itself had changed. He was a stranger to all the people living there. So, he desired to return to the palace under the sea. On reaching the sea shore, he called his wife. His voice echoed back to him but the princess did not appear. Driven by sorrow, but hope as well, he opened the box. A swirl of air flowed out. What the box contained was the years of his life. Suddenly, he became a wizened old man and fell down dead on the sea shore.

The desire to live long was what made the story capture my imagination. At night, when I felt lonely, I yearned for a deathless existence.

I had an irrepressible fascination for books. Besides reading the books from our school library, I borrowed from the Ayamkudi Mahatma Reading Room as well. I was more interested in novels. For some reason, during that phase, I was not drawn to detective fiction. I did not read the novels of Muttathu

Varkey,[49] or Kanam E.J.[50] I did read Varkey's *Mayilaadum Kunnu* ('The Hill where the Peacock Dances') when Chechi once brought home a copy. But what interested me were the works of Thakazhi, Kesavadev, Uroob, Basheer and M.T. Vasudevan Nair. The usual pattern was to read as much of a writer's canon as possible. Among them, my favourites were Basheer's *Balyakaala Sakhi* ('Childhood Girlfriend') and M.T. Vasudevan Nair's *Manju* ('Mist'); I even knew many parts of *Manju* by heart. Vilasini's *Niramulla Nizhalukal* ('Colourful Shadows') was another favourite. From Malayalam, I turned to Bengali novels and later to Tolstoy, Sholokhov and others. Besides, I read Nehru's *Discovery of India* and *Glimpses of World History*, H.G. Wells's *The Outline of History*, and Rahul Sankrityayan's works, and several others. Among these, the one that played a huge role in shaping my awareness about life was Kuttykrishna Marar's *Bharataparyatanam* ('A Journey through the *Mahabharata*'). What attracted me more than the analysis it contained was its moral compass. This, later on, led me to read the Bible, the Bhagavat Gita, the Upanishads and so on. It brought me to the conclusion that human life rests on universal values.

The annual function at school played a big role in helping me develop my aesthetic sensibility. It usually lasted two days. The students performed dance, music and solo acts. The most well-known singer at school was a tenth standard student named Yohannan. He had a booming voice. I remember when he sang 'Aakaashagangayude karayil', a song from the film *Kannum Karalum*, it was greeted with thunderous applause. I later came to know that this gifted singer had lost his mind and now led the life of a vagrant. Girls presented Kumaran Asan's 'Karuna' and 'Chandalabhikshuki', Changampuzha's 'Vaazhakkula', and G. Sankara Kurup's 'Chandanakattil' in dance form. Former students staged plays written by Ponkunnam Varkey and K.T.

Mohammed. Besides these, on the Chathayam Day celebrations conducted by the SNDP, Sambasivan, Edakochi Prabhakaran, Kedamangalam Sadanandan, V. Harshakumar and others presented kathaprasangam. I enjoyed them immensely and also the plays staged by the KPAC and the Kalidasa Kala Kendram.

It was when I was a seventh standard student that I acted in a play for the first time. The person who made it possible was the young vicar of Madhuraveli church. He used to stay in a building close to the church. He knew me since the time I was in primary school and was very affectionate towards me. Occasionally, he even gave me snacks. The vicar had written a short play based on the Bible, the Gospel according to St Luke in the New Testament, to be precise:

A man had two sons. The younger one told his father one day, 'Father, give me a share of the wealth.' The father gave him his share. Before long, the younger son gathered all his wealth and left for a faraway land, led a wayward life and squandered all his money. Around that time, the land experienced intense famine. He began to suffer greatly, and sought refuge in a house of a village where he was given the job of supervising the grazing swine in the fields. He desired to appease his hunger by consuming the pods of beans the swine were given to eat but no one offered him anything. When good sense finally dawned on him, he said to himself, 'All the labourers employed by my father get enough food to eat. They are even able to set apart a portion of it. On the other hand, here I am about to die of hunger. I shall go to my father and tell him, "I have sinned in the eyes of Heaven and you. I am not worthy of being called your son. Please consider me as one of your workers."' Eventually, the kind father forgave and welcomed him home.

When this story was rewritten into a play, the vicar chose me to play the role of the prodigal son. He directed it himself, and it was staged along with other cultural programmes as part of the Independence Day celebrations. I got good responses for my acting. Later, all the children who had participated in the cultural programme, as well as some others, were brought together to form a Mahatma Children's Association, of which I was made the secretary. The vicar was not only a patron of the organization but a fine mentor too.

Although the vicar was transferred to another place, the activities of the association continued for two more years. Thirty years later, the priest, by then an old man, happened to visit Madhuraveli. I was away at the time, working in the KSRTC (Kerala State Road Transport Corporation) office at Sultan Bathery. My family was going through a severe financial crisis then. They were staying in a thatched house with mud walls. It was to this house that the priest came in search of me. When he enquired about my job, Mani told him about my position as a clerk in the KSRTC. The priest was surprised I had not done better for myself.

When I was studying in the eighth standard, a girl in the seventh became infatuated with me. She belonged to a poor Christian family. She used to walk past my house on her way to school. I would invariably be either in front of or behind her. Although the acquaintance lasted two years, we spoke to each other only a couple of times. That teenage romance did not last. The tragedies at home forced me to keep away from such things. The girl, too, when she came to know about them, through village gossip, did not wish to become a part of the misfortune and opted to distance herself. It was impossible to act otherwise.

12. Shadow Lands

Our house had two rooms, a tiny anteroom that served as a toilet, and a kitchen. It had a tiled roof, its walls were painted with limestone solution and had wooden doors and windows. In those days, Pulayas who had a house with a tiled roof were rare. The majority of them lived in houses whose roofs were made of hay or woven coconut leaves. Amma had some ideas about better living standards. So, when we could afford to have cots, stools, tables, benches and other household items, she disposed of the old earthen pots and pans, replacing them with aluminium ware. In short, years back, even though we were not prosperous, we had fairly decent living conditions. My younger brother Baburaj was born in this house.

From the beginning of the 1960s, vegetable farming became very popular all over the village. Although Chaachan and Amma did manual labour at Neythassery Mana, they did not get enough that could cover daily household expenses and our tuition fees. So, we started vegetable farming too.

On Tuesdays and Saturdays, when the market opened, numerous people went there with headloads of vegetables. As it was possible to return before 8.30 in the morning, I accompanied Chaachan to the market regularly, even on school days. I was, as I've said earlier, quite a glutton. These trips to the market made possible visits to the tea shop to have two dosas and chammanti. During harvest season, when we had paddy in plentiful quantity, Amma would buy these from the shop for all six of us.

The main food during mornings and evenings was tapioca; the curry was invariably chammanti, made by crushing roasted chilly and onion on the grinding stone. Sometimes we got baked dry fish. Rice was cooked for lunch only on the days we went to school. The side dish was chammanti made from onion or bitter gourd. Believing our curry to be of inferior quality, I sat in a secluded spot away from my friends' line of vision and ate it. At home, we never had tea or coffee with milk and sugar. We went to the provisions store or to the market, bought the skin of coffee beans, added coriander seeds and roasted the mixture to made coffee. At tea time, in the evening, we ate jaggery. Amma grew purple yam, elephant yam and colocasia in our garden plot. Moderately well-off families did not consume banana flowers, banana stem, Chinese senna, jackfruit or colocasia stem, as they were considered poor man's food. As a result, only the Pulayas ate them. I think the basis of this hardworking community's robust health and long life was the food sourced directly from nature. In these modern times, such items have found their way to everyone's diet. Amma grew a lot of chickens. This ensured chicken meat once in a while. The chickens were sold at Kuruppunthara market.

One of my clearest memories of the time is of the Indo-China war. It occupied the newspapers, radio news, leaders' statements and even discussions in front of tea shops. No one gave serious thought to the Communists' pro-China stand. Everyone rooted for India and was against China. Even students could not escape being submerged in this ocean of emotions. The Prime Minister was 'Chacha' (uncle) Nehru to the children. Many solidarity rallies were taken out to proclaim allegiance to him. Newspapers brought to the readers stories of victory of our army. The result of these reports was that patriotism, along with an irrepressible desire to wipe out China from the face of the earth, arose in every citizen's heart.

Every day, the NSS High School at Kallara, where I studied, pasted newspaper reports of the war on a blackboard installed in its central playground. Crowds of boys and girls assembled there to read it in the morning. Reading it was the first thing I did on stepping into the school premises. In the evening, I re-read it in the tea shop or the barbershop, turning my patriotism to jingoism. I also happened to see at this time a play staged by some youth at Manvettom. The plot revolved around a young man who, fired by patriotism, sought the permission and blessings of his parents and joined the army. The play overwhelmed me so much that I too wanted to join the army and serve my country.

When this desire became very strong, I wrote a story. The subject was war. I tore three or four pages from a notebook and filled it with whatever my imagination came up with. I can't recall either its title or its contents now. What I do remember is that the word 'I' was repeated a couple of times in nearly every sentence. Written secretly, under the light of a kerosene lamp, when it was finally completed, I showed it to my classmate and friend M.S. Sasidharan Nair. He read the story and gave me positive feedback. The only publication I knew was the *Malayala Manorama* weekly. So, my friend and I went to a post office, bought an envelope, and sent it to the *Malayala Manorama* office at Kottayam. The following weeks passed by in sheer anxiety. I believed that the story would get published. Every week I would pick up the weekly and look for my story. Eventually, I realized that it likely would never see the light of day. Thereafter, not only did my hope vanish but my interest in literary writing too. But this did not affect my reading.

We faced a severe financial crisis when Ichaayan was doing his first year BA course in NSS College, Changanassery, and Chechi was in her first year pre-university course in Devaswom College, Thalayolapparambu. It became impossible to cover the expenses on clothes, textbooks and notebooks required for high school and college education over and above the daily needs of the family with the wages Amma and Chaachan got and our earnings from the garden plot. Chaachan saw a way out by selling our landed property. And so, a portion of the Kodukuthy parambu was sold. There was no other option.

Chaachan had allowed two men—Joseph and Devasia—to put up their shops in that part of our garden plot which was close to the road. He had done this on a purely humanitarian consideration. But a rumour soon spread that my Chechi and Joseph were romantically involved. Chechi later told me that this was not true. Raised under the watchful eye of Ichaayan, she could never have entertained such an idea. But there were some people in the village that weren't particularly fond of our family and Chechi in particular, and the rumour about the romance found fertile ground. The Thaithara family, which included us, was fairly prosperous, and more educated than many others. However, we were highly orthodox, submitting ourselves to very severe casteist moral rules. All our relatives became enraged when it was suspected that a member of this large family had a relationship that crossed caste boundaries.

One day when I was away at school, Valyaachan and other relatives came home and subjected Chechi to questioning. Chaachan even beat her in front of all of them. Chechi maintained her innocence, repeating to Chaachan what she had said after the relatives had left. A few days later, she started going to college once again. But Joseph followed her to her college, and threatened to commit suicide. Soon after, Chechi eloped with him to Kasaragod. Our relatives were furious. They even boycotted us. To everyone in the family, with the exception of Baburaj, who was a small child, Chechi's departure was unbearable. We all loved her dearly.

Chaachan was devastated. For a long time, he stopped going to work. He drank excessively, spent his time playing cards and smoking, and often quarrelled with Amma. Yet, amidst the family fissures, money had to be made to cover our daily expenses. The remaining plot at Kodukuthy had to be sold off too.

Eventually, Chaachan brought Chechi back and admitted her to a teacher's training course at a training school in Ettumanoor. Even before she completed her course she got a job as a teacher in Kasaragod. His interaction with the Communist party had made Chaachan indifferent to caste and religious differences. It was probably why he could defy the opposition of our orthodox relatives and bring back Chechi. Our love for Chechi was so deep that we were not only not prepared to disown her but also wanted to see her settle down in life and do well for herself. Chechi, for her part, felt an obligation to Chaachan which she honoured till the end of his life. Every month, she would send a portion of her salary to Chaachan. She did not miss once. Later, when she became head mistress of her school, she would send Chaachan Rs 300 every month.

---

13. Tree with Fallen Branches

What made tragedy a fixture in our family was Ichaayan's severe psychiatric illness. I was in the tenth standard at the time. The teachers had high hopes of me. The other such student in our class was Mukundan from Kallara. Despite the turmoil Chechi's departure had caused, I was determined to study and do well in life, and for that reason, I was sure I would earn a creditable pass. It was around this time that Ichaayan came back home mentally disabled.

One day, a group of students, Ichaayan's hostel mates at NSS College, Changanassery, brought him home in a taxi, his arms and legs bound. What we learnt from them was that Ichaayan had flung his lunch away and fled outside, roaring. They followed after him and found him lying on the ground with his head resting on the railway line. Though they were able to coax him somehow and bring him back to the hostel, they were forced to tie his arms and legs up when he became violent.

It was an unbearable sight. He wasn't merely the eldest sibling. He was like a guardian. Everyone, irrespective of age, used to call him 'Ammavan'. He was acknowledged throughout our village as the first Pulaya youth to do a BA course. Ichaayan incoherently muttered something and asked us to untie him. Those who were assembled there did not dare do so, fearing the consequences. A few among our relatives and fellow villagers who reached our house by evening suggested that we take him to the mental hospital at Oolamppara in Thiruvananthapuram. That very night, promising to give him a piece of our garden plot, we borrowed a big sum of money from Chackochan, our neighbour. One of our relatives arranged for a taxi for early the next morning. No food was prepared at home that night. No one slept either. Silence pervaded the entire house. It was as if a death had taken place. Ichaayan alone kept up a steady monologue.

Early the next morning, when the taxi appeared, Chaachan and three of his relatives took Ichaayan, still bound, to Thiruvananthapuram. On reaching there, Chaachan personally met the health minister, P.S. Sreenivasan and told him about what had happened. Not only did he lend a sympathetic ear, he even went to the hospital and spoke to the superintendent, Dr K.J. Jacob, a psychiatrist well known all over India. The doctor told Chaachan that Ichaayan was suffering from chronic schizophrenia. It was not completely curable but its intensity, they were told, could be brought down with care and medicine. It was when I read the doctor's series on mental illness in *Mathrubhumi* that I came to understand the seriousness of Ichaayan's condition.

Although Ichaayan was brought back home, after a long spell of treatment at Oolamppara, he never recovered fully.

Half a century back, *insanity* was not a mental illness but a curse. A swirl of superstitions and mystery surrounded it. There were a lot of interpretations about Ichaayan's illness. The most prominent one was that it was caused by too much reading. Another was that it was the result of disappointment in love! Yet another was that it had been brought on by a Brahmin's curse because Chaachan had plucked coconuts from the garden plots of Namboodiris and sold them. Amidst all this, not only the patient but his family too was feared and avoided. In most cases, such an attitude led to patients either being stripped naked, chained inside a dark and closed room, and left to defecate and urinate where they lay, without the comfort of care or treatment; or abandoned on the streets where they wandered unclean and unwashed, attracting everyone's disgust and hatred. Our relatives looked at Ichaayan and all of us not with sympathy but disdain. Our house became isolated, like a branch that fell off a tree.

Amma believed that Ichaayan's illness was caused by spirits that had possessed him. She consulted Moolethara Azhakan and asked him to exorcise the spirits. When this failed to cure Ichaayan, Amma suspected someone had poisoned him with the help of black magic. So Ichaayan was taken to the Thiruvizha temple near Cherthala, where after some special pujas he was given milk to drink from a very ancient, verdigris-lined bronze tumbler. The belief was that after drinking the milk, if the person vomited, he would be cured of the poison. When this failed to deliver results too, an astrologer was consulted, and on his advice and under his supervision, an extremely costly *homam*, or ritual sacrifice, was conducted. With that doing little good either, he was admitted once again to the Oolamppara hospital. Whenever he came back and took his medication regularly, he would have some peace. Later, when he refused to take them, we began to conceal it in his food. But gradually, that too became impossible to do, and Ichaayan completely lost his mind. He gave up brushing his teeth, taking bath or changing clothes, preferring to wander about here and there during the day, and spending sleepless nights singing old songs he remembered from plays and films.

Soon enough, we had no land left. With the dwindling of job opportunities in the agricultural sector and the inadequacy of the wages to meet the expenses of a seven-member family, we had to sell off what remained to cover Ichaayan's treatment.

As soon as it became public that land reforms were about to be implemented, people with surplus land quickly began to sell it. With the partial execution of land reforms in 1963, large-scale land ownership that was centralized in the hands of a few underwent a process of fragmentation into decentralized lands. The beneficiaries of this change were the middle-level communities comprising various types of lease holders. Most of them were Nairs, Christians and a few Ezhavas. What the Dalits got were ten-, five- and three-cent lands or houses in the Harijan Laksham Veedu colony—the One Lakh Housing Scheme launched in 1972 during the tenure of the C. Achutha Menon government—as per the rights accorded to hut dwellers. The process of landlords, including small landowners, switching from crops like ginger, tapioca and banana, which had repetitive agricultural cycles, to cultivating rubber, had been underway since before the Land Reforms Act was put in force, and continued thereafter. It took seven to eight years for landowners to earn a profit from rubber, so they had to suffer a financial deficit for a brief period. The result was that many opted for paddy cultivation as it yielded quicker crops. This new development grievously affected wage labourers.

Many paddy fields in places close to Upper Kuttanad became sites of conflict. Numerous people, including those from Harijan colonies, that were the residential places of Dalits, converged on the paddy fields for work. They spent the nights on the ridges of the fields and, disregarding the preventive steps taken by the landlords, began to work from early morning. It was when the landlords and their supporters tried to use violence in order to stop them from working that fights broke out at numerous paddy fields. Chaachan and Amma kept away from all this. The Kerala Congress broke off from the Indian National Congress in 1964 ostensibly with the aim of confronting the social conflicts erupting in the agricultural sector. Most of the landowners, as I said above, were from Nair and Christian communities whereas a good majority of the workers were Dalits and Ezhavas. The very purpose of the birth of the Kerala Congress was to not only protect the interests of the Nair and Christian communities but also to put down the Dalits who were agricultural workers. Such a stark truth was concealed so effectively that its birth was attributed to infighting within the Congress.

No conflicts between the Ezhavas and the Christians took place anywhere in the land as they usually did during the time of the Liberation Struggle. In fact, most of them were directed against the Dalits. The reason the Congress did not come forward to oppress the Dalits was that it had had to face widespread criticism over its inaction during the Liberation Struggle. The second reason was the election result following the Liberation Struggle. Although the Communist party and the independents who supported it got only 29 seats, the party garnered 36.8 per cent of votes and the independents, 6.2 per cent. What this revealed was that the Congress could not shake the Ezhava–Dalit foundation of the Communist party.

At around the same time, the Communist party too was

undergoing changes. The measures taken to bring in financial reforms by the government in 1957 benefited mostly the Ezhavas. With toddy tapping expanding almost like a service sector, the financial status of the Ezhavas improved considerably. They gained an upper hand in the toddy business. Over and above all this, capital investment in the coir, cashew and handloom sectors as well as government control in the form of corporations and boards, besides creating economic prosperity, also gave birth to an organized employment sector. The land reforms that subsequently came led to the inception of a class of landowners among the Ezhavas. When the Communist party split in 1964, it was the social and economic status gained by the Ezhavas that formed the foundation of the CPI more than its ideological positions. In short, the split in the Communist party brought about a political division within the Ezhava community. As the financially backward segments refused to integrate themselves with the prosperous middle class of the CPI, they aligned themselves with the Communist Party of India (Marxist).

The peasants' movement spearheaded by the CPI(M) in the state, however, did not conduct struggles that focused on economic rights. So, those who worked on the garden plots and fields of Neythassery Mana continued to be in the same state as before. At the same time, peasants, including those living in the colonies, entered the workforce on a massive scale as a result of the pressure in the agricultural sector. This had an adverse effect on the Ezhavas and the Pulayas who worked in a traditional manner at Neythassery Mana. They now had fewer days of work. Chaachan and Amma fell victim to this predicament. Maybe obsequiousness towards Namboodiris and the ownership of small land holdings had made them reluctant to work on others' fields and plots and become agricultural labourers. And the stress on the family, caused by Ichaayan's illness, came in the way of working in our own plot.

I felt that the cold climate of Wayanad would have a positive effect on Ichaayan's condition. Besides, the relocation would spare us the scorn of neighbours and relatives over the selling of portions of our land. So I suggested that we dispose of the rest of our property and shift to Wayanad.

14. The Spiral Staircase

I joined the second group (a combination of Physics, Chemistry, Botany and Zoology) at Maharaja's College in Kochi to do my pre-degree course. I wanted to become a medical doctor. That would be a solution to the problems at home, I felt. With dark clouds casting shadows on the lives of Ichaayan and Chechi, I was now the sole source of hope for the family. Given that I had secured high marks in the SSLC examination, and did not have any sharp edges to my personality, everyone believed I would indeed become a doctor.

T.V. Kunju, who was an alumnus of Maharaja's College, had suggested this institution to me for higher studies. I went along with Chaachan for the interview. We were accompanied by C.R. Ramachandran and his father Raman from Kappikkadu. This was my first trip to a city. I had never travelled beyond Kaduthuruthi and Thalayolapparambu and was overcome by fear and consternation. I would stand confused at intersections, unable to identify directions. And yet, while we walked from the railway station to college, the sight of the intertwining streets and the unusual vehicles in that huge city made me happy too.

Coming as I did from a remote village like Madhuraveli, the college was another world altogether. The buildings whose two storeys seemed laden with the past were interconnected in a square configuration. There was a uniqueness and a regal grandeur to the architecture of buildings of Maharaja's college. It was little wonder, then, that it evoked such nostalgia in its former students. The spiral staircase close to the Department of Botany, for instance, became a character in R. Prasad's story. The classrooms were of different sizes, and some were galleries. Pungent smells wafted from the laboratories.

Life in the college was a lot different from what I had known until then. I tried to focus my attention on studies as best I could, attending all classes, hoping to secure a job soon after my education. I was only one among the numerous students in the college. Hostel life was a totally new experience. At home I used to spread a pandanus leaf mat on the cement floor whenever I wanted to go to sleep. In the hostel we had a cot, a mattress and a mosquito net. The food served at the mess was good. Tea and breakfast was served in the morning. In the afternoon, fish, meat or egg and curries were served along with rice. In the evening, after our classes, we had tea and snacks. At night, it was chappati and chicken curry or dal. Chappatis were new to me, but I was glad to have them, and all the rest of it. It was a release from the life of half-starvation I suffered at home.

My roommates at the hostel were K.K. Sukumaran and another student. Sukumaran was from Mulanthuruthy. His father was a teacher who had been severely threatened by the police for his participation in an NGO—or non-gazetted officer—teachers' strike led by the CPI(M). Sukumaran was a CPI(M) loyalist himself. The student in the adjoining room was K.C. Vijayan from Kanjiramuttam whose father was an upper division clerk in the Education Department. My friendship with them was not due to political affiliations.

During my time here, I rarely read any books or magazines. I mostly read newspapers. It was almost as if I had forgotten the days when I used to read novels and science books at home. As I was a staunch believer, I made it a practice to go to the Shiva temple near the Durbar Hall grounds almost every evening. Occasionally, I even went to the Subhas Bose Park and listened to film songs at seven in the evening.

It was during my second year that things turned topsy-turvy. Initially, it was because of the prevailing circumstances in the college and the hostel. A fellowship developed here which was based on caste relations. Many students who came to Maharaja's College generally had high marks and were financially better off than the rest. The stipends as well as lump sum grants that the latter received marked out their caste. Instead of being recognized as constituting a right due to the community, the stipends and lump sum grants only served to create a feeling of inferiority among the Dalit students. Given that their parents were employed in agriculture, the Dalit students generally gravitated towards the Left.

Among the Dalit students, Sukumaran and I were the ones who wore our political affiliation on our sleeve. Not only did we participate in the meetings of the party and its feeder organizations that took place in the city, we also regularly listened to broadcasts of the leaders' speeches. When a demonstration of the party's plenum took place at Ernakulam, it was T.K. Ramachandran who led the students of Maharaja's College. We shouted slogans like 'EMS, AKG, Sundarayya Zindabad' and also 'Tata-Birla Constitution, Black marketers' Constitution / We don't want this Constitution' with equal enthusiasm. Alongside these overt activities we subscribed to the *Deshabhimani*, a daily owned by the Kerala state committee of the CPI(M), read the booklets distributed at party meetings and bought books from the Deshabhimani book stall. We kept up with information about the Communist movement, the paths of various struggles the party had taken, the Vietnam War that was raging against America, the headway made by the Communist parties the world over and so on. Not long afterwards, I abandoned the religious faith I had since childhood. On holidays, I returned home, an absolute rationalist. I spoke ardently about the non-existence of God in front of the ordinary people who came to the tea shop in our garden plot. None of their counter-arguments could shake my new belief.

The Students' Federation at college, which had the support of the CPI(M), was very weak. At a district meeting convened at the TDM Hall, in which K. Satchidanandan (he would later become a famous poet) participated, there were fewer than 30 students that formed the audience. In such circumstances, in the college union elections, it was the Kerala Students Union, of the INC, that won all the seats.

During a vacation, when I went to my village, I learnt that a peasants' union had been formed with Thacheril Chacko as president and P.K. Kochu as secretary. The union inspired a lot of hope and enthusiasm. It was led by the CPI(M), and a great majority of its members were Pulayas. I wanted to improve the lives of Pulayas, including those of the residents of the Harijan colony, who worked on garden plots and fields. Their demands—fewer hours of work, better salaries and one-eighth of patham—seemed just. A conversation I had with P.K. Kochu, who was my relative, revealed that the struggle had begun on the fields owned by the Neythassery Mana. Although my Valyaachan was the manager there and several of my relatives, Chaachan included, worked for the mana, I spoke to the secretary of my willingness to participate in the struggle. I was happy, not only because this was going to be my first stint in a struggle, but also because it was a peasants' struggle.

The number of people who came out to the fields of

Neythassery Mana for the strike was meagre. None of them were my relatives or even regular workers of the mana. Only two or three of them were from the same village, and they were party activists. The rest came from Kaduthuruthi, Ayamkudi, Kallara and other areas. When the strikers reached the venue, at about 7:30 am, the regular workers had already begun their work of tilling the soil. Valyaachan was seated on the ridge. As soon as they saw the red flag-holding strikers, the workers stepped out of the fields and clambered onto dry land. Thacheri Chacko spoke to Valyaachan and put forth the demands. At eight o' clock, as soon as P.K. Kochu waved the red flag, all the strikers, including myself, stepped into the field, holding our spades, and started working the soil. A little later, Valyaachan left. The union office bearers had made arrangements for our lunch. By five in the evening, when the party flag was waved at the ridge, we stopped our work. Later, the union president and the secretary went to the mana and held discussions with the junior Namboodiri as well as Valyaachan. All our demands were met.

Within two years of this incident, the mana divided its extensive garden plots and fields into small units and sold them. Thus, when, on 1 January 1970, it was formally declared that feudalism had come to an end, the Namboodiris who had always profited off their lands were no longer landlords. They had become owners of plots of land that were legitimate in the eyes of the law.

The paddy fields of Marangattu Mana at Kappikkadu were the next site of our struggle. This too was led by Thacheri Chacko and P.K. Kochu. The participation in my first struggle and its victorious conclusion had filled me with great zeal and I joined the next strike with much enthusiasm. There were no supervisors of the mana in sight that day. Our work started at eight in the morning with the waving of the red flag. Besides party workers, a few of the labourers who used to work for the mana too were involved in the strike. As decided by the union, the work had to come to an end at five in the evening, at which time the secretary duly waved the flag. But a little more of the tilling work still remained, and when the workers stopped at five, the president told them to finish it. Nobody objected, though clearly it would require an extra hour of work. And so, I remonstrated, 'The work has to stop!' The president and the secretary yelled at me. With the rest of the workers carrying on with the work, I flung my spade away and came out of the field. I did not bother to collect my day's wages. I later came to know that the party had taken up the field work on contract! I felt intense hatred, for both the union as well as the party.

The incident haunted me for several days. My faith had been betrayed. I had been humiliated and the peasants had been cheated. At around the same time, there were a few activists of the CPI(M-L)—the Communist Party of India (Marxist-Leninist), the Naxalite splinter group of the CPI(M)—in the neighbourhood too, but I did not establish contact with any of them. I prepared a notice titled 'Vilayiruthal' ('Evaluation'), expressing my opposition to the union and loyalty towards agricultural labourers. That was my first political article. Although I do not recall the details of its contents, I remember alleging that the peasants' union behaved like a landlord in making the labourers work like slaves; the American Blacks had been exploited in the same manner and their leaders were betrayers. The notice created a furore in the village. It seriously affected not only the peasants' union but the party as well. CPI(M) leaders put up stiff resistance, by propagating that the Naxalites had begun to rear their head in the village.

By the time I returned to college, my faith in the party had eroded completely. I discontinued my subscription to *Deshabhimani*, stopped reading party literature and attending the party meetings. It was in the midst of this turmoil in my head that I took my exams. I did not have the faintest hope of passing. But when the results came out, I found that nearly all the Dalit students had passed, including myself.

When I applied to Maharaja's College once again, this time for admission to the graduate programme, I had abandoned my desire to become a medical doctor. In my application form, I indicated that History was my first choice, Malayalam my second, and Botany the third. When I appeared for the interview, however, I was seen as a politician, and admitted thereafter to the BSc course in Botany—shackled to a subject that I had no interest in.

15. Fiction Writing and Facts

Once again, I joined the New Hostel. On the ground floor, next to the room that K.K. Sukumaran and I occupied, were P.V. Krishnan Nair, who had joined for MA in Hindi, and Melath Chandrasekharan who had joined for MA in Malayalam. Both of them were affiliated to the KSU and came from Payyannur. Krishnan Nair, with his warm, polite and sincere nature, earned everyone's respect. To all, including the seniors, he was Krishn*ettan*.[51] Chandrasekharan, on the other hand, was a man of few words. I was close to both and had free access to their room. I used to borrow money from Krishnettan all the time, and never bothered to pay back small amounts. He never asked me to return the more substantial loans either, but I repaid him, because I knew I would have to invariably approach him again in future. He was and remained a very good friend of mine. Many, many years later, it was only when Krishnettan became the secretary did I get an opportunity to participate in Sahitya Akademi programmes in my capacity as a writer.

The shelf in their room was full of books and periodicals. Most of Chandrasekharan's books were poetic anthologies. Krishnettan's collection had works on literary criticism. Besides, they subscribed to magazines like the *Mathrubhumi*, *Anveshanam*, *Yugareshmi* and so on. To me, who until then had known only about the *Malayala Manorama*, this was a revelation. I felt I might not be able to understand them as they focused on modern compositions. Precisely for that reason, I didn't bother to read them.

I once went to their room when Krishnettan and Chandrasekharan were away. There was a notebook on the table. I leafed through its pages for fun. They contained poems written by Chandrasekharan. The poems fascinated me not because of the new reading experience they afforded but because this was my first acquaintance with a poet. It gave me goose bumps. Mixed feelings washed over me. I wondered why I could not write such things myself. Poems and stories had not really been part of my reading experience. Until then, I had read only novels, scientific books and party literature.

Works of modernist literature—the stories of O.V. Vijayan, Kakkanadan, M. Mukundan and others, and the poetry of Ayyappa Paniker, N.N. Kakkad, M.N. Paloor—were unfamiliar to me. Such works usually got published in magazines. Chandrasekharan's collection on the other hand contained textbooks and the poetic works of Sugathakumari, Vylopilly, Edasseri, P. Kunhiraman Nair and others. In an effort to become a writer, I began to take books from this collection and read them. I also read plays and works of literary criticism. It was then that I came to learn of other teachers at the college teachers like S. Guptan Nair, M. Leelavathy and M. Achuthan. Among all of them, the most noteworthy and informative classes were those of M.K. Sanu Master. His classes, during which he went beyond prescribed textbooks and talked about contemporary and world literature using simple language, played a major role in expanding the horizons of my literary consciousness.

I soon began to purchase *Sameeksha*, *Kerala Digest*, *Gopuram*, *Anveshanam* and books I had become newly interested in at a cheap rates from second-hand bookshops on Broadway. Later, I would go to the Sahitya Parishad Hall to listen to lectures by Sukumar Azhikode and others like him. It was during this spring season of reading that I began to appreciate the intellectuals in the campus like T.K. Ramachandran and Satchidanandan. The latter's poem 'Megham' ('Cloud'), which appeared in the college magazine, was one that I used to recite frequently. I can still recall the first couple of lines of that poem. A work whose craftsmanship overwhelmed me was K.P. Nirmalkumar's 'Chelakkarayude Atheetha Swapnangal' ('Chelakkara's Dreams of the Past') which appeared in *Mathrubhumi*.

When I realized that reading Malayalam works alone was not going to be enough if I wished to deepen my literary sensibility, I turned to English literary works. I took books from the college library, the Ernakulam Public Library, and from students interested in literature. Soon I became familiar with Sartre, Camus, Kafka and T.S. Eliot. Sometime during these perambulations, I wrote a story titled 'Vazhi' ('The Path'). It was influenced by M. Mukundan's short story 'Radha Maathram' ('Radha, Only Radha'). I sent it to *Yugareshmi* in Thiruvananthapuram whose editor was E.N. Muralidharan Nair. It got published under the name KKK, and made me famous in college and my hostel. The stories and poems that I wrote subsequently came out in similar publications. In the poetry writing competition conducted in the college, when I got the second prize, I received P. Kunhiraman

Nair's poetic anthology titled *Thaamarathoni*. In short, I came to be recognized as a writer during my college days.

Meanwhile, student politics at Maharaja's was changing in form and essence. Students believed that the root cause of Congress's victory was power; those who got special consideration were the sons or relatives of either the rich, or high-ranking bureaucrats. When, following the military coup in Indonesia in 1965, thousands of Communists were massacred, these students held demonstrations and shouted slogans that threatened a repeat of what happened there. They even branded non-Congress affiliated Dalit students as Communists.

The aims of the Students' Federation were the obverse of those of the KSU. It sought to protect the EMS government—the second, formed in 1969—and counter the opposition of the KSU. They responded to the latter's slogans with creative ones like: 'If another Indonesia gets staged, remember the courageous Vietnam!' Other organizations could not maintain this absolute anti-Congress stand of the Students' Federation. This opposition was taken over by a group which included T.K. Ramachandran, N.S. Madhavan, Ashraf Padiyath, Nanu, Ayyappan, Jayakumar and others. The Dalit students, including me, aligned themselves with this group.

All Dalit students—whether sympathetic to the Students' Federation or not—were constantly harassed by the KSU. If there arose a complaint that the food served at the hostel mess was bad or inadequate, they would counter: 'Don't look a gift horse in the mouth!', 'Do you get enough to eat at home?' and so on. Even when such ridicule was tolerated in silence, the hurling of abuses continued. Dalit students on their way to drink tea or back from the mess at night were driven away. Gradually, such behaviour by the KSU spread to the college as well. The availing of stipends and lump sum grants openly invited scorn, the argument being that the Dalits were enjoying allowances that were provided for by the non-Dalits. The Dalit students, for their part, took care to collect the money when no one was around. They were financially disadvantaged, and could not afford to forgo the stipends. But the Students' Federation was not prepared to question this practice of shaming fellow students, let alone supporting the Dalits. The Communist awareness of the issue of 'class' did not problematize 'caste'. Besides, they didn't think they could confront the KSU on this issue.

And so, resentment was simmering within the Dalit students. Discussions in the hostel were largely about neglect, discrimination and aggression. But no one had any suggestion to put forward on how to put up resistance. Everyone wanted to oppose it. But how? It was P.K. Thankappan who crossed the line of restraint. He was known to be a firebrand. He had passed the SSLC examination with excellent marks and the pre-degree examination with a first class. He was from Kaninad in Ernakulam district. Thankappan beat up a KSU student on a veranda near the Zoology laboratory. He was alone at the time when a boy and four friends of his confronted him and said, 'Instead of tilling the fields this chap is here to collect his stipend.' The boy was a relative of a high-ranking police officer. Thankappan beat him up despite the latter being healthier than him. This was the first conflict in the college where the KSU had been ruling the roost for a very long time. Since the response was totally unexpected, the friends of that young man ran helter-skelter, and Thankappan walked away unfazed. Nobody stopped him or attempted to attack him. He came straight to the room that Sukumaran and I occupied, recounted the incident and warned us of a retaliation. He also cautioned us against walking alone in the campus the next day, and suggested that we move about in groups.

The news that one of the star members of the KSU had

been beaten up spread like wild fire on the campus. Whatever the reason for it, they could not tolerate what had happened. A counter-attack seemed inevitable. Sukumaran and I suggested that all the Dalit hostel mates, whether they belonged to the Students' Federation or not, should go to college as one group at nine in the morning. I had never been involved in a fight before other than minor ones between us siblings, which inevitably ended with a few slaps from Chaachan and Ichaayan. But now I had to face something graver. Since a fight was unavoidable, I mentally prepared myself to face it. I thought of it as an opportunity to express the resentment I had been nursing all along. Precisely for that reason, I genuinely felt no fear.

But nobody joined us at nine the next day. Some did not leave their rooms at all. A few others, who did go to college, snuck in through the northern gate. Even Thankappan, who had sparked the conflict, did not appear. Finally, only Sukumaran and I were left. We decided to go to college, and that if someone beat us, we would retaliate. At ten, we proceeded to the eastern gate. At some distance, a crowd of around 40 students stood waiting. A few among them were spectators too—including Students' Federation activists. As a fight was imminent, we decided to keep moving forward. If we turned back then, we would not have been able to continue our studies. For the KSU, beating us into submission was a matter of restoring lost pride. If not today, it would happen some other day in future.

Just as Sukumaran and I stepped through the gate and into the campus, several boys came screaming at us. What followed was a severe beating. We too began to throw our limbs. But then somebody boxed me in the ear and knocked me off my feet. Sukumaran was left standing, fighting even as he was getting beaten. The fight came to an end when Shanmukham, a Students' Federation activist, who had remained a spectator until then, came to our aid. Somebody took us to the General Hospital. They let us off after giving us first aid and we came back to the hostel.

This was not like the usual fights that take place in college campuses but a retaliation against caste-shaming. It was not one of the regular Students' Federation–KSU scuffles. It was an act of resistance against the savarna hegemony that had held sway both in the college and in the hostel.

16. Freezing Nights

Our move to Wayanad was reminiscent of the migration of refugees to faraway lands. In the midst of the various crises, our bronze kitchenware had been sold off, one by one. What remained were a cot, a table and a bench. When they too were sold, we were left with a mortar and a grinding stone which we gave away to someone. So when we set out on our life as emigrants, our entire stock of vessels could be held in a sack, and our set of clothes in a bundle.

The trip began in the evening. A small group, including our neighbours and Valyaachan, had turned up to see us off. K.K. Joseph, the CPI(M) leader, and Thekkedath Gopalan, who had spent some time in hiding in our house, were there too. Accompanying our family to Wayanad were Valyaachan's daughter's son, Kunjukuttappan, and another relative named Kuttan. As Ichaayan's illness had abated somewhat, we did not have much trouble on his account. But neither he nor Baburaj, a little child then, had any awareness of the stressful times we were going through. Amma was crying relentlessly. The rest of the family too felt overwhelmed by it all and close to bursting into tears. Chaachan suppressed his feelings as he faced everyone.

Through several generations the family had multiplied and spread. We had relatives all over the village. Uprooting ourselves and going to a faraway place was difficult.

'We'll return. Definitely,' Chaachan said, as he took leave of everyone. We hired a jeep and it took us through the Vaikom road (Aappanchira) to the railway station. We then boarded the evening passenger train to the Ernakulam South Railway Station to catch the Mangalapuram train at night to proceed to Kozhikode. The next morning, we took a private bus from the Palayam bus stand that dropped us at Kakkavayal, in Wayanad.

The road from Kakkavayal to Vazhavatta was not a tarred one. It was a laterite path, winding and full of thick mire that was knee-deep at some places. As neither buses nor any other vehicle plied that route, we had to walk the distance. Such small groups of immigrants with sleepy, travel-weary faces and wearing dirty clothes were a common sight in those parts. So there were no curious onlookers to stare at us. They must have surmised that another refugee family was arriving. One of the main reasons behind such migrations was backwardness. Since the people here had first-hand experience of it, we were not the butt of ridicule.

Vazhavatta was four kilometres from Kakkavayal. Karappuzha, where we had decided to stay, was another one-and-a-half kilometres away. There were not too many houses on the sides of the road. We walked past Thoneri estate with its coffee and pepper plantations, a small temple and a primary school run by the SNDP. Vazhavatta was a partially developed village. On both sides of the market were provision shops and tea shops run by a set of Muslim brothers. There was also a post office, two barber shops and a small shop that sold minor items of daily use. The richest man in the village was a timber merchant. The rest were small and big middle-class families.

We had bought a piece of land near the Karappuzha project

area. It was during the time of British rule that a decision had been taken to build a dam there. But since no measures had been taken for a long time, no one imagined the project would come through. The construction of houses, farming work and sale of property in that area went on uninterruptedly. But title deeds did not exist. The only proof of transference of property was a statement, handwritten on a piece of white paper.

The topography was uneven, with many crests and troughs. The place was surrounded on three sides by the Karappuzha river. A Christian family was the earlier occupant. The main source of income here was the sale of home-brewed arrack, made using the water from the river. In those days, arrack manufacture was like a cottage industry, patronized by many families in Wayanad. For a long time, many came to our house seeking arrack. It had been vacated three days before we moved in. The coffee bushes, for lack of pruning, had spread out as if in the wild. We made a small profit from the few pepper vines that grew in the plot. There were many mango and jack trees there too. Pumpkin, bottle gourd and tomatoes grew without anyone caring for them. Tapioca was cultivated at the top end of the plot.

Although the profit we got from the land was meagre, the plot had come cheap. But what attracted me to the place was the seclusion it offered as well as the presence of the Karappuzha river. When we had set out to look for a quiet place to purchase, the uppermost thought in our minds was the presence of a mentally ill individual among us. He had to be kept as far away from people as possible. Having been born and raised on the outskirts of Upper Kuttanad, which had a river and canals, I fell for the Karappuzha at first sight. Giant, thorny bamboo clumps on the sides of the river formed a canopy, and here and there were elephant bamboo thickets too. A huge wild jack tree that had fallen over the river formed a bridge across it. The south-eastern boundary of the plot was a steep incline. Down below, on the banks of the river, bamboo and creepers had overgrown. If we stood on the front yard of the house, we could get a clear view of the Cheengeri hills.

The house had a single long room, a kitchen and a veranda. It was thatched with hay. The floor was plastered with cow dung. The walls were made using bamboo stems and plastered over with clay. It was broken and crumbling at various places. I had been rather proud of our Madhuraveli house. The dilapidated condition of this one made me sad. I found relief in the thought that had it not been for certain unexpected tragedies this would not have been our lot. A small hut stood close to the house. All it had was a hay roof. There were no walls, only a floor and an encircling mud boundary that stood half-a-foot higher than the ground. We stored our vessels and firewood there.

We had no savings, having used up all the money we got from the sale of our Madhuraveli house to purchase the new plot. We could buy only very small quantities of rice and other provisions, and they would not last long. But there was no lack of vegetables or tapioca. Our life in Wayanad in fact gave us some reprieve from the life of half-starvation we had led in our village.

What troubled all of us was the climate. The shift from the heat of Madhuraveli to the chill of Wayanad was unbearable. Sunlight was available only during noon. By dusk, mist would begin to gather, making visibility extremely poor. We were unable to see each other, let alone the trees. By night, the cold would seep into our very bones. So, as soon as dusk fell, all of us would assemble near the small hut outside the house, start a fire using the logs of wood stored there, and sit or lie close to it. Nobody had enough clothes or blankets to cover themselves fully. Chaachan had bought a cheap blanket, black in colour with red borders, which barely covered our bodies. Baburaj and Shanta slept under it.

There was considerable improvement in Ichaayan's condition but the illness did not disappear completely. To our relief, he began to take the medication prescribed by the doctor at the mental hospital in Thiruvananthapuram regularly.

Besides our relatives, Kunjukuttappan and Kuttan, who had accompanied us to Wayanad, a man named Divakaran joined us here. People used to come from various places to Wayanad in search of work. Good wages were paid for picking coffee berries and peppercorns. And so, Wayanad was the Gulf[52] for job-seekers, who invariably came alone. Most of these men had secrets to hide. They never divulged details about their native lands or relatives. Divakaran was no exception. The reason for his closeness to our family was caste. Hindu Dalits were rare in Wayanad. Most Hindus had converted to Christianity and become Dalit Christians. They prayed at the Pakkam Church close to Vazhavatta. The lower primary school Shanta and Baburaj were admitted to was run by the church management.

We soon dismantled the dilapidated house in the plot we had bought and built a new one with mud brick walls, a little to the south of the old structure. It had two rooms, a kitchen and a toilet. Kunjukuttappan and Divakaran took the initiative for the job. As soon as the construction work was over, we shifted, leaving intact the little hut close to the old house. We had good relations with our neighbours that went beyond considerations of caste or religion. As an immigrant family, a crucial asset we lacked was relatives, a large social circle which was imperative to ensure participation in functions from weddings to funerals.

Kunjukuttappan eventually married Saramma, a Dalit Christian girl who was our neighbour. As soon as they were wedded, we gave them a small portion of our land for the purpose of building a separate house. Kunjukuttappan very rarely went out to do manual labour. But Saramma was a hard-working woman. She did all kinds of work—harvesting, picking coffee berries and so on. The couple could thus lead a trouble-free life. Kuttan, the other relative who had accompanied us, converted to Islam and married a Muslim girl. He continues to live at Wayanad.

The returns from our garden plot were meagre; coffee berries and peppercorns did not fetch much profit. Shanta and Baburaj were still in school. Burdened by the responsibility of leading the family through the crisis, Chaachan and Amma became manual labourers. The person our Wayanad life changed most drastically was Chaachan. Until then, he hadn't suffered any form of slight or deprivation. Even when he did work for the Neythassery Mana, sometimes merely as a formality, financial worries did not trouble him. So, he very rarely went to work on others' fields. Never once did he work for middle-class Christian families. He had also for a long time been associated with politics, and Chaachan therefore had the regard of people cutting across differences of caste and religion.

Chaachan very quickly established a good relationship with the middle-class people in the neighbourhood. He became a worker in their fields and garden plots. Amma did not suffer the crises that he did. A good harvester, she did all the work related to paddy cultivation. At the same time, she could mingle with the Adivasi Paniya[53] women and become like one among them. The absence of paddy cultivation did not mean there was no harvesting and threshing work. She went to the fields of the Kurumas[54] and worked there too. Both Chaachan and Amma were tied to the business of merely surviving. There was no room for dreams of becoming rich.

Ichaayan became very peaceful at our new home. The cold climate seemed to be having a positive effect on him. He now behaved and spoke normally. A vacation period thus sped by, and soon I returned to college.

---

17. The Period before the Struggles

On returning to college, to borrow C. Ayyappan's words, I threw the earthen pot of my student life to the ground. What was forgotten was my bounden duty to study hard, land a job, and bring an end to the misery that faced my family. With very few exceptions, the condition of other Dalit students associated with the CPI(M-L), or alleged to be so, was little different.

Even before the seven-party coalition (Saptakakshi Munnani) ministry led by EMS came to power in 1967, agricultural labourers' struggles led by the CPI(M) had begun at several places. The CPI(M), which was born following the split in the CPI, supported such struggles with the aim of widening the party's base. Agricultural labourers were mostly Dalits or poor Ezhavas. The financially better-off Ezhavas aligned themselves with the CPI. Therefore, the strike that followed did not enjoy its support.

The agricultural labourers' strike was opposed by Christians who were farmers and by a Christian–Nair alliance in certain areas. In central Travancore, mostly in the Kuttanad area and Christian-dominated places, the Kerala Congress had elbowed out the INC. In areas where the Kerala Congress had little influence, it was prominent Christians within the Congress that came forward to suppress the strike. Sukumaran told us about the incidents at his native Mulanthuruthy, where the Kerala Congress had no presence. Here, it was a Congress leader named Paul P. Mani who organized the farmers against the striking agricultural labourers. In the attacks unleashed against the strikers, many including Sukumaran's relatives were injured. The deep hatred and sorrow he felt as a result led Sukumaran to seek out another kind of politics.

Neendur is four kilometres from my village. Its paddy fields are very close to Upper Kuttanad. Neendur too witnessed the agricultural labourers' strike that swept all of Kerala. Taking retaliatory measures, some Christians of the Kerala Congress incited violence and killed three striking labourers named Ali, Vava and Gopi. Another murder took place at Vadayar, situated between Vaikom and Thalayolapparambu. Here too the Kerala Congress made a direct intervention. A man named Thankappan was stabbed to death. Besides these incidents that we learned of directly, there were daily news reports about attacks mounted and murders committed by the Kerala Congress.

It was a private army, called 'Thoppippala Sanghom' nurtured by Niranam Baby, a Kerala Congress MLA, which was behind the attacks made at several places including Kuttanad. This group torched the houses of Dalits and tortured their women and children. In the demonstration staged at Thiruvalla, the derogatory slogan its members shouted was '*Thambraan ennu vilupikkum, paaley kanji kudippikkum*' (Will make you address us as 'Lord' and make you drink gruel from a spathe).[55] The scene picturized in the song 'Balikudeerangale' in the film *Cheriachante Kroora Krityangal* ('Cherian's Cruel Antics') directed by John Abraham of Kuttanad, which features the flinging of the corpses of agricultural labourers into the lake, is a recreation of the tragic experiences that Kuttanad witnessed in real life.

The Dalit students of our college and hostel had seen and read about these incidents, as I had. They had agricultural labourers among their relatives, and they felt that the CPI(M) had not given proper leadership to the oppressed classes, nor prepared them to build up a resistance. Their dissatisfaction with the party was evident even in private conversations.

After the Neendur incident mentioned earlier, the party decided to bury the corpses of the three murdered men on the roadside, close to the house of the murderer, and build a martyrs' memorial there. Thousands of agricultural labourers flowed in from all over Kuttanad to attend the funeral at Neendur. Many from the Dalit colony in my village attended it too. Even as the funeral service was underway, a car pulled up at the spot. John Jacob—of the Kerala Congress and also a member of the assembly—and a couple of other men stepped out of it and said they had the High Court's injunction order prohibiting the burial of dead bodies at that site. The agricultural labourers of Kuttanad recognized John Jacob. Hundreds of men raced towards the car. But the CPI(M) leaders who had come to attend the funeral—K.R. Gowri, T.K. Ramakrishnan among them—stepped up and formed a protective circle around him. 'You'll have to kill us first,' they told the crowd, 'before you touch John Jacob.' The crowd was forced to withdraw, but a group of labourers left the scene extremely enraged. On their way back, they slashed the banana plants and coconut trees of the farmers. Many Dalit students had similar stories to narrate.

I learnt of another such incident years later when I was working for SEEDIAN. It was Aanjilithanam Prabhakaran who told me the story. Before his involvement in the activities of SEEDIAN, Prabhakaran had been a member of the branch committee of the CPI(M). Kerala Congress activists torched 36 houses that belonged to agricultural labourers in a single night at Prabhakaran's native village of Paral near Changanassery. At a party committee meeting, Prabhakaran and another (a Nair) member raised this problem and suggested that retaliatory measures be taken. Not only was the request not considered, they were even opposed. The next night, Prabhakaran and the other member set a couple of houses, belonging to Kerala Congress members, on fire. The other committee members had not been informed of this.

While these experiences were what caused Dalit students to

gravitate towards politics, non-Dalits like T.K. Ramachandran, Jayakumar, A.K. Ravindran, N.S. Madhavan, Ashraf Padiyath, Sankar Menon, Harry and others were drawn to it by their belief in Marxism, that held the promise of liberation.

The different streams that existed in Maharaja's College came together and formed a fellowship outside the SF. That was the true Left. It did not have an institutionalized organizational structure, a programme of activities, or leadership. Instead of a uniform and co-ordinated set of activities, different types of events took place at various points of time. But as this new Left fellowship was also opposed to the KSU and the Congress, I did not keep away from the confrontations that took place within the campus. In fact, on certain occasions, I even played a major role in them.

It was usual for state leaders to participate in the programmes conducted by the KSU, on the strength of the majority they enjoyed. These leaders were received on campus like luminaries in the fields of art and literature. The SF did not oppose such functions owing to a lack of organizational strength. Once, V.M. Sudheeran, the state president of the KSU, was invited to the campus. As soon as they got wind of the imminent visit, the Left students made it known that he would not be allowed to set foot in the campus, a call KSU ignored, given the support it enjoyed among the great majority of students. But on the day of Sudheeran's arrival, both sides were organized. There was unease in the air. The Left students may not have had strength in numbers, but they were determined. So when Sudheeran stepped into the campus flanked by the formidable contingent of supporters, the Left front students moved forward shouting 'Sudheeran, go back!' This set the stage for a real conflict. I joined Ashraf, Nanu, Ayyappan, Jayakumar and Sukumaran in meeting them head on. In the melee that followed, although Jayakumar and I did manage to get close to Sudheeran, we could not break the security cordon created by the KSU. In any case, Sudheeran was not able to deliver a speech in the college.

There was opposition too when news came that Prime Minister Indira Gandhi would be speaking at the college grounds. The Left front students approached the principal and demanded that permission not be granted for the Prime Minister to use the grounds, which, quite naturally, was turned down. A podium for her address was erected on the opposite side of the New Hostel. But the ceaseless agitations and confrontations in college had made the Left front students a power to reckon with. On the day of Indira Gandhi's visit, the Left students began to congregate in the hostel. As a result, all the hostel inmates, except a few who were from Lakshadweep, left the place. At one point, we noticed the Congress leaders A.K. Antony, Oommen Chandy, Vayalar Ravi, A.C. Jose and a few others walking along the street close to the hostel, on their way to have lunch. Immediately, the Left front students rushed to the terrace of the hostel and started flinging glass bottles and stones at them. They were forced to go back. The students, triumphant, stood on the terrace, shouted slogans, hoisted a red flag, and declared that they had captured the hostel. Later, as Indira Gandhi began to speak, cat calls and slogans ('Go back!') rose from the hostel. The police ran towards the hostel and beat up all those who had assembled in front of the building. Indira Gandhi herself intervened to stop them.

By early evening, INTUC[56] workers of the Port Trust, led by A.A. Kochunni, parked themselves in front of the hostel. When it became clear that violence would break out if either the students came out of the hostel or the labourers entered it, nearly 20 students left the hostel through its back door, crossed a stinking, garbage-laden canal, and reached Hotel Maruti situated close to the CPI(M) district committee office on the Shanmukham Road.

A prominent CPI(M) leader who they spoke to suggested that each of them should be armed with a pen knife!

Here's the story of the last scuffle in the campus that I was involved in: The Left front students launched a really serious fight in response to the series of brawls that had been breaking out from time to time. It was a pre-planned attack. Nearly 30 students participated in the discussions organized in the New Hostel. At the meeting, the students were divided into three groups, and a leader selected for each. We would enter the campus through all the three gates. We decided that, unlike in the past, we should arm ourselves with bicycle chains, hockey sticks and National Cadet Corps belts, with their heavy buckles, and attack every KSU member we came across in the campus. That was not all. We also assumed the role of moral police, a phenomenon that is all too common today, and resolved to beat up all those who had friendly relations with girls.

As the leader of one of these three groups, I had a bicycle chain in my hand as I entered the campus. I went into my classroom, and hit one of my classmates. He was not even affiliated to the KSU. But we were driven by a feeling of vengeance, and many bystanders had to suffer for it.

By the time all those who led or were at the receiving end of such attacks during that phase of student violence in campuses finally left college, the KSU was a spent force. The entity that made the most of this situation was the Students' Federation of India of the CPI(M), created in 1970. Without a tough opposition or fierce criticism, this organization established its dominance in Maharaja's College through propaganda and agitation.

18. Through the Struggles

A comprehensive description of Naxal involvement at Maharaja's College is impossible to give, for the simple reason that there's an absence of written records. So, let me retrieve the few scattered memories I have of it from that period. The entire history of the Naxal movement in Kerala centres on the attacks on the Thalassery, Pulpally and Kayanna police stations; the elimination operations conducted at Thrisillery, Thirunelli, Kongad, Vellathooval, Nagaroor and Kilimanoor; and people like A. Varghese, Kunnikkal Narayanan, Ajitha, A. Vasu and K. Venu. What took place beyond this—the blood spilt and the tears shed—remains in the memories of people. Since historiography neglects micro worlds, those are marginalized areas of intervention.

Going by the traditional interpretation, although we passed off as intellectuals, our inclination towards Naxalism was not founded on a deep knowledge of Mao Zedong's philosophy or the Naxalbari rebellion. Nobody had a clear idea about its party organization in the state or its leadership. The belief was that a revolution would take place in a swift manner and Communist rule would be established in Delhi. That was how we read Charu Mazumdar's observations. We believed that the spark would become a wild fire. In such circumstances, newspaper reports were the source of all our knowledge about Naxalism. Despite the contrarian views of the newspapers and the disappointing news they carried, all of us saw the leaders as courageous men, and concluded that revolution was a law of nature. T.K. Ramakrishnan played a crucial role in creating such an awareness in all of us, including me. He gave us basic information about the international Communist movement, the revisionist politics of CPI(M) and the Naxalbari uprising. As we had little contact with the party organization, which operated in stealth, all we got was a general picture.

The first Naxal leader to visit our college was Philip M. Prasad. I think he came to Maharaja's College with the aim of finding shelter, as he was in hiding then. Philip M. Prasad met T.K. Ramachandran, the student leader of our college, in the room occupied by C.K. Vijayan, the younger brother of C.K. Chakrapani, former MLA. I do not know what they talked about, but T.K. Ramachandran sent Philip M. Prasad to my room. During his time in student politics, through K.K. Manmathan, then an MBBS student at Kottayam, he had come to know about S. Rajappan, a student of NSS College, Changanassery, who was from my native village. I told him the way to his house. Although many Dalits in Rajappan's village had severed relations with the CPI(M) for its oppositional stand towards the agricultural labourers' strike and sympathetic attitude towards the farmers, they had not embraced the Naxalites. Yet, since Rajappan wielded considerable influence over the Dalits, Philip M. Prasad could be safely lodged in a Dalit house at Mundar. The area had many paddy fields and islands, and was difficult for the police to reach. After staying there for five days, Philip M. Prasad left for Chalakkudy, which was where he was arrested. With that, our passageway to the Naxalite movement was closed.

The link with the Naxalite movement was re-established with the arrival of V.S. Narayanan, a member of the state unit of agricultural labourers' union. He was nearly 40 years old. It was T.K. Ramachandran, then a student at the University of Calicut, who sent Narayanan to our college. Narayanan had been with A. Varghese and A. Vasu in their Thrisillery-Thirunelli struggles. We looked up to him. He was a party leader who had taken part in the action. In our eyes, that made him a hero.

Besides the students who stayed in our hostel, those from the

Scheduled Caste students' Post Matric Hostel as well as some other college students took part in the study classes. Our hostel was, in short, a strong centre of CPI(ML) activities for several months, and a hideout for many.

The most widespread and powerful struggles in the agricultural sector were the agricultural labourers' initiatives to secure rights to surplus land. They were suppressed ruthlessly, as never before, by the government led by the CPI leader Achutha Menon. Holding aloft the banner of another wing of Marxism, the Naxalites, by failing to expose the repressive measures adopted by the CPI–Congress coalition, became irrelevant in the eyes of the labouring classes. Only K.K. Manmathan could present the torture unleashed on the Dalits in the Kuttanad region as a political issue in a manner that differed from the party line. In his view, Dalits, who far outnumbered the working class that took forward the Russian Revolution, needed to be made the bedrock of an agrarian revolution. When such lone voices were ignored, it was the Dalit political fronts that spoke up about the violence meted out to Dalit agricultural labourers. It was this impetus that led, for example, to Kallara Sukumaran initiating the formation of the Kerala Harijan Federation in 1970. Without opposing Marxism, this movement put the Communist leadership in the dock. With the tide shifting, as if to wash away the sin of having supressed the Dalit labourers, on the instruction of the CPI general secretary, M.N. Govindan Nair, the Kerala Pulayar Maha Sabha (KPMS) was formed in 1970 with K. Chathan Master and P.K. Raghavan as leaders.

Even as I participated actively in the study classes, I was labelled a vacillating 'petit bourgeois' intellectual. The reason quoted to substantiate this was my inability to keep secrets. And so, although I took part in the study classes, I was never told about party activities, and also became ineligible for recruitment into the party organization. But there was another reason too that warranted such a conclusion—my reading habits and the doubts I harboured about Marxism as well as the mission of the party.

While the students in the group read and discussed only the writings of Mao Zedong and party documents, I used to read Malayalam and English books on several subjects, and talk about them constantly. Simultaneously, I read texts of Hindu literature, including the Bhagavad Gita and the Upanishads. Among the Upanishads, the one that attracted me the most was the *Kathopanishad*. Another text I read most carefully was the Bible. In the Old Testament, Yahweh asks Cain, who had killed his younger brother Abel, 'Where is your brother?' The reply Cain gave was, 'Am I my brother's keeper?' On the basis of this conversation, I wrote a short play titled *Anthyam* ('The End'). Written on the lines of Samuel Beckett's *Waiting for Godot*, it won the second prize in the literary competition conducted by *Mathrubhumi* in 1971. The Naxalites were totally opposed to such reading and writing exercises. I was singularly ineligible for becoming an armed guerrilla!

What also characterized my life at this time were some youthful addictions. Sukumaran and I were very close friends. We rarely went to college, and when we did, we attended only a few of our classes. We talked all night long, and often climbed out of the window of the hostel dining room, jumped over a parapet wall, and went to see films. Our favourite theatres were Lakshmana at Ravipuram and Padma on the MG Road. We took the cheaper seats and watched Hindi, Tamil and Malayalam movies. A theatre at Fort Kochi screened soft porn films, which students from the hostel flocked to. Since others believed us to have better taste, and since we were self-conscious about our image, we kept away from them. Our interactions with girls were no different. Girls were not part of the Naxalite movement or the Left front fellowship that had existed earlier. They did not associate themselves with the SF either. Therefore striking up a friendship with them was considered a weakness. The man–woman relationship presented in the film *Kabani Nadi Chuvannappol* ('When the Kabani River turned Red'), directed by P.A. Backer, and produced by Pavithran—which depicted the Naxalite movement—offered a realistic glimpse of cross-gender relationships that existed during those times.

And yet, despite it all, I continued to contribute to expanding the study classes. A few attempts I made with the help of certain friends in the eastern region of Kuravilangad met with failure. I spent my holidays in the houses of my relatives but this link with my folks did not help draw any of them to the party. I surmised that even though my relatives loved and trusted me, and wished to see the Naxalite movement be successful, they were unwilling to be part of it. This realization was what led me to the conclusion that CPI(M-L) was not a mass political movement.

K.K. Mohanan, who was part of the gang that destroyed the statue of Gandhi in Thiruvananthapuram, came first to my room. The younger brother of K.K. Manmathan and an employee in the Postal Department, Mohanan urgently needed shelter. I shouldered that responsibility. Before both of us set out for my house at Vazhavatta, I gave the address of my neighbour, Kollipparambil Vasu, to Thankappan. I returned home two months before my course came to an end. I told my family that Mohanan was an MA student in my college, and that his name was Raghu. I told the truth only to Divakaran who was a Naxal sympathizer.

---

19. Scattered to the Four Winds

When I reached home with Mohanan, the situation was quite messy. Ichaayan's illness had worsened. He wandered around during daytime and was sleepless at night. Although he was not very violent, our neighbours began to persuade us to hospitalize him. As the pressure from them mounted, Chaachan and Kunjukuttappan and a couple of neighbours took him in a jeep to the Government Mental Hospital at Kuthiravattom in Kozhikode. By the time I came back, Ichaayan had already been admitted.

Mohanan had nothing to do in Wayanad. But he soon became part of the family and spent most of the morning hours reading below the bamboo thickets that grew by the side of the Karappuzha river. In the evenings we went to the market along with Divakaran, and returned by dusk. Mohanan was very close to Baburaj, to whom he narrated stories. He discussed general political matters with Chaachan, taking care not to bring in his political beliefs into the conversation. Even as the police search was on in full swing, he exhibited no fear or anxiety. During his conversations with Divakaran and me, however, he spoke of his decision to turn to a full-time political life of struggle. His intention was to conduct party activities in Kuttanad in regions where he had many friends and relatives. But fate had other plans for him.

Months later, Mohanan was arrested in Thiruvananthapuram and put in Poojappura jail. He was kept there for two-and-a-half years. Eventually, he was acquitted for want of evidence. But by the time he was released, the party was not there to receive him. All the friends of his past life had scattered in different directions. With all the doors thus closed on him, he took up teaching at a private institution at Attingal. He married a woman who studied there. She was already a mother. Later, a child was born to the couple. For some reason, the marriage ran into rough weather. Subsequently, when the tutorial institution closed down and Mohanan became jobless, a few friends stepped up and offered support. He sought out Baburaj occasionally at the Mahatma Gandhi University for financial help.

I saw him last on the day of my sister Shanta's wedding. When he had been in hiding at our house he had promised Shanta that he would definitely attend her wedding, no matter where he was at that time. We had not informed him of the wedding, which was conducted in a simple ceremony. But he kept his word. I later came to know that he had abandoned the path of revolution and converted to Buddhism. After some time in the company of Buddhists in Thiruvananthapuram, he had joined a Buddhist ashram in Nepal and become a monk. I don't know whether this bit of news is true or not.

One-and-a-half months after Mohanan had been living at our house, I got an inland letter written by Thankappan, addressed to Vasu, my neighbour. It revealed that many students had been arrested from the college hostel and also that I too would soon be taken into custody. Thankappan mentioned that he had written the letter in secret. As soon as this information reached us, Mohanan left. The police did not come to my house for a week, and I began to feel confident that no action would be taken against me. But the news of my friends' arrest was distressing. After an uneventful week, two policemen appeared in mufti. I was lying on a mat in the veranda of my house reading the history of Communist Party of the Soviet Union (Bolsheviks) written by Stalin. Chaachan and Amma were not back from work yet. Only Mani, Shanta and Baburaj were at home. Without protest, I walked out with the policemen.

People in the market came to know from these policemen that I had been taken into custody. A small crowd assembled to watch the scene. The villagers were not unfamiliar with Naxalites. Sasimala Raman Nair, who had taken part in the Pulpally police station attack in 1968, was a native of Vazhavatta. A good-natured man, he was a Congress worker. No one could believe that he had a Naxalite connection. When, during a police attack, Kissan Thomman was severely injured in a bomb explosion, the party decided to put an end to his agony. The coup de grace was administered by Raman Nair. On 30 October 1971, the Kozhikode Sessions Court acquitted those accused in the police station attack case. On returning to his village, Raman Nair eked out a living through manual labour. He later came to learn from a newspaper report that following an appeal filed by the government he had been sentenced to life imprisonment. This happened when he was at the tea shop of Jose Joseph at Kattithanam in Wayanad. He decamped immediately, and to date the police have not been able to arrest him. Neither the family nor the villagers know where he is.

I was taken in a bus to Kozhikode and put inside a lock-up at Nadakkavu for the night. The police left after that. It was the first experience in my life. I felt suffocated by anxiety and loneliness, my only relief being the fact that I had no actual links with the party. Nor did I know where those in hiding were lodged. The next morning, two policemen came and took me to Ernakulam in a bus. In the evening, I was put in a lock-up at Kasaba. The police guard was a middle-aged man. I sought some water from him to drink. After leaving me there for the whole of the next day and night, at 11 o' clock in the morning I was taken to the Crime Branch office on MG Road. The Crime Branch officer wanted to know where V.S. Narayanan, K.K. Manmathan and K.K. Mohanan were. Although a number of students from the college and hostel had been arrested, I was not asked about them. Since I had left Ernakulam for home many months back, I had no information to divulge. But, having taken upon themselves the responsibility of wiping out the Naxalite movement, they subjected me to torture and questioning. I was let off after seven days with the instruction that I was to report once every week at the Deputy SP's office at Kozhikode. I went there once to affix my signature. Thereafter, I excused myself citing financial difficulties and the troubles involved in travelling from Wayanad.

The torture, the lack of food and the absence of provision for bath or even a change of clothes had made me physically weak. It was in this condition that I reached the college hostel. There was no one associated with the movement there. Someone told me that my box and clothes had been transferred to Pavithran's room. Pavithran was sympathetic, and permitted me to stay there for the night as well as the next morning. He also gave me money to cover the bus fare to Wayanad. I think it was his sympathy for the Naxalites in the hostel that inspired him to produce the film *Kabani Nadi Chuvannappol*.

This was what I learned about what had happened at Maharaja's since I left. The ruckus in the college hostel during Indira Gandhi's speech was what had drawn police attention to the place, the hostel then coming under the radar of the Secret Police. Moreover, they received information that the hostel had become a hideout for Naxalites. Vellathooval Stephen was in hiding at the house of one of K.K. Manmathan's relatives in Kadavanthara at the time. On Stephen's insistence, it had been decided that a state committee meeting be held in a house at Aluva. The responsibility of escorting the state committee members to the venue was that of Thomas, an MA Malayalam student in the college. Although many members made it there, Thomas, who swam across the Aluva river to bring the rest, got caught in a whirlpool. He was a powerful swimmer but he sank and died. As Thomas went missing, the meeting did not take place. After his body was brought back to his house, following the post-mortem examination, many handwritten posters were found in his room. The police propagated the story that Thomas was killed by the Naxalites, to intensify their manhunt.

When police action became certain, Sankar Menon and A.K. Ravindran took Vellathooval Stephen to Thiruvananthapuram in a taxi. The wrist watches of four people, including Jayakumar, had to be sold to raise the amount required for the taxi fare. Widespread arrests began when the police became convinced that students had contacts with men like Stephen whom they branded as hardened criminals. The first to be arrested was Sankar Menon in front of the post office on Hospital Road. On hearing about this development, many students left the college, choosing to end their studies. The police arrested those who stayed on in the college and the hostel even in the middle of this crisis, and remained actively involved with the movement. In the vengeful violence that was meted out, Dalit students suffered the most. The affinity that many of them had for the Naxalites was only at the level of personal friendship. But the intention of the police was to suppress the Dalit students. Which explains why numerous students at the Post Matric Hostel suffered torture at their hands. All of those students, except V. Padmanabhan and K.M. Salimkumar, were innocent.

A month after my return home, we received a notice of the discharge of Ichaayan from the Mental Hospital at Kuthiravattam. We brought him back but there was no noticeable improvement in his condition. It seemed to have become worse. He would disappear and return after two or three days, his dress stained, his body unwashed, his teeth unclean. One day, Ichaayan slapped one of the villagers. The man filed a case at the local police station as a result of which the sub inspector of Kambalakkad came home to enquire. He suggested that Ichaayan be put in chains. He was chained in the hut close to our house, and this marked the beginning of the inevitable conclusion to the tragic tale of his life.

Having been tagged as a Naxalite, I was feared by the villagers. They refused to interact with or even speak to me. Gradually, however, things changed. I came to be identified as a writer rather than as a politician. Those who were interested in literary topics began to pay attention to what I had to say. Our casual meetings in the evenings turned into discussion sessions. Those who used to read long stories in weeklies like the *Malayala Manorama* or the *Mangalam* and the pulp fiction of Muttathu Varkey were drawn towards serious literary works penned by O.V. Vijayan, M. Mukundan, P. Valsala, Kakkanadan and others. Discussions about films began to focus on not only Adoor Gopalakrishnan and G. Aravindan but classics in world cinema as well. Amidst all this, it was the members of the labouring class who grew close to me. Most of them were Adivasis, particularly Paniyas. My circle of friends expanded to include sellers of spurious liquor, sex workers, barbers, masons and labourers who came from neighbouring districts to work in middle-class households. Many started approaching me for help in sending requests and application forms to the government, village office, panchayat office, taluk office or the police station. When distillers of arrack were caught by the excise officials, it became my responsibility to get them out on bail.

But while I was able to strike organic and extra-political relationships with people around me, the troubles at home kept mounting. Chaachan and Amma laboured to help keep the hearth fires burning. But that didn't bring in enough money for us to be able to buy new clothes or household utensils.

What troubled me the most during those days was the fact

of my unemployment. I had not completed my graduation. My educational qualification was essentially a matriculation. I was eligible only for Class III[57] jobs. Unemployment among the educated youth, even qualified ones, was a fact of life in the 1970s and a major cause of the growth of an atmosphere of conflict in the land. This has been dramatized in the literature and cinema of that time. In K.G. Sankara Pillai's poem 'Nishabdatha' ('Silence') we get a picture of an unemployed youth who stands on the railway platforms of Delhi and Calcutta, suffering the heat. Civic Chandran's play *Akshauhini* is about the insecurities created by unemployment. A character in it asks, 'Let us cast off the skin of this false sense of honour, and pick up spades. Where is the sky against which we can hold our heads high? Where is the earth on which we can plant our feet firmly?' Adoor Gopalakrishnan's film *Swayamvaram* is about the selfish survival of the unemployed. This problem of unemployment had its effect on mainstream political movements as well. The youth wing of the CPI led a struggle against it. Their slogan was 'Employment or Imprisonment'. As a result of this agitation, the C. Achutha Menon government initiated a 'Half a Million' Employment scheme, and recruited many in government service directly.

It was around this time, when I was facing an uncertain future in both my personal and political life, that Varghese Vaidyan, the CPI(M) leader from Meenangadi, came home and invited me to join the party. With all other paths blocked, after a couple of days of thought, I saw connection with the party as an opportunity to work amidst the masses. I became a branch committee member, but remained so only for a few months, during which time I took active part in meetings and agitations in Wayanad. In the course of these activities, I was introduced to Johnny, a party worker and son of Kottayam Kunjukunju. He was from Vazhavatta and belonged to a fairly prosperous middle-class family. He had studied only up to pre-degree. Both of us participated in nearly all the meetings and struggles that took place at the time.

The Theneri estate was a small estate located between Vazhavatta and Kakkavayal. It had coffee and pepper plantations. Less than 150 individuals worked in the estate, most of them Muslim women. The trade union there was led by Swatantra Thozhilali Union (Independent Workers' Union) (STU)[58] of the Muslim League. Compared to the other estates in the region, Theneri offered lesser wages. The conditions of work too were pathetic. As a result of several days of relentless intervention, Johnny and I managed to bring all the employees under the banner of the CPI(M)'s Centre of Indian Trade Unions.

Johnny and I shared a warm relationship that went beyond common political interests. As he came from a financially sound background, he covered all my expenses when we participated in struggle. I had open access to his house (he was a bachelor), and he often shared meals with me. He owned some property at Gudalur, close to the forest. Johnny met with a grisly end, crushed underfoot by a wild elephant, while engaged in some farming work there. It was a tragedy that caused me considerable pain.

My views were taken seriously at the branch committee meetings when the party planned its agitations. But beyond that, no ideological or political discussions took place at that forum. At around this time, a murder took place at Swargathilkunnu in Vazhavatta. A man (not a local resident) who was employed at a house where arrack was distilled got into an argument with a few customers and was killed in the scuffle that followed. But it was made to appear that he had hanged himself to death. Although there was clear proof that it was a murder, the Kambalakkad sub inspector, succumbing to pressure from prominent Congress and Muslim League leaders as well as bribes, reported the death as caused by suicide. My demand that an agitation be led against it—which I raised at a branch committee meeting—was not accepted. It was argued that any struggle against the rich and politically well-connected was bound to fail.

Sometime after, I heard that a member of the Kozhikode district committee of the youth organization spoke denigratingly about Che Guevara while conducting a study class. When I took this up with the party and raised an objection to it, a quarrel broke out between us. I was asked to get out. I did, and that brought my brief association with the party to a close.

20. The Paths Taken

In his autobiography, the famous French thinker and litterateur Jean Paul Sartre wrote, 'I began my life as I shall no doubt end it: amidst books.' Although a huge gulf separates Sartre and me, there was always a fairly good collection of books at my home too. I did not consider it a crime to buy books. That was why in writing *Kerala Charitravum Samooha Roopikaranavum* ('The History of Kerala and the Formation of Society') published in 2012, I purchased all the required books from the book stalls of various publishers not only in Kerala but in Coimbatore, Bengaluru and Chennai too. I also took photocopies of all the necessary books from the Kerala Sahitya Akademi bookshop, the Public Library, Ernakulam, the Calicut University Library, the ICHR Library, Bengaluru and so on. Many individuals helped me in these efforts, like Dr K.S. Madhavan of Calicut University, Mr Salim of Sir Syed College at Thalipparamba, John Joseph, a public worker, and many more. Those who extended financial support included T.K. Mohandas, an officer with the Motor Vehicles

Department and member of the Prathyaksha Raksha Daiva Sabha (PRDS),[59] and J.M. Jayachandran, who lives in Bengaluru. That was how I could rescue Dalit writing from the mere empirical plane and co-ordinate it with the knowledge system.

Even in penurious circumstances, I never hesitated to buy books. Baburaj is like me in this regard. I have lost many rare works because of the pathetic condition of our house and also because friends who took my books on loan failed to return them. But that is another story. I was once at Thrissur, where I bought a copy of *Kaliyugam*, written by Ponjikkara Rafi and Sebeena Rafi. I could not help wanting to read it. It was a book I felt could help me find an explanation for the conflicts then raging in my mind. I was not left with enough money to cover my travelling expenses. I left Thrissur and reached Kozhikode, where I took a ticket to Vythiri, but Kakkavayal, where I had to go to, was another 20 kilometres away. I had not eaten anything on the way. I was ravenous. The only solution I could think of was selling the umbrella I had with me. I had a meal with the money I got by selling it at a stop in Vythiri before proceeding home.

Vazhavatta was a backward village. No books or magazines like the *Mathrubhumi* weekly were available there. Little magazines, which enjoyed a spring during those days, were practically unheard of. The library in the neighbouring village of Pakkam stocked only a few books and that included detective fiction. No one here took reading seriously. Though not undertaken with this end in mind, my travels became a search for knowledge. Had I not travelled, I would have been burnt on the pyre of my inner conflicts. Or I might have led a humdrum life, in defiance of the desire in me to learn. Through my travels, I not only read books and magazines but also picked up elementary skills in journalism, learning also about cinema, painting, drama and music.

My primary destination used to be Kozhikode city. I have

lived there for some time in the course of several short stays. What attracted me to the place was not its political or cultural prominence. Rather, it provided a refuge away from home. Although Kozhikode was home to more political workers, writers and artists than any other city, I did not know anyone and felt that even if I tried to befriend them, none would be interested. So, I did not make any attempts at all.

Since I had little money on me, I could not afford to stay at a lodge in the city, participate in the richness and the luxury the city afforded or watch a film without financial help from someone. I used to borrow money from home or from my friends to cover my bus fare to Kozhikode, where I would put up at the homes of local acquaintances. I required nothing other than a place to stay, some food and a few beedis.

The first person who shared his quarters with me in Kozhikode was U. Phalgunan. I cannot remember who introduced him to me. Phalgunan was then working as a reporter for the weekly *Kerala Sabdam* and occupied a tiny room at the end of Ramdas Vaidyar's Ayurvedic treatment centre. He welcomed me with an open heart. Never once did he show the slightest hint of displeasure towards me. He had come to know me through my writings and, as a native of Thalipparamba, he had connections with the Naxalite movement, though he never actively participated in their programmes. Phalgunan was aggrieved at the implosion of the movement in the 1970s, and felt that reorganizing it was impossible. And so, there were no Naxalites to speak of in his circle of friends.

To Phalgunan, journalism went beyond a mere means of livelihood. It was part of social work, and provided scope for cultural interventions. I felt that he was trying to accomplish with the help of journalism what he could not through politics. He looked at the labouring class with genuine sympathy, and this peculiarity helped him maintain a strong link as much with the cultural side of the city as with its common life. I learnt my first lessons in journalism from what I saw and heard in that single-room quarter of his. The report Phalgunan prepared on the sex workers of Kozhikode and the serialized report 'Akalangalile Manushyar' ('People in Far-off Places') by K. Ravindran that got published in the *Kaumudy* weekly became templates for me to emulate.

Many years back, the spectacle of women of all ages waiting on the sides of dark as well as well-lit streets of Kozhikode was a common one. Men would select any one from among those streetwalkers and disappear behind buildings. In most cases, the utterly poor and helpless women were subject to violence at the hands of the police and the goondas. Phalgunan looked at these women with compassion. Through his investigations, he discovered that most of them, who came from different parts of the district, belonged to the Kumbharan (potter) community. When aluminium vessels invaded the markets, these women were robbed of their traditional source of livelihood, and flung into the mire of the city. This happened because, with the disappearance of traditional occupations, which were caste-bound, there were no openings available in others.

Muslim women formed another group that was pushed to the darker corners of the city by poverty and unemployment. Their piteous condition came to light when, in the wake of the Gulf boom in the 1970s, men went to the Middle East in search of jobs.

Phalgunan used to dictate his sentences and I would write them down. I had access to some of his handwritten articles also. That was what gave me the material to write about Adivasi women who worked as prostitutes in broad daylight in the forests behind the KSRTC depot in Sultan Bathery in my column in the SEEDIAN weekly.

Phalgunan was very close to K. Ravindran (aka Chinta Ravi), whom I called Raviettan. Theirs was a deep bond that transcended mere friendship based on their common professional journalistic interests. Raviettan had a huge circle of friends in the city that included political activists, writers and artists. Phalgunan and Raviettan usually met at the playwright and artist Vasu Pradeep's room. On most days, the famous singer, Kozhikode Abdul Khader, would join them. Common topics of discussion were literature, films and plays. Although I did not really participate in them, those conversations played a big role in shaping my sensibility. I used to take part in the city's cultural activities too, either in the company of Phalgunan or on my own. Those experiences gave a cultural orientation to my social and political activities.

Another place of stay in the city was the Post and Telegraph employees' lodge at Puthiyara. Devanand and his brother Ramesh's room at the lodge, to be precise. Devanand was a close friend of mine in college. He had a clear head that helped him look at issues dispassionately. He had Leftist views and was closest to Pavithran. More interested as Devanand was in cinema and literature than in politics, he was a regular at my room in the hostel. He scored very high marks in all his exams, from SSLC to graduation. So, he got a job immediately after completing his studies, and since he belonged to a fairly prosperous family, Devanand did not have financial troubles. I met him at the Town Hall at some function, and renewed our acquaintance. There was a pretty good collection of books in his room at the lodge and I had plenty to read. Although this later became my new place of stay, I continued my friendship with Phalgunan.

I started going to Ernakulam after Raviettan became the editor of the *Yatra* ('Travel') magazine. Its publication was begun by the novelist V.T. Nandakumar. *Yatra*, which was not a small magazine, focused more on literature. It was when

Yatra was taken over by a man called Kalleli Padmanabhan that Raviettan became its editor. Subsequently, politics and cinema also made their entry into its contents. Raviettan made good use of his friendship with politicians and writers. Before long, the *Yatra* office became a magnet for well-known writers. When *Yatra* slowly began to emerge as a prominent magazine, Kalleli Padmanabhan approached Raviettan with the demand that his novel be published in it. At the very first glance, it appeared to be a work without any quality and not worthy of publication. Raviettan returned the typescript, which caused a rift between the two men. Subsequently, Raviettan resigned.

With Raviettan's exit, I established contact with C.I. Ummen, and started staying at the Dalit students' Post Matric Hostel. I was given the responsibility of taking his book *Muthamudakkillatha Thozhilukal* ('Jobs Without Capital Investment') to the bookshops in Thiruvananthapuram. I had never been to the city before. It attracted me just as any other city. Ummen gave me only enough money to cover my travel and food expenses.

The evening I reached the city, I knew that staying the night was going to be a problem. I suddenly remembered Prabhakaran. He hailed from Chalakkudy and had been a student at Maharaja's College. Although he was a KSU sympathizer, I enjoyed a personal friendship with him. He was a law student at Thiruvananthapuram. By the time I reached his hostel, it was late night. He welcomed me heartily. His next door neighbour was Natarajan, who would go on to become an IAS officer. He admonished me for stopping my studies and being involved in a job that paid me no regular salary. What occasioned it was a fellow-feeling towards another Dalit. Many, many years later, a long conversation that A. Arun and I had with Natarajan was published in the *Mathrubhumi* as a service story.

In Thiruvananthapuram, I stayed for a long period with

Krishnakumar, the painter. As a student at the Government Arts College, he was in the forefront of students' struggles at the institution. He stayed at the University College hostel. Since food was not available in the mess there, we had to depend on local eateries. But he had financial difficulties. On most days, he had very meagre food. But Krishnakumar's warm friendship made up for this lack. He knew a lot about painting and sculpture as well as the famous painters of the world. While in Ernakulam, although I would go to 'Chitrakoodam', Raviettan's house, where all kinds of artists would converge, I knew very little about painting. It was Krishnakumar who helped widen my horizons. He opposed the Raja Ravi Varma[60] school of painting, worshipping and following modern art instead.

Although he was a Marxist in terms of ideology, he was an iconoclast in spirit and hated all systems. He had lofty and idealistic notions about aesthetics and was never ready to compromise on them for the sake of profit or success. The weekly *Kala Kaumudy*, recognizing his genius even while he was a student, invited him to paint for its issues. Reluctant to commercialize his talent, however, Krishnakumar left the job after a short while.

Films were another passion of his. It was in his company that I watched the classics, screened by the film clubs in the city. He used to analyse the films in depth and thus helped me not only enjoy and evaluate films but also understand the art of film making from an aesthetic point of view. He taught me that films are not ideological products but philosophical explorations into the human condition. Although we were the same age, I listened to him very carefully. He was a prodigy of Indian painting, but before he came to the end of his youth, Krishnakumar sought refuge in suicide.

As must be obvious, I was not in the habit of staying at any place for long. The main reason was financial. And I did not wish to be a burden on anyone. Although I had come to be recognized as a writer, I hadn't shaken off the tag of being a Naxalite yet. So, I never sought out my Naxalite classmates from college. Besides, barring a few, the rest had distanced themselves from their past and now led private lives. Nobody wished to remember the old days. Those who had landed government jobs feared that old life. The rest, being unemployed, had to depend on their families. The families despaired for them, and so, they looked upon old contacts with fear. Even when I did get in touch with them, there were no topics we could talk about. The condition of the Dalits students was no different. Most of them had abandoned politics altogether.

---

21. With the Adivasis

I was particular about reading the newspaper, even at home, for which I used to go to the market each morning. After my return, I either slept or did some reading. Those were lonely mornings, and my heart ached when fragments of songs from plays from the shackled Ichaayan's lips made their way to my ears. The only way I could overcome this unease, and the political uncertainty of those times, was through composing poems or stories. It was these works of my imagination, which contained my inner conflicts and hopes, which I published in small magazines.

I had another circle of friends in the market. Most of them came from other districts and there were a few unemployed youths besides. Some of them smoked marijuana and drank liquor. For the first time in my life, I smoked marijuana with one of them. That happened on the morning of a holiday in the Pakkam school grounds. I felt extreme physical discomfort rather than any euphoria. Even till afternoon, I was sweating all over, and my head throbbed. I somehow managed to make my way back home. I never tried it again, despite the many friends who smoked marijuana. But I drank liquor with some of them. It was mostly distilled arrack. I would wander about in their company, returning home late at night. But only once did I drink excessively. I spent the entire day in a stupor on a bench inside Sukumaran the barber's shop. I came to abhor the habit, not because I felt it would taint my reputation but because in no way did it help me overcome my inner turmoil.

I had just returned to Vazhavatta one day when I heard that an Adivasi named Chettan Muttan, who belonged to the Paniya community, had been beaten up. The incident had occurred a week earlier. Prominent Congress, Muslim League and Marxist leaders of the locality had done it. This is what had happened: High on distilled arrack, Chettan Muttan picked a quarrel with his relatives. Threats were made on both sides. When the local leaders found out they promptly arrived at the scene. Everyone except Chettan Muttan decamped. They asked him to go back home but he shot back aggressively. Nobody in the market tried to stop the beating it resulted in. The local residents usually ignored such things done to the Adivasis. Their reasons were many—they were drunkards, disorderly and untrustworthy! The Adivasis never organized themselves to resist such acts nor did they lodge complaints with the police. They were illiterate. Besides, the attackers invariably enjoyed political clout. In the eyes of the Adivasis, these political leaders were like the aristocracy of old times. And so, they silently suffered the exploitation and violence inflicted upon them.

The next day I went with Divakaran to meet Karvarnan. Besides being a native of Vazhavatta, he was the nephew of

Madhura, an MLA and member of the Kuruma community. Karvarnan was a graduate from the Regional Engineering College, Kozhikode and president of the Adivasi Swayam Sevak Sangh that was active in Wayanad. This organization was formed on 22 November 1970 with K. Allen, a Class IV employee of Kalpetta Sarvajana High School and member of the Paniya community, as president, and C. Prabhakaran (Alanthatta), a resident of the Cheengeri Settlement Colony, as convenor. All the different sects of Adivasis—Kurichiya, Kuruma, Paniya, Naykar and Urali—were represented in it. P.T. Vijayan was its general secretary. A native of Thalassery and member of the Thiyya community, he had been a Forest Department official in Maharashtra. It was after he read B.R. Ambedkar's works that he resigned his job and became a member of this Adivasi organization.

Vijayan was an undisputed leader as far as the Adivasis were concerned. In other words, he was a demigod to them. This was because of the struggle he had given lead to. St Mary's College at Sultan Bathery is situated on Adivasi land on Kuppady hill. Before the college was established, this vast land was occupied by retired army officers and members of the Kuruma and Paniya communities who had received seven-and-a-half acres each from the government. The college committee that worked under the church did not bother the army officers but sought police help to drive out the Adivasis to government-owned wastelands on either side. The Adivasis were helpless against this organized attack and it was the Adivasi Swayam Sevak Sangh led by Vijayan that gave an ordered structure to the resistance and converted it into a struggle. As part of it, they blocked the Sultan Bathery–Kuppady road. In the lathi charge they were subjected to, several individuals including, Alanthatta Prabhakaran, were injured. It was feared that those who did not retreat after the lathi charge would be shot at. But eventually a compromise was struck. Many of those who had been evicted were given back their lands, and the rest received revenue wastelands. The Adivasi Swayam Sevak Sangh became a force to reckon with.

Let me return to Vazhavatta. Divakaran and I told Karvarnan that a struggle should be organized to protest against the torture inflicted on Chettan Muttan. At first, he pleaded helplessness because the opponents were not only rich but politically powerful too. Besides, the Adivasis were unorganized. Eventually, at the end of a long conversation, he agreed to lead a demonstration and hold a public meeting at Vazhavatta. So, I accompanied Karvarnan to Sultan Bathery, met P.T. Vijayan and convinced him of our plan. On his instructions, it was decided to hold a demonstration and a public meeting and to have Madoor Kesavan, Alanthatta Prabhakaran, P.K. Kelu and K. Allen, besides Vijayan himself, as participants at the meeting. Following the decision, we went to each and every hut that belonged to the Adivasis and requested them to attend the function. Since Karvarnan knew the language of the Adivasis this message was easily communicated. All the leaders invited to the meeting kept their promise. Nearly a hundred people participated in the demonstration. Most of them belonged to the Kuruma and Paniya communities. It was with this meeting that I became an activist of the Adivasi Swayam Sevak Sangh.

The leaders of this organization were members of different political parties but the organization itself worked independently, affiliated to none. Most of the cases it handled concerned illegal acquisition of land and instances of torture. Vijayan sought solutions to all these problems through court action and the intervention of various government departments. Most of the victims were members of the Paniya, Kuruma and Naykar communities. Many Adivasis owned land back then. But they did not possess title deeds, and often gave their lands away to immigrants in return for small amounts of money, affixing their signatures or thumb impressions over revenue stamps on pieces of white paper. Since the Adivasis were illiterate, they never knew what the conditions of sale or the prices were. Many immigrants gave them lesser amounts than promised on paper. The members of the Adivasi Swayam Sevak Sangh brought all this to light. In most cases, it was while pressurizing the Adivasis to demand the lands back that the Sangh members themselves had come to see the bigger sums promised on the sale deeds. It was against this swindling that we sought action through the government departments concerned and the police station, and organized struggles too. Sometimes the problems were solved through compromises.

Among those who rendered yeoman service to the Adivasi Swayam Sevak Sangh was a Dalit named Velikrishnan, a Taluk Welfare Officer. He also gave all the support necessary for the writing of civil rights activist K. Panoor's well-known *Keralathile Africa* ('Africa in Kerala').

Political parties were indifferent to the exploitation and suppression of Adivasis and avoided taking measures to put an end to it. It was because they feared losing the support of immigrants, who formed a majority in the region. The Adivasi Swayam Sevak Sangh took the lead in the much needed struggle.

During those days of struggle, I stayed in the house of P.K. Kelu in the Cheengeri Settlement Colony. He was from Manandavady and belonged to the Kurichiya community, also known as the Hill Brahmins. P.K. Kelu was ostracized (forced to cross the Manandavady river) by his community. As a mail carrier at the Manandavady post office, he happened to have a meal at a hotel. This was what provoked the punishment of ostracism, a practice which was in force until recently. Several years back, a young woman who had been subjected to the same treatment went to Panamaram. There she was gangraped by a group of miscreants. When she was admitted to a government hospital at Vythiri, already in a horrible condition, she was subjected to gangrape again by the hospital staff. This incident made headlines across the state and provoked widespread discussion. Subsequently, the *moopanmaar* (elders) of the Kurichiya community decided to put an end to the practice of ostracism.

Although consumption of alcohol was common among the Adivasis, it did not affect the family to the extent that it does now. They drank wash/arrack (*chaaraayam*) and distilled arrack (*vaattu chaaraayam*), both of which were cheap. Arrack was usually sold in small one-room shanties. Customers were not permitted to sit there for long. Distilled arrack was sold secretly in houses. Sitting in houses for long too was not possible either. This brought an element of control on alcohol consumption among the Adivasis.

Family ties among the Kurumas and Kurichiyas were very strong. They did not depend on other communities because community-living, joint ownership of land, insistence on following traditions and the practice of rituals kept them bonded. Things were different in the Paniya community. Owning no land, they had to do manual labour for a living. Besides, many women from the community were also pushed into sex work. Paniya women engaging in sex work in the desolate areas of Manandavady and the wooded areas of Sultan Bathery behind the KSRTC bus depot were a common sight. These were directly perceived facts of life 40 years ago.

Naxalite attacks led by A. Varghese played a significant role in creating unmarried mothers among the slave communities in Thrisillery and Thirunelli. This is not an accusation against Varghese. It is an observation about politics pursued in an immature manner, without a pragmatic approach. Following Naxalite attacks, these above-mentioned places were identified as Naxal-infested areas and, as a result, a camp of the Madhya Pradesh police was set up there. The policemen threatened the innocent Adivasi women and exploited them sexually. By the time the camp was wound up, local men had taken over where the police had left off, continuing sexual exploitation of women, thus causing the number of unmarried mothers to grow.

---

22. The Colour of Death

P.T. Vijayan and family lived in a mud-walled, thatched house close to the paddy fields on the eastern end of St Mary's College. This house had been returned to a member of the Kuruma community after the struggle. Since the organization did not have membership fees or a monthly subscription, as a full-time activist of the organization during its initial period, Vijayan needed the support of the Adivasis. In course of time, with a decline in resources he used to be provided with, he had to face abject poverty. Vijayan then had to take up a job to make a living. He bid goodbye to Wayanad when he got appointed as the manager of the Janata Steel Mill that had been established in Kozhikode. This brought the activities of the Adivasi Swayam Sevak Sangh to an end. With most of the leaders belonging to separate political movements and trade unions, organizational activities could not be taken forward.

My house was now my only refuge. But I was miserable, and securing a job became a matter of paramount importance. And so, the sending application forms to the Public Service Commission and waiting for the postman became my overriding preoccupation. I had not retrieved my pre-degree marks card or a certificate attesting my completion of the BSc course from

Maharaja's College. I was, as I've mentioned before, basically a tenth standard pass.

While at Thrissur on a trip from Ernakulam to Wayanad, I had once bought *Prasakthi*, a magazine edited by K.G. Sankara Pillai. Before the bus reached Kozhikode, I had finished reading it from cover to cover. K.G. Sankara Pillai's poem 'Bengal', an article titled 'Yuvaakkalum Viplavavum' ('The Youth and Revolution') and a report by the Calcutta-based human rights organization, Association for Protection of Democratic Rights, about the torture suffered by Naxalite prisoners in the prisons of Bengal led me to overcome my political indifference.

I began reading about the Naxalites engaged in struggle, including party literature, and shared what I learnt with friends. With this, a small group with an affinity towards the Naxalite movement came into being in my village. None of its members, however, were prepared to establish contact with the party or participate in its activities. My interventions were thus confined to Vazhavatta. Nevertheless, I believed that the experiences gained from one region could provide a model for initiating a people's revolutionary movement. I kept in constant touch with Civic Chandran who, without making direct contact with the Naxalite movement, gave leadership to anti-establishment cultural activities.

It was *Akshauhini*, a play that was staged on the initiative of Meenangadi High School teachers in 1974, which gave political content to anti-establishment activities in Wayanad. Written by Civic Chandran, its plot revolved around the unemployment crisis and the responses to the problems faced by the youth, which form the flashpoint for a revolution. The posters that were exhibited at Meenangadi and various other parts of Wayanad to publicize the play were very novel. Done in the style of modern art, they created a unique visual experience. Even before the play began, the thatched talkies building in Meenangadi was filled to overflowing. The play itself created quite a stir among the spectators. I had not only helped organize the play but taken along some people from Vazhavatta to watch it.

It was during this period Ichaayan passed away. It was a tragedy that deeply affected me. To borrow words from M.T. Vasudevan Nair's *Mist*, 'I am living my own life / And the lives of those after me / I am dying my own death / And the deaths of those after me'. No one deserves such a life, or death. Had he not become mentally ill, he would have become a writer or, as the first bachelor of arts from the Pulaya community in our village, likely a government servant. Our family would have been spared long years of misery. It was life, not death, which we suffered. It is probably why I remember that death decades after it happened.

When it became certain that neither medicines nor care would bring him back to normalcy, Ichaayan was put in chains. It was not possible to accommodate him inside the house, which had only two rooms and a kitchen. So he was confined to the tiny hut with its hay roof, with one end of the chain around one of his ankles and the other a pillar. Since the hut had no walls, he was exposed to the bone-chilling cold climate of Wayanad. He was given a woollen blanket, a plate to eat in, and an aluminium tumbler to hold water for drinking. He sat there all the while, stark naked, never standing up or walking, staying awake even at night, urinating and defecating at the same spot. It was a picture that vaguely resembled the fate of Kuppuachan in O.V. Vijayan's novel *Khasakinte Ithihaasam*. Neither Amma nor Chaachan even looked in that direction. Chaachan was almost indifferent.

Our troubles reached their peak during the rains. The relentless downpour, squelchy garden plots and the insufferable cold made it impossible to stir outside. With work on garden plots and fields difficult to come by for Amma and Chaachan, our main food was tapioca. Chaachan used to take tapioca from the neighbouring houses to Ambalavayal, four-and-a-half miles away, to sell. Balancing a load of it on his head, he had to walk along the slippery ridges of the paddy fields and swim across the canals on the way. The toughest part of the trek was climbing the Cheengeri hill. One slip along its steep slope would send anyone hurtling down 15 or 20 feet. The pittance he got from selling tapioca was what kept the family fed.

Four or five decades back, when modern treatment methods were not available, insanity was not a disease. It was a curse, a terrible fate. Many stories, including M.T. Vasudevan Nair's *Iruttinte Aatmavu* ('The Soul of Darkness') and films including Lohitadas's *Thaniyaavarthanam* have presented such tragic lives. The family to which the patient belongs becomes brittle, the future of relationships uncertain. A tragedy that can be compared with it is suicide committed by unmarried young girls. The family of the girl has to live under a cloud of shame. The warmest of human relationships can break under the stress sometimes. I'm reminded of these lines from a poem by Satchidanandan:

Plant a casuarina tree here,
In memory of mad grandmother.
Plant a lime tree here,
In memory of father who died, dry-lipped.[61]
Plant an Asoka tree here,
To big sister, snatched by suicide.

What Ichaayan's insanity destroyed utterly was the future of Mani and Shanta. With a looming financial crisis and a stormy atmosphere inside the house, Chaachan could no longer pay attention to his children's education, like he had done before. Besides, I too had discontinued my studies. Mani took charge of Ichaayan's care. Before leaving for school (at Meenangadi, three-and-a-half kilometres away), he would serve food and water to Ichaayan. In the evening, after coming back from school, he removed the waste from the hut and wiped Ichaayan's body with a wet cloth. He also trimmed Ichaayan's hair and beard. His education was sure to suffer, with these heavy responsibilities on his shoulders. He could not study beyond the tenth standard.

Shanta's situation was little different. She took on the full responsibility of running the household. The first thing she did when she got back from school was to walk half a kilometre to Oliyil and collect water required for the day. Then she prepared dinner. With no scope for rest, after all these duties were performed, she hardly had time to study. Like her brother, she gave up her studies after her tenth standard. Baburaj, a talented child, cultivated the habit of reading very early in childhood. He was the only person who escaped this fate.

Ichaayan died on a rainy day. I was at the Dalit students' Post Matric Hostel at Ernakulam at that time. I didn't really have a job, or any money on me. I ate the food the students offered me and took money from friends working in the city to buy beedis. My family had no idea where I was. So there was no way for them to tell me what had happened. But that day, I woke up with a vague sense of foreboding. As time passed, my uneasiness grew. The students had gone to college and I was all alone in a room. I tried to read but could not concentrate. I stepped out of the room. There was a small amount of money in my possession. I wandered through the busy streets feeling drained of all strength. I decided not to go back to the hostel. But where else could I go?

By the evening, I had decided to go to my Ammavan's house at Thalayolapparambu. I took a private bus and on alighting there was informed by a neighbour that Ammavan and Ammayi had left for Wayanad. Kunjukunju's (Ichaayan's) condition had worsened. He asked me why I was not home. What gripped me then was an unimaginable sense of dread. I was sure it wasn't his condition that had deteriorated. He had probably died. Along with sorrow, I was gripped by an acute sense of uneasiness. Did I think frequently that death was preferable to the present condition of life? There was no running away from ties of blood though.

I did not have money to pay the full bus fare to Ernakulam. So, I borrowed a small amount from that neighbour and left.

I reached the city by dusk but did not have enough for the journey to Wayanad. The students in the hostel would obviously have only small amounts of money with them. So, like a maniac, I wandered about from one place to another hoping to collect some. The first person I sought out was C.I. Ummen. He was not available. So, I went in search of the manager of the Ceylon Bake House who had been introduced to me by Raviettan. But he too was out of station. Suddenly, I remembered K.G. Bhaskaran who stayed at the Law College hostel. He didn't hesitate to help out. I then dashed towards the south railway station where I found a train bound for Mangalapuram. I bought a ticket and hopped in just in time, for in a few minutes, the train left the station. All I had had to eat the entire day was a meagre breakfast at the college hostel. But I wasn't hungry, or thirsty. Besides, I knew that if I spent money on food, I would not have enough to take me to Wayanad.

I reached Kozhikode very early the next morning. Without any delay, I boarded a state transport bus for Sultan Bathery. I had only as much money as would buy me a ticket up to Vythiri. I purchased the ticket and sat at the end of the bus. When we reached Thamarassery, it began to rain, which had turned into a storm by the time we reached the foothills. All the window shutters had been rolled down as the bus trudged along slowly through the mountain pass. There were very few passengers inside. At Vythiri, the rain only became stronger. I did not step down. Instead, I pretended to have fallen asleep.

By the time I alighted at Meenangadi, it was close to noon. I had to walk four kilometres in the relentless rain to reach home, wading through knee-deep mire on the untarred road. It was deserted as I walked along on it, wet and dripping. One-and-a-half kilometres along, after climbing down a hill, one had to walk on the ridges of paddy fields, but the whole place was so flooded that the ridges themselves lay submerged. Although I was used to walking in the area, I slipped and fell several times. A bridge that stood half-a-kilometre from there had been washed away. But as the canal was narrow, I had no difficulty swimming across. I finally reached the bank of the Karappuzha river. Its current was strong and muddy water was overflowing the banks. There was a garden plot on the other side. I could avoid swimming across the river and instead walk another half a kilometre to get to the bridge. But I had to reach home as quickly as possible. It didn't cross my mind that this could prove to be dangerous. I jumped into river, swam against the raging current and managed somehow to reach the other side. I then ran up and down the hill to get home.

Ichaayan had passed on the previous evening. The shackles had been removed two days earlier and he had been brought into the house. As his legs could not be straightened, we had to order a taller coffin. Around the corpse sat Ammavan, Ammayi, Chaachan, Amma, all their children and a few neighbours. They had been waiting for me. I was drenched and dirty as I stepped in. Amma, Chechi and Shanta were weeping. The others were impassive. The skeletal corpse covered by wrinkled skin was buried in the southern side of the house even as the rain continued to drizzle. There were no rituals of either the religion or the community. That was how Ichaayan's miserable life came to a close.

Amma was greatly distressed that Ichaayan had been laid

to rest without the observance of any traditional rituals. She believed that his soul would wander listlessly. So, she picked up some earth from his burial site and preserved it in a plastic container. Later, even when we relocated to Vakeri, and still later when we returned to our village and put up residence at Kappikkadu, she did not lose it. On Amma's insistence, an astrologer was consulted. He suggested various kinds of votive offerings at different temples. With that done Ichaayan's soul was granted peace. For my part, I dedicated my book *Kalaapavum Samskaaravum* ('Rebellion and Culture') to this elder brother of mine who had hand-held and raised me into the world of knowledge and independence struggles.

That same year, I landed a job as a lower division clerk in the Public Works Department.

---

23. MELSA

My first job appointment was at the Kannur office of the PWD Minor Irrigation Department. I needed that job for financial security and in order to help my family. I also wanted to be employed. Since I had responsibilities and financial obligations, I was content for several months. When I got my first salary, I bought some good blankets for everyone at home. However, this period of my life didn't last very long. The middle-class atmosphere that prevailed inside the office was stifling. The routine life—of taking a bath, getting dressed for office and leading a regimented existence—became unbearable.

I stayed at the MELSA (Marx, Engels, Lenin, Stalin, AKG) Lodge at Thana on the Thalassery route, nearly one-and-a-half kilometres from the city. It was an old building with a tiled roof and had two rooms, a hall and a kitchen. Four men from Kollam district, who were lower or upper primary school teachers, were the other inmates. All of them were hardcore followers of the CPI(M) and activists in the teachers' organization. But the atmosphere in the lodge was a cordial one.

Arguments and counter-arguments that were conducted in order to make me a member of the CPI(M) and the NGO Union had the effect of removing the ash from the embers of my political ambitions. Neither the CPI(M) nor the CPI(M-L) were acceptable to me, on ideological grounds and because of their organizational structures. I turned to reading in order to discover a different political path.

I started by reading *An Advanced History of India* written by R.C. Majumdar, H.C. Raychaudhuri and Kalikinkar Dutta. While in high school, although I had read Jawaharlal Nehru's *Discovery of India* and H.G. Wells's comprehensive volume on world history, *A Short History of the World*, those readings were not oriented towards any single aim. In the account of India of the Middle Ages in this major book on the history of India, mention was made of the many agricultural laws that had come into being at various points of time. It also revealed that each of these laws had formed as the result of a violation of law carried out through agrarian revolutions. Reading this convinced me that an agrarian revolution would take place once again, and that its success was inevitable. This made a study of the Communist party—the frontline warriors of the agrarian movement—very relevant.

Although the eventual aim was to get to the emergence of the CPI(M-L), I decided to write about the Communist party from 1921, the time of its formation. I began composing it under the title *Tashkent muthal Siliguri vare* ('From Tashkent to Siliguri'). Four chapters of the book, which began from

Harappa and Mohenjodaro, were published in the SEEDIAN weekly under the pseudonym T.K. Balan. The fifth was to be on what constituted Indian nationalism. It would be based on A.R. Desai's *Social Background of Indian Nationalism*. This text was the immediate inspiration behind the Communists', including EMS's, adoption of the concept of working-class nationalism. I wrote the introduction to the fifth chapter but could not take it forward. The ideas in my mind were so confused that it was impossible to string the rights words together. I read the book several times but it did little to help. I was like a child at a crossroads, unable to figure out which path to take. There was no alternative but to abandon the project, which was what I did. Although K.S. Das, the publisher, repeatedly followed up, I was helpless. It was only much later that I realized that the Communist party's concept of nationalism was what had created the obstacle. It took me many, many years before I was able to give shape to a different concept of nationalism on the basis of my understanding of subaltern life.

I was attracted to Dalit literature that had taken shape in Maharashtra too, and as far back as this period in my life, I came to recognize that Marxism and Dalit literature converged at a certain point. With this realization came the desire to start a magazine for establishing Dalit literature. I went to the Kannur Collectorate and put in an application for the declaration of a magazine with the name *Spartacus*, with the MELSA Lodge as its address. The inspiration behind the choice of the title was a film on Spartacus, who led a slave revolt that shook the Roman Empire, sometime before the birth of Jesus Christ.

As I waited to receive the declaration, P.K. Damodaran Master came to see me one day. I had been in touch with cultural activists at Wayanad, but this was the first time that a CPI(M-L) activist had approached me. A bespectacled, mild-mannered man, he was a school teacher in Kozhikode. I discovered that he was a representative of the party that was newly reconstituted at the initiative of K. Venu. He requested me to co-operate with the party.

He spoke mostly about the correctness of the ideology promoted by the party and the relevance of Charu Mazumdar. With absolute confidence, he spoke about the inevitability of the success of an armed revolution. The conversation extended well into the night. At one point, I asked him, 'Can't we build the party among the Adivasis?' His reply was, 'They won't understand ideology.' Those words not only irritated me but also caused me to lose faith in the party. Later, when I told him about my intention to start a magazine titled *Spartacus*, he told me that there was already a Hindi magazine under the same name, and also that since I was a government employee, there was no likelihood of my receiving the permission. Subsequently, he suggested that both of us collaborate to publish a magazine. Agreeing to it, I suggested that it be named *Yenan*. The name was inspired by the place where Mao Zedong had delivered a famous speech on art and literature.

It was V.C. Sreejan who put in an application for the declaration of the new magazine with the MELSA Lodge address. I had not been introduced to him. P.K. Damodaran Master's influence might have made him get involved. It was in a similar fashion that Civic Chandran became a member of the editorial board. While I too was a member of the editorial board, I was not given the main responsibility. The authority vested in the party. The magazine was printed at Bharat Press in Thalassery. I soon came to know that K. Venu was staying in a lodge there to run the magazine. The printing and the distribution too were done by the party. I had no part to play in any of it.

The expenses for travel among the other tasks related to the running of the magazine that I did perform led me to a financial crisis. I could not pay the rent at the lodge or send money to my family. I requested the PWD for a transfer to Kasaragod because that would make me eligible for additional income by way of a transfer allowance. There was another reason too for making this decision. The visits of people like P.K. Damodaran Master in association with the publication of the magazine led the inmates of the MELSA Lodge to believe that I was conducting Naxalite activities with the lodge as my hub. They were dyed-in-the-wool CPI(M) followers and objected strongly, asking me to vacate my room. The difficulty involved in finding new lodgings in Kannur was the other reason for seeking the transfer.

Around this time, I contracted chicken pox. It had worsened by the time I got back home. A week later, I returned to the MELSA Lodge along with Mani. By then the issue of the magazine which was in print when I had left had reached its readers either by post or through party contacts. A few copies awaited me at the lodge. I gave some of them to Mani for distribution in Wayanad. The rest I distributed by myself.

When I reached the office, my transfer order was ready. I took it, collected the transfer advance, paid back all my loans at Kannur, and joined the Kasaragod office.

24. The Emergency

The office at Kasaragod was a small one with an assistant engineer and another member of the staff. I was to occupy the post of the lower division clerk which had been vacant for a long time. Finding a place of residence was not very difficult. The NGO Union leader at the office helped me find a room at the NGO Home. Teachers and employees of various departments lived there. Food was supplied by the canteen. I placed my clothes, magazines and books in the tiny room and settled down. A few days later, the Emergency was declared.

I was troubled greatly by the newspaper reports on 26 June 1975 about the declaration of the Emergency, and the ban orders on 26 organizations, including *Yenan*. Later, as a result of censorship, newspapers carried only government declarations. That was when the absence of a people's movement really hit home. Although I was not a member of the NGO Union, one of the largest service unions of the CPI(M), I was so opposed to the Congress and the Emergency, that I participated in a meeting conducted by the Union, along with its leader. He said that we should accept the changed circumstances and conduct organizational activities following the rules. This attitude was grating to my ears. The meeting convinced me that no substantial reaction could be expected from the middle class, which included me as well. Since then, I have stopped attending such meetings.

In the early days of the Emergency, the *Deshabhimani* carried a few articles about the political situation in the country. It was through these that I came to know about the prominent central and state leaders that had been put behind bars. But there was no news report about Naxalites, either in the *Deshabhimani* or any other newspaper. With the censorship becoming worse, no news was available. The atmosphere was suffocating. My contact with cultural leaders all but ended. The only source of news was a leaflet titled *Kurukshetra*, published by the Rashtriya Swayamsevak Sangh (RSS), which Shanta picked up from her school. Another was a copy of *Inquilaab*, of which K. Venu was the editor.

The latter was supplied by Divakaran, who was associated with Madhu Master. What it contained were reports of Naxalite activities in various parts of the country and the declaration that the programme set forth by the party was indeed the correct one in these altered circumstances. There was no analysis of the Emergency or any instruction about the propaganda activities against it. However, when Civic Chandran decided to bring out an anthology of stories of revolt, and another, of poems, I contributed to it by sending a story titled 'Devu' written a long while back.

One afternoon, while I was at work in my office, two young comrades came to see me. Several years later, I learnt that they were Chandran and Rajan, both natives of Kannur. We spoke at a vacant spot at a little distance from the office. Rajan informed me that although the CPI(M-L) had been banned, its activities were on in full force throughout the state. The organization had been revamped because of the Emergency. The party now worked as three units—the first, at the ideological plane; the second, to execute armed revolution; and the third, to garner financial support for the party. I was asked which unit I preferred to work with. I remained silent for a long time. Finally, I asked, 'Those who handle ideological issues are the ones who build the party organization, aren't they? And the second group, isn't it involved in the party programme of elimination and attacks on police stations?' The answers to both were in the affirmative. Since the party was not a mass movement, I was not interested in joining either of those units. So, I promised to be part of the third group and contribute financially to the party every month.

But I did let them know what I thought of the party's strategy. Marxism offers a concrete analysis of a concrete situation, I said to them. What the party should do is take the initiative to arouse the masses against the Emergency, and not take forward its own programme at the moment. It was for the party to decide how it was to be done. I was interested in being part of such a mass movement rather than getting involved in political activities that demand the sacrifice of one's life. They merely read back the party line to me but we parted on cordial terms. The next month, when Chandran came to see me, I gave him some money. No one approached me after that.

The police took me in custody too during the Emergency period. One evening, a high-ranking officer accompanied by a few policemen from Kannur came to the NGO Home at around 7 pm. They parked their vehicle outside, walked up to my room, and asked me to accompany them. I put up no struggle. While I changed my clothes, they examined my collection of books and magazines. There were no publications that could connect me with the CPI(M-L), even a copy of *Yenan*. Most of them were little magazines that contained my articles and poems. They picked up only those.

It was past 10 in the night when we reached a room inside the Kannur Collectorate. The officer who had come to the NGO Home did the questioning. He behaved decently. The first questions were about the connection between me and the *Yenan* magazine. I told him that I was a member of the editorial team along with V.C. Sreejan and Civic Chandran, and that I had the responsibility of reading whatever matter I received and making selections from it, and that the party was in charge of printing and distributing the copies. The next query was about my connection with the Naxalites. There was no cross-examination of the explanation I gave. The officer asked a policeman to take me back to the NGO Home. It was three in the morning when we got back to my quarters. Even as I was getting ready that morning for office, the leader in charge of the NGO Home asked me to vacate my room. He didn't ask me a word about why I had been taken away. That evening, after I returned from office, I picked up my mattress, clothes and books and shifted to another lodge where I stayed for two days. Later, with a colleague's help, I shifted to a lodge at Thalangana which was occupied by madrassa instructors and a few Muslim teachers.

During those days, I was put under surveillance by the Special Branch of the state police. A policeman who was on the verge of retirement used to appear regularly. He never revealed to the other hostel inmates that he was a policeman but took care to talk to them outside the lodge. Most of his questions to me concerned personal matters. When I spoke to him about the financial situation at home and about my parents who did manual labour, he was full of sympathy. A couple of times, he asked me to move out of the area. The reason he cited for his concern was that if he received the order from above, he would be compelled to take harsh measures against me.

The man who replaced him did not take a liberal view of things. From our conversations it was clear that he considered me a criminal who could be arrested any moment. Moreover, every time he came, he asked me about my movements and the people who came to meet me. Eventually, I realized that the situation was not favourable. I resigned, put in my papers with the superintendent and went to the Kasaragod railway station to take a train bound for Kollam. This was in October 1975. The other reason for resigning was that my name had appeared in the rank list of clerks to be appointed in the KSRTC. I had taken the entrance test at the Sarvajana High School at Sultan Bathery and was confident of landing the job.

On reaching Kollam, I headed for the room occupied by C.R. Ramachandran, a Railway Mail Service employee from my village. He had once been my classmate. What drew me towards him was thus a personal bond, more than any political connections. I had no clear-cut political duties to discharge, and so I did not need to go into hiding. With no direct links to the party organization, I felt the possibility of arrest was remote. And so, I did not go by any other name. But as a long stay there was not advisable either way, I bid goodbye to Ramachandran, returned to Madhuraveli and spent a few days with my relatives there. Soon, however, rumours spread that I, a government employee, was in hiding. I returned promptly to Vazhavatta.

Although not a conscious decision on my part, being away from Vazhavatta for so long was what helped me avoid arrest and jail. Certain events that took place in Vazhavatta confirm this conclusion. During the initial days of the Emergency, there were no widespread police measures in Wayanad. Although V.C. Sreejan and Civic Chandran, members of the editorial board of *Yenan*, were questioned by the police, they were not arrested. The cultural activists and those who were involved with the play *Akshauhini*, on stage and off it, were safe too. Things changed completely, however, when, as per the party's district committee's decision (while in hiding), Madhu Master led the Mani action at Manandavady. When the party's involvement in it came to light, all the party workers and loyalists all over Wayanad were taken into custody by the police, tortured and jailed. The cultural activists were not disturbed though.

I returned to Vazhavatta unaware of all these developments. I got a fairly rough sketch of them at the market. On the way home, Chaachan said, 'This place is not safe. Why don't you go somewhere?' The thought of remaining safe, when everyone in my circle of friends was suffering torture and imprisonment, filled me with an acute feeling of guilt. 'I'm not going anywhere,' I replied, full of self-hate. 'If they want to arrest me, let them!' The facts that I learnt later were as follows.

Subsequent to the Mani action in Wayanad, Madhu Master was arrested. The rest went into hiding. One night, during this period, the police surrounded my house, made a forced entry, woke up Divakaran, and took him into custody. He had links with the district committee through Madhu Master but had not taken part in the Mani action. Yet he was arrested under the

MISA (Maintenance of Internal Security Act), put in Kannur jail, and released only after 19 months.

After arresting Divakaran, the police began their search for me. Chaachan told them that I was working in Kasaragod. In fact, I had resigned my job and left Kasaragod by then. But I had not informed my family about my whereabouts. The police surrounded the house like the night they arrested Divakaran several times thereafter. Chaachan thus advised me to stay away.

By the time I returned to Wayanad, the Naxal hunt was over. But since the Emergency had not been lifted, the threat of police action hung over our heads like the sword of Damocles. We spent our morning hours cooped up inside Kunjukuttappan's hut within our compound. The KSRTC appointment letter had reached my house a couple of days earlier but I had not learnt of it. As I had not joined duty within the allotted period, a show cause notice had been dispatched asking me why my appointment should not be cancelled. I went to Civic Chandran at Amabalavayal. He took me to the superintendent of a government agricultural farm and got him to draft a reply. I sent it to the KSRTC's managing director, and awaited a fresh appointment letter.

During that time of waiting, an unexpected problem came up one day. Someone had driven a stake into the anus of a cow owned by a farmer in Kallupady, one-and-a-half kilometres from Vazhavatta. This happened at night. By the morning, a crowd had assembled there. The culprit was a Paniya youth. When he came to the tea shop in the area, the crowd began to question him. The youth pled innocence. A barber who had a shop at Vazhavatta happened to be present there. He pushed his way through the crowd. He said the youth would not confess to the crime if all they did was question him, and slapped him. Fortunately, someone stopped him immediately after and the youth was not tortured further.

In the afternoon, on hearing the news, Kuttan, who was staying in my house then, Vanchala, a Paniya youth, and I went to the barbershop and asked him why he had beaten the Paniya youth. 'Who are you to question me?' he hollered to my face, rushing towards us with a pair of scissors in hand. Kuttan grabbed the scissors from him, and Vanchala and I beat him up. He closed his shop immediately after and, vowing to teach me a lesson, went to a local CPI(M) leader and got him to lodge a complaint against me at the Kambalakkad police station. The sub inspector knew me. He had been my senior at Maharaja's College. When he came home to see me, I was away. So, he left word with Amma that I report at the police station. Amma was distraught when I got back home. She yelled at me and told me to go to the police station. To calm her down I said that I would, but I went to Civic Chandran's house at Ambalavayal instead and spent the following two days there. The case was not political and was not pursued further.

By now, my life at Vazhavatta had returned to normal. There was no police action against me, and the local people came to realize that I didn't have any connection with the Naxalites. I never spoke publicly about my political beliefs, which confirmed their belief. It was during this time that the apart from being friends Jose Joseph and I also became political allies.

The Communists and Socialists, who earlier opposed the Congress, were now silent. A group of youngsters was very uneasy about the silence. Jose Joseph, who kept in touch and interacted with these young people, gave concrete shape to their belief that the Emergency had to be opposed. It was when I got involved with this fellowship that I began to see the Emergency as a political problem. But they had neither a clear ideological perspective nor a framework of programmes with which to confront the issue. Nonetheless, we decided to convert this fellowship into a study group. In the meetings that we had, the main topics of discussion were Naxalbari and CPI(M-L). But there was no real political alternative in sight.

---

25. A New Path

I got a letter appointing me a lower division clerk at the KSRTC Ernakulam depot on 4 February 1976. We were still living under the Emergency, but I faced no serious threat. The situation at Wayanad was similar. But the Kayanna Police Station attack, only a few weeks later, on 29 February, led to a sudden turnabout. With the aim of completely uprooting the Naxalite movement, the government gave carte blanche to the most notoriously violent police officers. As a result, camps were set up in several places, including Kakkayam, and many were arrested.

I came to learn about the Kayanna incident when a bus conductor on his return after his trip to Kozhikode spoke of it the next morning. However, he had no details to share. I continued my work in office. My duty got over only at nine the next morning, after 24 hours.

Three days later, I reported for work again. But just as I was wrapping up the day's work, a police officer in mufti appeared and told me that I should meet him on my way out. I co-operated, and went to him after leaving office. He pointed to a vehicle parked at a distance from the office. Three or four policemen in mufti were inside it. They took me in that vehicle to the Crime Branch Office on MG Road. After presenting me to their officer, the policemen withdrew. The officer began to question me. He was harsh and threatening. He wanted to know about my relationship with the party, about the people who sought me out, and about where the leaders in hiding were. I kept my anger to myself and replied to all his questions. The truth is, had I actually had any connections with the party, I would likely have been more insolent. That was the extent of hatred I felt for the man. The questioning did not last long. He asked me to leave, instructing me to present myself at his office whenever summoned.

By the time I stepped out into the street, I was not the same person. My brain felt crowded. I could not hear the sound of the relentless traffic. In a fit of madness, I had lost all sense of time or space. Why were the police hounding me? I asked myself. I was sweating profusely in the terrible heat. Back in my room, I went into deep thought. For a long time, I had had no official connection with the party. Why then should I be subjected to this? I felt. All the policemen who had come in search of me, barring a few, had been inhuman sadists who behaved little better than goondas. I was overwhelmed with emotion when I thought of the torture that political workers suffered at the hands of the police carrying out the dictates of the government. I hadn't been subjected to a fraction of it.

Simultaneously, I felt sorry for those unfortunate men. I realized that they were being led by the wrong kind of politics. Their future was dark and dreary. I began to feel that if no one else was going to do it, I had to give the right kind of lead to this movement in which I had put such faith. To lead the labouring and farming people of India through a class struggle, I felt the need to rescue the CPI(M-L) movement from its middle-class leadership and re-organize it as a people's revolutionary party. In a way, I can say that my political experiments, or my political life, began that day.

While I didn't know any ideology other than Marxism, Leninism and Maoism, my knowledge of the original works was limited. That was the major challenge that I faced. In the days that followed, I began a careful study of their works. Whether in my free time at the office, inside my room in the lodge, or while travelling, I could be found reading *Das Kapital* and the selected works of Lenin, all purchased from Prabhat Book House and the Deshabhimani Book Stall. Simultaneously, I read about the Russian, Chinese and Cuban revolutions and the history of agrarian revolutions in India, especially in places like Telengana. My inability to indulge in literary compositions troubled me during those days, but I focused on my study.

Changes that occurred in national politics were what paved the way for my political life. On 19 January 1977, Indira Gandhi made an unexpected announcement that general elections would be held in March that year. Subsequently, all prisoners except Naxalites were set free. Following the elections, the Naxalites too, barring a few, were released. Divakaran, who had been arrested from my house under MISA, was freed from Kannur jail. After he came back home, I brought him to Alappuzha, where I was working then, so that he could get over the fatigue and boredom of imprisonment. Although he had no desire to remain in the CPI(M-L) any more, he did not agree with my political views. But disagreements over my criticism of the party did not affect our personal friendship. I did not get emotional about such things. That was why I took the initiative to give shape to the Communist Youth Forum on 1 August 1977. I was guided by Lenin's advice to the youth.

In April, I sought a transfer from Alappuzha to Sultan Bathery in order to become an active political worker. But Jose Joseph, along with others who had been with me, was not interested in working for a political party. They were opposed to the Naxalite principle of eliminating class enemies, and were more interested in public activities. Besides, they were unwilling to undergo any further jail terms.

As a Congress worker, Jose Joseph had also been a direct witness to the tragedy of Vazhavatta native Sasimala Raman Nair, an accused in the Pulpally police station attack case. Raman Nair, who had been acquitted by the court and later sentenced to life imprisonment, was a regular customer at Jose Joseph's shop whenever he was in his native village. Since he had been marked as a revolutionary, nobody interacted with him. Even political leaders kept away from him. Thus isolated, he had to do manual labour to eke out a living. This experience was what kept the youth of Vazhavatta away from the Naxalite movement. And yet, the political failure of movements like that of the CPI(M) and their reluctance to be associated with people's struggles had made these youth sympathetic to the CPI(M-L). They wanted a people's revolutionary movement that was led by the ideology of the Naxalites without joining the party. I did not think differently from them.

The argument I put forward was that the interpretation of Marxist-Leninist and Maoist thought had not taken the Indian context into consideration. The basis of this observation was the CPI(M-L) document that recommended swimming against the current. This document sought to show that Charu Mazumdar's ideological perspective had been right. My observation was that the methodology had gone wrong, and that only the right ideology could make the right methodology possible. If the methodology was wrong, it proved that the ideology was wrong too. Therefore, after studying Charu Mazumdar's argument, a Communist Youth Forum was created with Jose Joseph as its convenor. The aims of the organization were to propagate Marxism-Leninism and Maoist thought in order to re-organize the CPI(M-L), conduct struggles against state oppression, support workers' and farmers' agitations, and participate in the cultural field. The Communist Youth Forum was the first organization that acknowledged Naxal politics and yet existed without any support from the CPI(M-L).

The first activity of the organization involved the publication of a four-page leaflet that contained quotations from the works of Marx, Engels, Lenin, Stalin and Mao. Created along the lines of Mao's *The Little Red Book*, the leaflet was titled *Chuvarezhuthukal* ('Graffiti'), and its aim was to help propagate ideology with the help of illustrations and graffiti. Through the distribution of this pamphlet, the organization came to be known in CPI(M-L) circles.

It was at around this time that Civic Chandran, with the support of the CPI(M-L), took the initiative to give shape to the Wayanad Cultural Forum. I did not concede to the demand for co-operation with this organization. I saw it as a petit bourgeois grouping. Besides, I had already created a People's Art and Literature Forum in Wayanad, with the same office-bearers as those of the Communist Youth Forum.

In the same year—1977—I got married. The bride's name was Omana. She was from Thalayolapparambu. But that relationship did not last long. Too many irreconcilable differences came in the way, and we separated with mutual consent. I later married a girl from Thrissur named Usha.

---

26. At the Forefront of Struggles

I virtually abandoned my writer-persona. My reading continued as before, so the fact that I did not write was not as big a problem. In the course of a casual conversation, a friend once told me that I should focus more on writing than public life. As far as I was concerned, I replied, *jnana* (knowledge) and *karma* (action)[62] are one and the same. I still feel that jnana and karma cannot be separated from each other. My life of action was always driven by an opposition to poverty and violence. I did my work without any pressure from outside, and I kept to it even in times of financial trouble and domestic stress. An incident that remains undiminished in my memory is associated with labour problems during the initial stages of the Karappuzha Irrigation Project and the eviction of people from the project premises.

The contractor for the building activities under the project was one Kunjumoyin, from Kasaragod. He used to come with his son in a jeep from Kasaragod, accompanied by a few workers, and he brought all the necessary tools like spades, pickaxes, hoes, baskets and so on. Around 40 labourers from Vazhavatta and neighbouring areas came in the hope of long-term employment. Those who came from other places were provided food at the work site. Within a couple of days, two workers came to me with a complaint. The contractor's son and his lackeys were forcing the labourers to work harder, and threatening them too. Besides, the afternoon meals were of poor quality. When a worker named Velayudhan enquired about the wages, there were no clear replies. The workers resented such outrageous behaviour. Most of them had even begun to quit.

Come Saturday evening and it was time for giving the weekly wages. The contractor's son and his assistants sat on a bench in the veranda of a closed shop on the roadside. The shop belonged to a man named Muthirakkala Pappachan. The male and female workers went there in a group to collect their wages. These were fixed at nine rupees for men and six for women. This was way below prevailing local rates. Not only did the workers refuse to accept the payment but they demanded more. When this was turned down by the contractor's son, the workers began to protest. That was when Velayudhan came home and explained matters to me. I approached the contractor and told him that his rates were low, and that he must pay what the workers demanded. By then, local residents who had heard about the matter assembled there. The crowd, a fairly large one, lent full support to the workers. As the pressure mounted, the man requested that the workers accept what was being given for the moment. The outstanding amount would be paid after getting consent from his father. The workers were unwilling to accept his condition.

By now it was 9 pm. The workers who had laboured hard all day long had begun to lose their patience. Complaints began to give way to threats. It became certain that violence would break out any time now. So, as a last resort, I suggested that the workers' demands be conceded fully. 'Leaders like you are out to grab our money!' the contractor's son shot back. I began to shiver with rage. I grabbed his hand, pushed him from the bench, and threw him on the floor of the veranda. Just then, quite unexpectedly, Chakkala George appeared armed with a stick. Another labourer came rushing with a knife, screaming, 'I won't spare him!' But the crowd, including women, formed a ring and prevented them from doing any harm. Realizing that things were getting out of hand, the man conceded to the workers' demand.

How are the events of that night to be assessed? The prevailing atmosphere seemed to be in sync with the Naxalite principle of elimination, that is, the killing of the intermediaries, like landlords, between the masses and the state. What we had overcome was the possibility of an act of political indiscretion that could have hurt a struggle which had evolved naturally, without the benefit of organizational planning and without any thought about how to resist any reversals. Had things gone out of control, this is what would have happened: with colourful versions of the event circulating in the news from the very next day, a picture would have been presented of an institutionalized form of Naxalite violence, bringing in its wake government-sponsored terrorism, causing numerous people to suffer police atrocities, and families to be destroyed. The path of Naxalite elimination always ends with the helpless cries of the common people. That was why the movement sank into history without much impact.

However, unexpected things happened at the project work site. Sunday was a holiday. On Monday morning, as I was getting ready to go to office, a labourer came home and informed me that the contractor and his men had decamped, taking away all the tools. I went to the work site along with the labourer. A small crowd had gathered there. When some more people joined us, we held a demonstration and proceeded to Vazhavatta market, shouting slogans all along. There we asked the Communist Youth Forum activists to send a telegram to the Collector of Kozhikode and make arrangements for a direct meeting with the Circle Inspector of Vythiri. For the next two days, we held demonstrations and conducted public meetings. At this point, other political groups too began to intervene. Consequently, the Labour Officer convened a meeting at the Kalpetta Travellers' Bungalow, and a decision was made to restart work. As I had taken unauthorized leave, during those eventful days, it was one month before I could rejoin duty.

Another strike I got involved in concerned the eviction drive at the Karappuzha project site. Although my family was to be evicted too, I sought another way to align myself with the labouring classes. When the residents got wind of the impending eviction, there was a virtual torrent of political leaders and peasants' organization activists to the site. Nobody was opposed to the eviction per se. Everyone believed that they would get adequate compensation for their land as well as the produce under cultivation there. The calculations had given people the hope of receiving handsome amounts. As a result, the political and peasants' groups had only one slogan: 'Fair Price to Farmers'. With this aim in sight, a meeting convened by a commonly acknowledged leader—the vicar of Vazhavatta church—and attended by leaders of various political parties, including the Congress and the Communist parties, gave shape to a farmers' organization. All the farmers of the region participated enthusiastically in the meeting and *welcomed* the eviction.

We put forth a couple of queries to the political leaders and the activists of farmers' organization. Farmers who owned a lot of land and made substantial profits from their produce could afford to purchase arable land elsewhere. But would agricultural labourers, owners of small bits of land, landless peasants and Adivasis, we wondered, be able to solve their livelihood problems with the paltry sums given as compensation? Shouldn't they be given special consideration? Why were political leaders silent on this issue? If these caused a bit of a furore among the farmers, they raised enthusiasm among the poor. Under the prevailing conditions, local leaders of all political parties were invited to Vazhavatta Talkies for a convention of the evicted masses. None of them attended it. The labouring classes of course did.

The convention put forth various demands: granting of adequate compensation to evicted farmers; award of one acre of land and financial help to construct houses to agricultural labourers and owners of small bits of land; granting of land and relocation of Adivasis to ensure that their joint family system is not affected; provision for jobs to local residents in the project activities, and so on. We also created an organization called Karshaka Thozhilali–Adivasi–Daridra Bhoorahitha Karshaka Samithi ('Agricultural Labourer–Adivasi–Poor Landless Peasant Committee') to co-ordinate agitation programmes and submit these demands to the authorities concerned. In the following days, we organized a number of demonstrations and public meetings. This new organization had to face strong opposition from farmers' and political organizations. Their primary allegation was that Jose

Joseph and I were causing a rift among the people who were being evicted. This opposition followed us right up to our homes.

For the first time, Chaachan asked me to put an end to my public activities. The other option he gave me was to leave home. I tried to convince him by talking about the legal issues associated with eviction and damages. What came as a relief was an official order that instructed the revenue authorities to look compassionately into the demands we had put forward and to take appropriate measures. I do not recall whether we got the order from the Kozhikode District Collector or the Revenue Minister. The Revenue Department officials who arrived to evaluate the land and the price of the produce were very cordial. The distribution of compensation money in the initial stages of the eviction took place without any complaints. With the money that my family received, we bought a plot of land at Vakeri.

Soon afterwards, however, problems began to appear. The evicted people were scattered to various neighbouring places. With the increase in the demand for land, prices shot up uncontrollably, making it difficult for people to find plots close to motorable roads, or land that had sources of water and was arable. Only barren plots and those with fewer conveniences were available. If a hefty sum was paid to purchase such land, a large amount had to be set aside to put up a house there, and also to take care of expenses until the land began to give yield. As a result, most lost the facilities they enjoyed in the Karappuzha region. Additionally, when the compensation money had to be divided among members of a family, even owners of surplus land were left with only small bits. Those who lived on them and eked out a living through manual labour found few job opportunities in their new places of residence. Cordial relationships that had existed among neighbours for years became strained.

I write all this in order to give an experiential account of what happens to people when they are evicted in the name of development. Had it happened today, I might have opposed the Karappuzha project and the subsequent eviction.

When it became evident to me that a reorganization of the party was impossible, a veil of darkness began to envelop my Communist beliefs. In a bid to overcome this situation, I turned back to writing but that effort met with failure. I found myself slipping once again into a turbulent state of mind.

It was during this time of personal, organizational and political crises that the Naxalites eliminated Madhathil Mathai at Kenichira on the Panamarm route, four kilometres from Vakeri. The next morning, as I was travelling to my office, police vehicles stopped the bus and conducted a search. A friend had informed me about the killing of Madhathil Mathai as I had boarded the bus. But it hadn't bothered me much since I had no connections with the party.

Despite a month-long hunt, the police were unable to trace those involved in the elimination. Rampant arrests followed. The first to be subjected to police excesses were the local youth and labourers. With little information forthcoming, workers from other districts who had come to Wayanad to eke out a living began to be arrested. That was how Ravi, who was staying in Karappuzha, was taken into custody. Jose Joseph, too, who had contacts with Ravi, was subsequently apprehended. Both of them were first taken to the Sultan Bathery police station for questioning. By then, several people from Kenichira had been arrested and subjected to cruel torture. The complaint registered against most of them was that they shouted slogans seeking a change of government, held demonstrations, and were involved in seditious activities. They were later remanded to custody in Kannur Central Jail. After the remand period was over, Jose Joseph and Ravi were released on bail by the Manandavady court on the condition that they appear at the police station every Monday and affix their signature there. As I was in my village, busy negotiating marriage alliances for Shanta at the time, I escaped arrest.

Jose Joseph and Ravi did not have the remotest contact with the Naxalite movement. I therefore saw their arrest as a violation of human rights and citizens' rights. Yet a people's struggle was not possible, because that would have been construed as sympathy for Naxalites and their policy of elimination. Besides, our organization was weak. It wielded little influence in the interior of Wayanad, beyond Vazhavatta. A struggle launched by us was not likely to attract the notice of very many people. It was under these circumstances that legal redress was considered.

As I understood it, Jose Joseph and Ravi were arrested under the Travancore-Kochi Preventive Detention Act with the aim of preventing sedition. My argument was that with the attainment of political freedom and the adoption of the Constitution, this Act had become invalid. I spoke about this to Advocate Soman P. Paul, and considered filing a writ petition in the High Court in this regard. Paul did so with the help of his brother, Sajan P. Paul, a senior advocate at the High Court. The judge who pronounced the verdict stated that demonstrations and struggles had taken place before and after Independence demanding change of government and that they were not instances of sedition. He demanded that sections that legitimized such accusations be proscribed, and asked the government to withdraw all steps taken against those who were arrested on the basis of this section. Not only did this lead to the release of many who were arrested in association with the Kenichira case, many such cases were brought to a close.

But the police action that took place in the wake of the Madhathil Mathai murder case had had a serious impact as much on the Communist Youth Forum as on the Naxalite movement. Ordinary activists were no more willing to participate in such dangerous missions. Fearing that their political activism could hurt their jobs and families, most lost interest in organizational work. This caused the Communist Youth Forum to disintegrate on its own. Its end to me spelled the failure of the grand narrative of Marxism.

27. The Release of Political Prisoners

When the perpetrators of the Kenichira Madathil Mathai murder were arrested, all the fire and fury that had raged until then subsided. The manhunt mounted by the police came to a stop. All of Wayanad was relieved. Much later, a people's protest convention was held at Kalpetta under the leadership of K.N. Ramachandran, the state secretary of the CPI(M-L). Its aim was to protest government excesses. I knew little about the details or anything about the behind-the-scenes activities, but I drew up a statement demanding a boycott of the convention conducted by a party that had not sought the release of political prisoners. I sent the statement to Jayachandran, the *Mathrubhumi* reporter from Wayanad, for publication in the newspaper. But after reading it he said it could not be published.

Jayachandran not only covered the convention but also conducted an interview of K.N. Ramachandran. It was carried in the edit page of *Mathrubhumi*. I have a hunch that Jayachandran may have handed over my declaration or conveyed its contents to Ramachandran. Whatever be the case, it was on Ramachandran's initiative that a co-ordination committee was set up for the release of political prisoners.

In the context of widespread public anger over the disappearance of P. Rajan,[63] following the withdrawal of the Emergency, and the terrible torture that was perpetrated at the Kakkayam camp, many political prisoners were released. Yet others—M.N. Ravunni, Bhaskaran, N.V. Chandran, Vellathooval Stephen, Somadathan, K.K. Damodaran, M.A. Alexander, Appukuttan and Rajendran—were still behind bars. Many of them led very difficult lives to begin with. One of them whom I knew personally—M.A. Alexander, a Dalit Christian from Muttappally—had to spend the night at a bus stop after his release.

Among those who were incarcerated, a few including M.N. Ravunni created local headlines by escaping from jail. I did not have any links to the prisoners. Nor did I see eye to eye with them on ideological grounds. The government argument—intended to not release political prisoners at all—was that life imprisonment meant imprisonment until death. Therefore, release after 15 years behind bars was not possible. To me, that was a violation of human rights and prevailing practice. However, living as I did in a small village like Vazhavatta, and working in a small organization, I could not lead a struggle at the state level. Institutionalized political movements like the CPI(M) would not take up such a cause either. That was the reason why, with the aim of exerting pressure on the Naxalite movement, I had drawn up a statement demanding the boycott of the people's resistance convention. I never found out if K.N. Ramachandran knew about it. He never spoke of it even when, much later, we worked together as state-level leaders in movements such as the Anti-Caste Secular Forum or the struggle for freedom of expression. Be that as it may, Ramachandran invited me to a meeting he convened at the CMS High School hall. It was presided over by K.V.K. Warrier, and the main subject of discussion was the issue of treating the release of political prisoners, irrespective of party affiliations, as a humanitarian problem. An agitation committee with Warrier as chairman and Ramachandran as convenor was later constituted. I too was elected to the state committee of that body. Civic Chandran, Advocate Premachandran and I were given the responsibility of preparing a pamphlet for distribution among the masses.

I drafted the pamphlet. In it, the release of political prisoners was presented more as a political issue than a humanitarian one. My reading of the history of the nationalist movement of India was what inspired me to take such a perspective. The operative forces behind the nationalist struggle had been not only the Congress, the Socialist and the Communist parties, but revolts led by armed guerrillas too. They were branded as terrorists by the colonial administration even as the public saw them as freedom fighters. From the people's perspective, those who fought to remove an unjust system and establish a different political order were not criminals. It was this kind of evaluation that made the agitation for the release of those whom the British government had thrown into jail a part of the freedom struggle. I submitted the draft of the pamphlet, written from this point of view, to Civic Chandran. Advocate Premachandran added legal clauses to it, and Chandran made certain other amendments and gave it the title 'Those Who Sacrificed Their Youth for Their Beliefs'. Tens of thousands of copies of the pamphlet were printed and distributed. There were no other pamphlets in circulation throughout our agitation. It paved the foundation for a unified set of ideas that were propagated everywhere.

Those who joined forces for the release of political prisoners were not only Naxalites, present and past, but activists of political parties and even those who had until then never participated in public life. It was this broad representation that gave a public face to the agitation. Many agitation committees cropped up at different places, even without the state committee taking the lead or initiative; customary forms of demonstrations, public meetings, vehicle rallies and so on were organized. Poetry-reading sessions and cultural programmes were conducted as well. Among these, the most significant contribution was made by the actor and playwright, Surasu, who staged a song-and-dance show throughout the state. When the protestors held a demonstration in front of the Secretariat in Thiruvananthapuram by walking in shackles, it made for a novel spectacle and attracted a lot of attention. The arrival of the Speaker of the Legislative Assembly, Sankaranarayanan Thampi, underscored the mass appeal of the agitation. Many litterateurs, including M.T. Vasudevan Nair, came forward, expressing solidarity with the common people who had joined the struggle.

These activities at the grassroots level had their impact on institutionalized political movements as well. Under the leadership of M.N. Ravunni, who had been consigned to solitary confinement following his indictment in the Kongadu case, in which the Nair landlord had been beheaded, those who had been sentenced to life imprisonment began an indefinite hunger strike. M.V. Raghavan, the CPI(M) state committee member, went to the jail to pay a visit to the satyagrahis. His statement that Ravunni be released unconditionally was published in the *Deshabhimani*, which subsequently also published a signed declaration making the same demand. The signatories included many prominent people from the political and social arena, including Chathunni Master, a Rajya Sabha member.

Neither EMS nor the CPI(M) took a favourable stand on the issue. In EMS's view, the prisoners, including Ravunni, were men who had committed murders. They had not killed people to protect the interests of the labouring and farming classes. He also branded the state-wide agitations as propaganda work cranked up by mainstream newspapers. Although the CPI(M) turned away from the agitation on the basis of this ideological stand, we submitted a memorandum to the governor and the chief minister which had been signed by 81 MLAs, of both the ruling and the opposition parties. Eventually, in the wake of this massive agitation, all political prisoners were released in November 1985. To me, who was not part of the Naxalite movement, this agitation for the release of political prisoners was a chapter retrieved from our nationalist movement.

---

28. Dalit Life

While the struggle for the release of political prisoners was going on, we sold off our house and property at Vakeri and returned to our native village. We had bought some land at Kappikkadu, a region close to Madhuraveli—a one-acre garden plot with coconut trees and a half-acre paddy field adjacent to it. We made a decent income from selling coconuts. Besides, as water was plentiful here we grew a lot of vegetables too. On the western side of the garden plot where Upper Kuttanad ended, there were vast paddy fields. It was upland on the rest of the sides. We put up a house with brick walls and thatched roof, and started living there.

It was ownership of land that shaped the Dalit perspective on politics and society that I hoped to evolve. Although we owned land in Wayanad, Chaachan and Amma had worked as wage labourers for a long time and later as farmers. Since the condition of our neighbours, and the rest of the residents in the area, was not dissimilar, I made no attempt to view our landownership differently. But back in our native village, things changed drastically. Chaachan and Amma did not engage in wage labour. We suffered acute financial hardship because I was often either on long leave or on unauthorized absence from work because of political activism or because of personal problems. But the income from our vegetable farming offset our troubles somewhat. The lesson I learnt from this experience was that ownership of land and wealth held the key to self-reliance, which was so important to Dalit life. It was the reason I argued so strongly for Dalits' wealth, authority, status and culture.

Although I was no longer addressed with a caste label appended to my name or kept away from interventions in social life, I was identified as a Dalit (Pulaya) and my relationships had not overcome these boundaries. If politics and class had once been important determinants of identity, now I was in an exclusively casteist space. The majority of the caste and religious communities, including the Ezhavas, had acquired a land-owning middle-class status. The SNDP, the NSS and the Christian churches wielded influence on the individuals and families that belonged to their respective communities more than ever before. Political affiliations were asserted only during the time of elections.

The changes in the economic sector were key to these developments. Decentralized land ownership took the place of centralized possession of property. Thousands of acres of land that were once the exclusive possession of the Neythassery Mana were now fragmented and in the hands of many different individuals. Very few people owned more than five acres of land. The uplands on the eastern side were swallowed by rubber plantations, the level grounds on the western side were largely coconut farms. The small fields in the possession of individuals produced paddy. Tapioca, banana, ginger and other crops were rarely cultivated. When land began to be set apart for cash crop cultivation, excess wealth flowed into the educational and commercial sectors. On the completion of education, jobs in government institutions, private educational establishments, private hospitals and other firms now became accessible. Many could go overseas and take up employment there after mortgaging their lands with nationalized and co-operative banks and other financial establishments in return for huge sums of money. With increasing income from cash crops, tiled roofed structures began to give way to concrete buildings. The financial progress of a substantial section of the population brought about a corresponding change in the very landscape. There were tarred roads everywhere, bus services had grown, markets saw the mushrooming of textile, stationery and bakery shops. In short, what I observed was that one-and-a-half decades had transformed life here completely.

On the other hand, I also noticed that the Dalits had been excluded, ostracized even, from this good fortune. With this realization, a new communitarian and political perspective began to take shape in my mind.

Dalit life was the darkness within the light of the region. Very few individuals had even small pieces of land in their possession. The majority of them lived on very tiny plots. And as the numbers in the families grew, more huts came into being in the neighbourhood, thatched with woven coconut leaves or just hay. Virtually none of them had toilets. Besides work on the paddy fields and garden plots, rubber tapping and coconut plucking became newer sources of livelihood. Another job was inland fish farming where the workforce was largely women. Dark, sunburnt women leaving the village early in the morning to catch fish in faraway regions like Kumarakom was a common sight. They fished on an empty stomach, often without even drinking water, took their catch to the markets by three or four in the evening, and sold them there.

Dalit life in the Harijan Laksham Veedu ('One Lakh Houses') colonies was the most pathetic. There were several houses built on ten-cent plots granted by the panchayats. Life there was so piteous that many families began to occupy the sides of roads and canals as well as wastelands. Before rubber plantation took over, since there was the practice of inter-crop cultivation, job opportunities had been better. But when jobs began to dwindle in the agricultural sector, road and house construction work became the source of livelihood for many. Complaints then arose that agricultural labourers were not available for work on the paddy fields in Kuttanad. The fact was that since there was no income to be gained from paddy cultivation, the fields were left fallow.

The social relations within the Laksham Veedu colonies became the cause of fights within and among families, and such areas to become the breeding grounds for criminals. As no one was willing to marry the girls who lived here, love affairs, break-ups, weddings and divorces were confined within the colonies. This led to the impression that the women here had loose morals.

When private firms closed their doors on the literate members of the Dalit community, a small number of them gained government jobs with the help of the reservation policy. But the salary did not permit them to lead comfortable lives. That was because the responsibility of the entire family was invariably on their shoulders. I myself was one among the low-salaried people who stood as guarantors in financial institutions to secure loans for relatives and friends. The kind of poverty and misery that the Dalits suffered was not the same as that which members of other communities endured.

Although I was not with the CPI(M), I attached value to the peasants' struggles of the 1960s and the '70s in which the Dalits took part in a big way. I had thought that the struggles would bring about a change in the lives and the level of awareness of the Dalits. But this belief could not withstand scrutiny. Those who participated in the struggles with great zeal, even enduring torture in the process, led miserable lives now. This first-hand experience was what occasioned my own interpretation of terms like 'peasant' and 'peasants' struggles'.

All the Dalits of the land aligned themselves with the CPI(M) with a kind of maniacal enthusiasm. They formed a substantial presence at demonstrations and public meetings. People who got involved in fellowships like these did not think about the conditions of their own life. Neither they nor the party appeared to desire an alleviation of their pitiable condition. And so, they never put forward the demand for ownership of land or wealth. The party made much of the Land Reforms Act, which granted 10-cent plots as well as the meagre peasants' pension institutionalized by its government. The Dalits refused to recognize that the kudikidappu right was not equivalent to land ownership but only meant the right to put up huts, which could be razed anytime, subject to the whims of the landlord. Thanks to party propaganda, the Dalits became slaves to the party but received no benefits either of political education or of individual and family reform. The result was that when the party foisted its political enmities from outside, it contributed to the Dalits becoming class conscious and suppressing their religious faith—whether Hinduism or Christianity.

The party stood for the interest of the farmers. It even created and propagated a theory to suit it. According to this view, as the financial status of the farmers improved, the 'class consciousness' among the peasants would grow and improve their bargaining power. The main responsibility of its leaders was to shepherd the Dalits to make them participate in demonstrations and public meetings and also to make suicide squads to fight their political enemies. As far as the Dalits were concerned, not only EMS and AKG but local leaders too were paternal figures. With such hero worship, they were prevailed upon and easily made to believe that those among the Dalits not aligned to the party but with intelligence and leadership skills were either Naxalites or followers of the Congress. Naturally, the Dalits among the CPI(M) nursed intense hatred for people like me.

What I learnt from this personal experience was that work had to be done to ensure that the life of the *Dalits*—more than that of the entire community—improved, their rights were secured, and the other depressed peoples brought together under a political umbrella. In order to achieve this goal, the CPI(M), which had enslaved the Dalits, both socially and politically, had to be opposed ideologically as well as organizationally. I felt this was the bounden duty assigned to me by history. Defying the Marxian hypothesis that linked freedom to historical inevitability, I arrived at the belief that what constituted real freedom was recognizing one's own life's condition and working towards changing it. Thereafter, all my *karma* (action) was led by this *jnana* (realization).

---

29. The Jaathi Viruddha Mathetharavedi (Anti-Caste Secular Forum)

It was when the issue of caste overrode Marxism in Dalit communitarian and political forums that the Kerala Stipendiary Students' Association (KSSA) organized an agitation-cum-propaganda procession against caste, pollution and servitude in 1983. It was inaugurated at Vaikom by Dr K.K. Manmathan. A few days after the procession concluded in Kottayam, K.N. Ramachandran met K.K.S. Das, the general secretary of SEEDIAN, and proposed the formation of a secular forum that would include organizations like the CPI(M-L) and SEEDIAN.K.K.S. Das who was also the Kottayam district secretary of the Kerala Rationalists' Association (KRA)[64] agreed to it, and suggested that the KRA be included in it too. On the basis of this agreement, a preliminary meeting of the representatives of the SEEDIAN, the CPI(M-L) and the KRA took place at Paikadas College in Kottayam.

I was not a member of any of these organizations but attended the meeting in my personal capacity. The point K.N. Ramachandran put forward was that a secular movement was being formed because the National Democratic Party (NDP), formed by the NSS, and the Socialist Republican Party (SRP), formed by the SNDP, were weakening Left Front politics. Rajagopal Vakathanam, who represented the KRA, did not have a different opinion. But what the SEEDIAN members—Dr K.K. Manmathan and K.K.S. Das—and I argued for was an anti-caste secular forum. This idea was later taken up, and subsequently, I was included in the state committee of the organization.

It was this organization that, refuting the claims of the nationalist movement and reversing the Communist party's attempts at erasure, made the Renaissance and its leaders a component of the rich past not only of their respective communities but of everyone else as well. Back then, the Communist party opposed these re-readings, alleging that they abetted casteism. That was the reason why the Communist parties were kept away from the activities of the anti-caste secular forum, the Jaathi Viruddha Mathetharavedi.

The forum came into being as a state organization with K.N. Ramachandran as chairman and K.K.S. Das as organizing secretary. The first state committee meeting, presided over by the chairman, decided to: (1) create district committees in all districts, including Kottayam; (2) organize seminars on Renaissance movements like the Vaikom Satyagraha at Vaikom, and on leaders like Sree Narayana Guru at Cherai, Ayyankali at Sachivothamapuram in Kurichi, Sahodaran Ayyappan at Kalavoor in Alappuzha and so on; and (3) conduct the first state meeting at Thalayolapparambu.

The reason for explaining the programmes of the Jaathi Viruddha Mathetharavedi here is to point out that we sought to retrieve the social renaissance from the communitarian and political history of Kerala through the above-mentioned activities; to repudiate the claims made by the institutionalized Communist parties; and, above all, to highlight the initiatives taken by the Dalits.

It was decided that the first seminar should be on the Vaikom Satyagraha, conducted at Vaikom. I had suggested the idea at the committee meeting, and there was a reason for it. Even before the JVM was created, I enjoyed a good relationship with SEEDIAN activists. That was an acknowledgement of my status as a Dalit writer. Kallara Sukumaran[65] and Paul Chirakkarode were leaders of a huge organization called the KHF (Kerala Harijan Federation), but since they did not have a clearly-defined anti-caste stand and were strongly opposed to the Communist party, SEEDIAN activists did not look favourably upon them, unlike me, who they considered an intellectual. One day, P.O. John and M.D. Thomas of SEEDIAN came to see me. At a Temple Entry Proclamation Memorial Meeting conducted by the RSS at Vaikom, certain speakers had claimed that the Temple Entry Proclamation was the result of struggles led by Hindu leaders, including Mannath Padmanabhan. Such propaganda agitated John and Thomas, and they wanted me to contribute an article on the Vaikom Satyagraha in the SEEDIAN weekly.

I did not know much about the Vaikom Satyagraha. In the works on the nationalist movement that I had read, the Vaikom Satyagraha had been hailed as part of the legacy of the Congress and Gandhi. In the history books of the Communists, however, it was not a subject of discussion at all. Since, in my reckoning, the Congress and Gandhi were in the enemy camp, and the Communists had not given the issue any serious consideration,

I never thought of the Vaikom Satyagraha as a subject worth studying. But the request from the SEEDIAN activists could not be turned down either. So, I decided to write the article. Although I read many works on Kerala's history as part of my preparation, I didn't have a very comprehensive picture. That was when I read an experiential account written by E.V. Ramaswamy, titled 'You and I'. Its content was different from all that I had read before. What attracted me to his article was the view he had on the Vaikom Satyagraha.

As far as the Congress leaders were concerned, the Satyagraha was meant to achieve the right to worship for the subaltern classes, including the Dalits. Consequently, all commemorative meetings at Vaikom resounded with praises of the magnanimity of the royalty and the caste-Hindus. It was argued that all Hindus were equal inside the temple premises, and that temple entry would create a religious unification of the Hindu community, overriding caste distinctions. With the exclusion of people like Barrister George Joseph, Sebastian and Abdul Rahman from the leadership of the struggle, thanks to the intervention of Gandhi, the struggle had effectively become one for reform within the Hindu community rather than a fight against a social evil. E.V. Ramaswamy's stand, on the other hand, was not about such matters. As far as he was concerned it was not a struggle aimed at securing the right to worship for the subaltern classes. It was instead a fight against the caste system which denied humans the right of way, a right that even by birds and animals enjoyed. That was the reason he said, 'Vaikathappan[66] is a stone, and it is good for washing clothes.'

Besides, E.V. Ramaswamy's participation in the Vaikom struggle contradicted the claims made by the Congress. This was his account: With the Congress leaders, including K.P. Kesava Menon, punished and jailed at the very beginning of the

Satyagraha, the pavilions at the protest site became empty. While in jail, K.P. Kesava Menon wrote a letter to E.V. Ramaswamy, president of the Tamil Nadu Congress Committee, to take over and lead the struggle. As soon as he received it, Ramaswamy came with his wife Maniamma, both dressed as prisoners. And this was how the struggle progressed.

The Satyagraha went on for a long time, but it yielded no results. The Backward Classes, including the Ezhavas, now began to prepare for religious conversion. This culminated in a meeting of Ezhavas at Edavanakkad in Vypin and their conversion to Islam. This was what led to the Temple Entry Proclamation.

Although I read Ramaswamy's description in conjunction with reports about the activities of the Congress, I got an account of Dalit participation in the struggle only in a book titled *Mathrubhumiyude Charitram* ('The History of the Motherland'). On the basis of the news reports of the time, the book pointed out that even before the Congress deputation, comprising K.P. Kesava Menon, K. Kelappan and Kuroor Neelakantan Namboodiripad, reached Vaikom, a Pulaya Maha Sammelanam was held at Ullala near Vaikom. It became a satyagraha with the intervention of the Congress leaders. Besides, there were reports that when a 100-member savarna procession led by Mannath Padmanabhan reached Shastamcotta in Kollam, they were received by 3,000 Pulayas. Over and above this, labourers were involved in the struggle too. In a study by Prof Robin Jeffrey, there is a reference to 50 members of a newly created labourers' organization in Alappuzha reaching Vaikom in a boat in the evening and participating in it. My article, 'The Historical Relevance of Vaikom Satyagraha', which included accounts of the participation of Dalits, subsequently came out in the SEEDIAN weekly.

It was K.N. Ramachandran who presented the subject at the

seminar. But he could neither evaluate the Vaikom Satyagraha historically nor point out its social relevance. He spoke like an ordinary political activist, making only a superficial narration of events, and complained that Dalits and the Backward Classes, instead of taking the path towards agricultural revolution, had aligned themselves with revisionist movements. When I rose to speak, I rejected his perspective, and stated that the Vaikom Satyagraha had played a major role in starting an anti-caste struggle as well as in forging unity among the subaltern classes. The speakers who came after me supported my argument.

It was the Dalits who gained the most from the seminar, from the point of view of ideas, because the seminar could indisputably establish the historical fact of the participation of the Dalits in the Satyagraha which until then had been considered a Congress legacy that had gained a firm footing through the proactive engagement of Nair and Ezhava leaders like Mannath Padmanabhan and T.K. Madhavan. On the 75th anniversary of the Satyagraha, the *Madhyamam* weekly carried an article of mine. The same issue had an article by Sunny M. Kappikad that established the leadership of E.V. Ramaswamy in the satyagraha. It was this unveiling of Dalit participation, which the nationalists and the Communists had sought to conceal, that made the participation of Kanshi Ram at the anniversary function possible. The Congressmen held a demonstration and a public meeting asking for the arrest of Kanshi Ram, for his criticism of the subversive attitude of Gandhiji in the course of his speech there. Kanshi Ram paid a visit to the house of Amachadi Thevan who, for the crime of having participated in the struggle along with K.P. Kesava Menon and T.K. Madhavan, had his eyes lined with limestone paste and rendered partially blind. Kanshi Ram also made a contribution towards the building of a memorial in the plot where Amachadi Thevan was laid to rest.

Kunjapi, a Dalit, one of the three individuals[67] who initiated the Vaikom Satyagraha, finds no mention in history, except as a mere name. Details about the place of his birth, his links with organizations, and his circle of relatives and friends are all unknown. There is no information in any written record either.

30. Retrievals

I still cherish memories of the seminar on 'Ayyankali in Kerala History' that we organized under the auspices of the Jaathi Viruddha Mathetharavedi at Sachivothapuram Welfare School near Changanassery in September 1985. To me, the seminar was a matter of self-surrender. I was actively involved in conducting it from start to finish. There was a specific reason behind conducting the seminar at Sachivothapuram. It was a mark of respect to T.T. Keshava Shastri, the first (and last) warden appointed to ensure the welfare of the residents of the government colony set up here, the first in Kerala, and to bring their complaints to the notice of the authorities concerned. He was Ayyankali's son-in-law who went on to become an MLC and Deputy Speaker of the Tiru-Kochi Legislative Assembly. Another reason was the historical relevance of the colony, which came into being in 1938. Here is what happened.

A local resident named Anandan Isaac, who was a community worker, set out on foot from Kurichi, reached Thiruvananthapuram, and with Ayyankali's help, submitted a request to Sir C.P. Ramaswamy Iyer, the Diwan of Travancore. On the strength of his request, a 112-acre plot was set apart for the establishment of the colony. With the welfare of the king's subjects in mind, the authorities gave each family a 25-cent plot with a two-

organizations, consisted of black pants, red shirt and a cap. Each person carried a short cane stick. The aim of the organization was to reintegrate Dalits and bring them under the purview of Dravida laws and culture. Maintaining an uncompromising stand against savarna authorities, they had become the protectors of Dalits who were subjected to abuse. The demonstration concluded with a public meeting at Ettumanoor at which certain derogatory remarks were made about the Pope, which provoked some of the listeners. A gang of miscreants led by a goonda, including Dalit women who sold fish at the Ettumanoor market, attacked the DCUF activists. Although the victims went back immediately, they reappeared a few days later. They, nearly 15 in number, conducted a meeting at the very spot where they had been manhandled earlier, where the goonda-led gang attacked them once again. The leading goonda got stabbed and killed in the melee and the followers scattered in all directions. A hartal was observed in the city the next day in protest. Shops were kept closed. At the all-party meeting that took place in the evening, a few prominent Christians demanded that Dalits coming to Ettumanoor should be driven away.

The SEEDIAN representatives and I raised the Ettumanoor issue at the state committee meeting of the JVM and decided to organize a people's resistance convention in order to counter the threat against the Dalits. The convention was held in the Hindu Matha Padhashala Hall. At a meeting organized in the evening, representatives of various organizations declared that attacks on Dalits would provoke a strong retaliation. That checked the assaults on Dalits, who could now move unhindered in the city as before.

The police registered cases against 15 individuals in the Ettumanoor murder case. Throughout the trial, the DCUF activists appeared in court in their uniform, causing some amusement to the judge, the lawyers, the court employees and the journalists. After months of litigation, all the accused were acquitted for want of evidence.

---

31. Preparations

In 1986, I was one among the invitees to the state meeting of the SEEDIAN Service Society conducted at Kaduthuruthi. The other two were Kallara Sukumaran and K. Venu. At the end of the meeting, unexpectedly, Dr K.K. Manmathan suggested my name for inclusion in the central committee and to the post of editor. None of the representatives raised any objection to it.

A year before the doors of the SEEDIAN opened for me, I had published an article titled 'The Challenges that the Depressed Classes Should Overcome' (1985). The view I spelt out in it constituted the foundation of my work as a Dalit activist. It was based on my reading of the Dr A.R. Desai-edited *Peasant Struggles in India*, Dr R. Prakasham's *Keralathile Trade Union Prasthaanathinte Charithram* ('The History of the Trade Union Movement in Kerala'), K.K.N. Kurup's *Colonial Capital Investment and Proclamation of the Abolition of Slavery*, E.V. Ramaswamy's 'You and I' and *History of the Motherland* [sic] as well as Dr A. Ayyappan's *Social Revolution in a Kerala Village*. Based on Father Fuch's article 'Missionary Movements', included in A.R. Desai's book, I established that the Dalits had gained nothing substantial from missionary work. At the same time, Ayyankali was found to be the initiator of an awakening among the Dalits. I presented him not as a stormy petrel as he is commonly portrayed to be but as a historical figure who tethered the struggle for rights to the struggle for self-respect.

In many of my subsequent articles, I tried to show how economic and social factors like the financial crash of 1850, the formation of the Public Works Department in 1860, the genesis of the plantation business, the spread of cultivation and so on were the foundational stones of the Renaissance, including the Ayyankali movement. On the basis of the American social scientist Kathleen Gough's work, I analysed the savarna hegemony in the Communist party too. Here's what I wrote:

> In the absence of a unified Dalit movement, the Communist party and the peasants' movement did not allow, as a continuation of the struggle for self-respect, either the removal of a cultural malaise like racial consciousness, evil customs and sub-caste systems or the transformation of a depressed people into a single community. In the other communities, however, that task had been completed by the NSS, SNDP and the Catholic Congress. As far as the depressed people were concerned, that duty remained suspended with the disappearance of the Ayyankali movement.

When I returned to Wayanad, I had a few copies of the JVM bulletins in my possession. It was when G. Harilal, the Public Works Department overseer, saw a copy of the bulletin that I got introduced to him. He was from Kunnamthanam near Changanassery. A member of the Vishwakarma, or the goldsmith sub-caste, he was a discerning reader. He was of the opinion that as a result of modernization, members of the Vishwakarma caste were losing employment. He realized, too, that his community was still shackled to the caste structure, and none of the existing organizations were able to unify the various sub-castes. It was this similarity in our views that became the foundation of our friendship. Harilal stayed at the PWD quarters situated 150 metres behind the KSRTC bus station. As it had three rooms and a kitchen, and he was the sole occupant, I was invited to stay there.

The days went by pleasantly. We read, held discussions, saw movies and travelled. Gradually, I began to make contact with the cultural life of Sultan Bathery. Both of us worked together to canvass nearly Rs 3,000 from the Pulpally region for funding John Abraham's movie *Amma Ariyaan*. We co-operated with the Thedal Film Society formed at Sultan Bathery. Harilal's quarters attracted the cultural activists of the place and became a popular venue for informal discussions among them. When Babu Mailambadi, a South Indian Bank employee, bought a 16 mm projector for the film society, it was kept safe at Harilal's house.

In 1986, P.N. Sukumaran, a native of Nayarambalam in Vypin, joined the Bathery depot as a clerk. Although we were meeting for the first time, he had heard about me. During his graduation course at SN College at Malyankara, he had been a member of the Kerala Harijan Students' Federation (KHSF), but he was neither a sympathizer nor a member of the Communist party. Later, even as he took up teaching at a tutorial institute, known locally as Sukumaran Mash (sir), he was famous all over the Vypin island as a good speaker and theatre activist. He was in great demand as a speaker at public functions, cultural programmes and during Onam celebrations. Though he had no official links with the Naxalites, the person he was closest to and had great respect for was V.C. Rajappan, who had endured terrible police torture in the 1970s for being a Naxalite. They lived in the same neighbourhood, separated only by eight or ten houses. When, during the Onam season of 1982, 77 people lost their lives after consuming spurious liquor, it was not the Naxalites but Sukumaran Mash who initiated an agitation against the tragedy. He contacted Rajappan as soon as he heard about it. The next day, when the CPI(M-L) Nagi Reddy group sympathizer, Mandalam Mohammed, and a teacher named Joseph Majali (who was not a politician) joined the frontline of the agitation, it spread throughout Vypin island. The agitation lasted a week with Naxalites from various places subsequently visiting Vypin to lend their support to the cause. All of them were given refuge by Sukumaran Mash and V.C. Rajappan. Sukumaran Mash created a new model in the history of agitations. I introduced him to Harilal and shortly afterwards he too began to stay at latter's quarters.

A month after Sukumaran joined duty, a labour strike in which both of us took part began at the Bathery depot. Many trade unions co-operated in this agitation, demanding an adequate number of chairs and tables for the clerical staff in offices. It ended with an officer getting roughed up, as a result of which many employees, including myself, were suspended. After five months of suspension, I was appointed once again at the Bathery office. The case dragged on for four years. Finally, the court acquitted all the accused because there was no proper evidence.

32. As Editor

It was during the period of my suspension, when I returned home from Bathery, that SEEDIAN's Dalit activism grew stronger. The publication of the SEEDIAN weekly too now became serious business. The SEEDIAN was a cadre-based organization, similar to the Naxalite groups. As it shared ideas with the CPI(M-L), SEEDIAN was perceived to be revolutionary group among the public. The slogans raised and the statements made during demonstrations and at the strike venues as well as at public meetings only served to reinforce that impression. This was further underscored by its image as an organization of intellectuals because members sought to spread their ideas through sharing book-reading experiences, conducting symposia and organizing seminars. The fearlessness shown by the members coupled with their inattention to sartorial neatness also contributed to the common belief that SEEDIAN was another Naxalite group.

Among the three members of the central committee, Dr K.K. Manmathan was a medical doctor practising privately, and K.K. Das was an officer in the Department of Education. Only a couple of members of the state committee were government employees. The rest were common people, largely wage labourers.

The challenges and crises that SEEDIAN faced were far more numerous than those other Dalit organizations in the state had to encounter. Since its members had a deeper engagement with Marxism than Dalit studies, they interpreted things with a Marxian perspective, not only in public meetings but in private conversations as well. Which is probably why they faced the staunchest opposition from the CPI(M), in whose eyes the SEEDIAN members were anarchists and Naxalites. As Dalits constituted a substantial CPI(M) vote bank, SEEDIAN as well as the Indian Dalit Federation (IDF) were objects of disdain. The Communist party was soft, however, towards caste organizations that did not have a clearly defined political orientation and were slavishly loyal to institutionalized political parties. The complaint against me was that I had given up my job to undertake organizational activities. Against Baburaj, the charge was that despite a post-graduate degree, he chose to remain jobless.

The perennial problem that SEEDIAN activists faced was a lack of funds. Dr Manmathan and S. Rajappan, who was an officer in the Canara Bank, were our sole benefactors. The rest, including members of the state committee, were in no position to spend money, which thus had to be sourced from business establishments and private individuals. Those who donated gave only small sums because they had to worry about objections raised by caste organizations. The meagre amounts we got were completely used up in our organizational work. What that meant was that members had to forgo food, compelled often to travel on foot to keep things going.

When I took my first steps in Dalit activism, nearly all the members of SEEDIAN were Dalit Christians. For that reason, Hindu Dalits did not patronize it. However, as the organization was against the Christian church and the funding organizations of the Dalit Christians, it did not have the latter's support either. Despite backing the demand that Dalit Christians be included in the list of Scheduled Castes and granted the benefits of reservation, it did not attract them into its fold. On the contrary, this move only provoked the opposition of the Hindu Dalits, conveyed through their caste organizations. Generally speaking, as far as Dalit organizations are concerned, bureaucrats often play a big role in providing leadership, executing organizational activities, and ensuring the availability of funds. But there were very few of them in SEEDIAN, owing to the fact that not only was the organization seen as a Naxalite group, they themselves saw bureaucrats as belonging to the petit bourgeoisie. SEEDIAN was thus an organization of a few frontline workers who carried out its ideological and social activities.

The first meeting I attended was a joint central and state committee meeting conducted at Paikadas College in Kottayam. What I understood from the celebrations that took place there was that the SEEDIAN had not formulated a proper Dalit epistemology and also that due to the limitations of its organizational structure it could never become a mass movement. And so, I hoped, by using the practical experiences gained through organizational work and disseminating ideas through its weekly, to give shape to a Dalit epistemology. Had it not been for this aim, I may not have been able to work in SEEDIAN for the years that I did.

The following days saw measures being taken for the publication of the weekly. The first step involved an examination of the earlier issues. During my college days, since I used to read *Sameeksha*, *Anveshanam*, *Yugareshmi* and nearly all the little magazines as well as political publications like *Inquilaab*, *Street* and *Nirnayam*, and national publications like the *Economic and Political Weekly*, *Frontier*, *Liberation* and so on, I realized that the SEEDIAN weekly did not have an impressive layout. The unattractive design and the unsystematic presentation of matter clearly pointed to the absence of good editorial intervention.

The SEEDIAN weekly was similar to all the Dalit publications that used to come out at the time. Its contents—articles, reports, stories and poems—were more Marxist than Dalit in spirit. Since they were products of first-hand experiences, complaints about the attitude of the Communist party stood out prominently in all of them. Nevertheless, as it contained some excellent pieces, albeit rarely, the SEEDIAN weekly was different. The issues edited by my predecessor V. Padmanabhan were distinctive vis-à-vis the previous ones. The last issue he edited carried the editorial titled 'Naxalite Prisoners Should Be Released'. Another noteworthy piece was a chapter from Mary Tylor's book *My Years in an Indian Prison*.

As editor, I wished to bring about substantial changes in the magazine's appearance and content, to make it appealing as much to the general public as to the Dalits. Towards that end, I decided to use works like Kumaran Asan's prose writings, the history of the SNDP Yogam, Sahodaran Ayyappan's poems, his biography, previous issues of *Mithavadi*[68] and *Vivekodayam*[69] as well as studies on the formation of modern society in Kerala.

Furthermore, I drew up a framework in order to include studies on women's liberation, and introduce Dalit movements taking place in other states like Maharashtra. Articles and reports written in English were translated into Malayalam by P.O. John. We did not give much importance to organizational news. It was limited to two columns under the title 'The Seventh Page'.

Although the weekly was the mouthpiece of the organization, neither Dr K.K. Manmathan, the managing editor, nor K.K.S. Das, the chief editor, interfered in deciding its contents. And the junior cadres were largely ignorant about these matters. I thus enjoyed total freedom in selecting what would go into each issue. I had the full co-operation of P.O. John, M.D. Thomas, K.O. Raju and others who worked as a single team. Another peculiarity of the weekly was that it received no financial support from the organization, which therefore became my responsibility. In order to bring out the first issue under my editorial supervision, I had to use my daughter's stipend money (she was then studying at Kallara NSS High School) and pay it as an advance to the press. Either John or Thomas would always be with me during the printing. So, I got their help not only in improving the appearance of the weekly but in proofreading the copies as well. By the time the issue came out, Dr Manmathan and S. Rajappan took some of the financial burden off my shoulders. I had to take care of the outstanding amount only.

The SEEDIAN weekly took over the duty of converting the crises faced by a community into the written word. The earlier issues hadn't been either creative or vibrant. The issues that came out with the collective effort of my team, during my tenure of editorial midwifery, gave voice to the problems and challenges of an entire community. It was because the weekly succeeded in setting aside the miseries and conveying a ray of hope that it became a subject of academic research to scholars in later years.

33. November Books

The publishing firm named November Books, with its tagline 'To Change the World, to Reconstruct Life', was established not by me but by K.K. Baburaj, my younger brother. In its life span of five years—from 1984 to 1989—it published 17 books. I was associated with it because of ideological affinity as well as political and financial reasons.

Those who advocate new ideas are often frontline members of renaissance movements, within their own communities if not all of Kerala. The key forces that gave a social orientation to Thunchath Ezhuthachan's bhakti movement, initiated reforms in Malayalam, and transformed it into a group strong enough to make political claims, were enlightened members of the Nair community. Vaikunta Swami[70] introduced the world of Dravidian wisdom, which included the *Thirukkural*. Mithavadi C. Krishnan and Sahodaran Ayyappan revived Buddhist thought. The Thangals of Malabar propagated liberal views of Islam during the middle of the 19th century, and Parammekkal Thoma Kathanar[71] and Hermann Gundert[72] initiated reforms within the Christian community. *Vivekodayam*, the mouthpiece of the SNDP, carried reviews of the works of Wordsworth, Shelley, Keats, Byron and other famous poets of Europe. (One of the four volumes of *Vivekodayam*'s founder Kumaran Asan's prose writings was dedicated to reviews of books written by the above-mentioned authors.) Such a spring season of ideas came to an end when these fellowships of the Renaissance period became institutionalized movements. When the communities ossified those ideas through the process of ritualization for the sake of financial, social and political gains, the spirit of argumentation within the communitarian movements was lost.

Some new ideas that emerged in various parts of India and the world in the 19th and 20th centuries were replanted among the public in Kerala by the intellectuals on the Left. Having rejected Renaissance ideas, they redirected the masses to another sphere of knowledge. Marxism and Socialist thought thrived as systems of thought such as Gandhism were pushed aside and replaced by these ideologies, particularly when the organizations propagating them became all-powerful.

The mid-1960s witnessed the birth of a movement led by figures such as Bertrand Russell which was intended to bring an end to the long-drawn-out American war against Vietnam. The anti-war sentiment that emerged in America became a powerful mass movement when those in the backwoods of society—like the Blacks, women and sexual minorities—joined hands with progressive democrats and created history. This caused an anti-imperialist wave and simultaneously politicized the people occupying the margins of society. Following the withdrawal of America from Vietnam, with the Black and feminist movements getting stronger, established systems of knowledge began to be razed to the ground. Such a discursive space was chiefly critical of the Marxist streams of thought. Following this, there was widespread demand for the political participation of the Blacks and an outcry against sexual discrimination against women. This was transformed into an ideological domain with the realization that Marxist militarism had been a failure in the anti-colonial struggles taking place all over the world. The setbacks suffered by the Communist parties in Indonesia and Chile, the defeat of Che Guevara in Latin America, the limitations of the Cultural Revolution in China and the new interpretations of Marxism made the formation of different ideological spheres inevitable in order to confront oppositional forces within nation-states. The agricultural revolution and the Dalits' anti-Brahmin struggles that spread in various parts of India were all part of a search for an alternate ideology. Enlightened individuals, small groups and institutions—many fated to crumble—internalized the new ideas, both that of the Marxists and those that followed, and infused them into society. It was this space that November Books occupied.

When Baburaj was an undergraduate at Maharaja's College, Ernakulam, a Left Front had come into being, with members both inside and outside the Students' Federation of India (SFI). It was neither aligned with the Naxalites nor showed any subservience to the institutionalized Communist parties. K. Sunilkumar from Mulanthuruthy and Abhimanyu from Kodungalloor were members of this fellowship. They read the works of authors whom the established Left practically ignored, like Pablo Neruda, Nicolas Guillen, Lorca, Gabriel Garcia Marquez, D.D. Kosambi, rather than Marxist literature. Baburaj aligned himself with this group. Works of literature produced in different parts of the world were easily available to these students through the Eloor Lending Library, which stocked books like these.

In the beginning of the 1970s, the CPI(M-L) state committee published a Malayalam translation of Charu Mazumdar's complete works. In September 1983, the Janakeeya Prasidheekarana Kendram (People's Publishing Centre) at Kottayam brought out two volumes of Mao Zedong's works. Another publishing firm established in Kodungalloor tried to give a new direction to the Naxalite movement by releasing books like Mohan Ram's *Indian Communism*, Suniti Kumar Ghosh's *The Indian Big Bourgeoisie*, Debi Prasad Chattopadhyay's *Indian Atheism* and so on.

As I had read the works of these authors and publishers, I could see beyond traditional Marxian hypotheses. The result was that I was not unwilling to accept new ideas. Baburaj returned home accompanied by the poet Shelvy, who had become famous through a publisher named Mulberry Books. They came with a proposal to join hands with Mohandas of Guruvayoor and start a book publishing firm named 'Shikha'. The first books they planned to bring out were Bertolt Brecht's *The Good Woman of Szechwan* and Garcia Marquez's stories (he had not won the Nobel Prize yet). Although I encouraged them to go ahead with the project, I was not in a condition to help them, financially or otherwise. My salary had to be used to cover our domestic expenses. Besides, my attention was divided between work and my public activities. Although the above-mentioned books were published with Baburaj's co-operation, that association did not last long. It was after both he and Shelvy left Shikha that they broached the subject of starting a publishing firm on their own. This was how November Books came into being.

I could not lend financial support, but I co-operated with the project wholeheartedly. I was convinced of the power of books to help bring about changes in our lives—social, political and cultural. Besides, I felt that Mani, who was reluctant to work as a wage labourer, would be able to earn something by working in it. There was also the hope that profits from the firm would improve the condition of our family. I became the general manager of November Books and Baburaj its editor. The emblem was designed by the writer V.M. Unni. The name was chosen in order to point to the Left orientation of the firm.

Among the books that Baburaj chose to publish first was journalist Ralph Schoenman's report on America's war crimes in Vietnam, prepared by the International War Tribunal, the Hague, with Bertrand Russell as chairman; it also contained Russell's radio address as a frontline pacifist to the American people. If Schoenman's report carried an honest picture of the inhuman violence perpetrated by colonialism, Russell's speech conveyed not only his anti-imperial sentiment but also humanity's irrepressible desire to create a war-free world. Russell's speech was also a call to the American citizens to do their duty of defeating America for the sake of democracy. Baburaj completed the translation in a matter of days and gave it the title 'Yuddhathinte Mukham' ('The Face of War').

Baburaj stayed for some time at a hostel in Ernakulam to solicit funds for the publication of the book. He got Hariharasubramanian to design the cover page. The book was printed at the best press in Kottayam—Changanassery Sandeshanilayam. Since we didn't really have an office, all the work was done at home. Mani was in charge of sales, which he discharged well, making good use of the contacts that Baburaj and I had. He also went to educational institutions, offices and individual houses to sell it. We had no worries on his account. He had absolutely no hesitation talking to the topmost political leaders or litterateurs wherever he went, as a result of which he soon became a familiar figure in political and cultural circles. His own contacts came in handy identifying Dalit and non-Dalit individuals interested in the Jaathi Viruddha Mathetharavedi, the struggle for freedom of expression and SEEDIAN.

November Books hoped to make book-reading a political act. Its aim was to create a broad Left front and bring together anti-imperialists and secular, progressive minds under a single umbrella. Thus, a lot of care went into the choice of books to be published under our banner. Along with the ideological relevance of each work, we also considered its saleability. It was with this in mind that we brought out *Vishwasavum Janathayum* ('Belief and the People'), a collection of articles edited by Baburaj. It included the writings and speeches of Lenin, Stalin, Mao, Che Guevara, Bertrand Russell, Antonio Gramsci, Pablo Neruda, Gabriel Garcia Marquez, Jean-Paul Sartre, Mulk Raj Anand and Charlie Chaplin, along with an editorial note by Baburaj for each of them. Besides introducing the piece, it would also contain a Marxian analysis of the particular period of time in which it was written. I wrote the preface titled 'Kalaapavum Samskaaravum' ('Rebellion and Culture'). The book was special in that we introduced names and works that were not very familiar among the reading public in Kerala—Gramsci and Marquez, or Chaplin's speech in *The Great Dictator*.

It was the same reason we published essays like D.D. Kosambi's 'The Sociology of the *Bhagavat Gita*' and Dr Nirala's 'The Economics of the *Bhagavat Gita*' as they represented ideological opposition to attempts at resisting reformation in Hinduism. The translations were done by Dr M. Gangadharan. Although Kosambi was not a recognizable name among the Malayalis, copies of the book sold out easily.

November Books, which became a part of this alternate history, did not have an independent existence. It was inextricably linked to the family, the SEEDIAN weekly and our organizational activities.

---

34. Struggle for the Freedom of Expression

Although I had to rejoin duty at Sultan Bathery after my suspension period was over, Baburaj and Mani took forward the business of November Books well. All the three books published by the firm received great reviews from readers. This was the primary inspiration behind the genesis of the November Book Club. When it became possible to sell books (published by November Books as well as other publishers) at cheap rates and send them via VPP (value payable post), we started receiving orders not only from within Kerala and outside but from the

Gulf countries and the US as well. Some readers encouraged us by sending in small donations along with the cost of the books.

Mani, besides being in charge of sales, succeeded in inducting new members into the Book Club. As a result, November Books became a profitable business. Not long afterwards, we could take a house, situated one-and-a-half kilometres from ours, on rent and convert it into our office. It had four rooms and, as one was set apart for me as the general manager, I could now do the editing work of the SEEDIAN weekly too properly. With the business thriving, we could alleviate our financial troubles somewhat, as well as those of Shanta.

The fourth book published by November Books was a collection of Mao Zedong's poems. They may not have had much literary value, but we decided to bring them out because they showed the self-awareness of a famous revolutionary. The translator was K. Satchidanandan. The next book was V.C. Sreejan's *Yadevisarvabhudheshu* ('O Mother of all Beings'). It was a collection of articles that were published serially in the *Kala Kaumudy* during the Emergency period, and given to November Books because by then, despite its small catalogue, it had acquired a reputation as a publisher of good books. Its second edition was brought out by DC Books. At a time when Hindutva forces were consolidating their power, we published a part of Paul M. Sweezy's compendious work giving it the title *The Economics of Imperialism and Fascism*, to clarify our stand in discussions about the evolving communal atmosphere. It was translated by Baburaj. Given our view that Hindutva politics was aimed at protecting Brahminism, which was opposed by Dalits all over India, the politics that he set forth through the book argued for the Communist party taking into its fold all the religious and communitarian sections that were anti-Brahmin.

Such an interpretation was based on the views upheld by

the SEEDIAN and the Jaathi Viruddha Mathetharavedi. No other publisher has brought out more than two editions of this book, the premise of which remains relevant even today. The Communist parties, including the CPI(M-L), ignored these new interpretations of Marxism.

When a controversy arose over the play *Christuvinte Aaraam Thirumurivu* ('The Sixth Holy Wound of Christ') by P.M. Antony, a playwright accused in a Naxalite elimination case, I was at Sultan Bathery. But since this was not reported in the local editions of newspapers, I did not hear about it. It was when I stopped at the office of the magazine *Samskarika* on my way home and read a small news report about the controversy in *Mathrubhumi* that I found out. Although I didn't know Antony personally, I had seen a play called *Spartacus* directed by him at Wayanad.

I had gone to the Alappuzha KSRTC office on a personal errand. Here I succumbed to a friend's insistence and saw the new play, which was not as artistically brilliant as *Spartacus*. So, the crusade against it didn't seem justified. The play reflected the writer's ideological perspective, which was different from what was commonly read about Jesus. Had the church leaders not raised Cain over *Christuvinte Aaraam Thirumurivu*, the play would not have gained the place in history it did. When I got back home, I decided to write a report on the play.

With my mind set on exposing church hegemony, on the basis of the resistance shown to the play, I went to Alappuzha to interview P.M. Antony. Just as I arrived at his house, I saw that he was getting ready to go to Fort Kochi. I did manage to speak to him for a brief while though. We later boarded a bus from the KSRTC stand. Antony took a ticket to Thoppumpadi. On the way to the place, he spoke about his political and theatre-related experiences, answering questions raised by me every now and then. And I made sure to remember everything he said. By the time he alighted at Thoppumpadi, I had all the material I wanted from him. I decided to include the interview along with the report on the play.

Back at the November Books office, I prepared the report and gave it the title 'Oru natakam kurushil' ('A Drama Crucified'), focusing more on the propaganda and the agitations against the play than the play itself because that was my intention. I sent the report along with my interview of P.M. Antony to the *Kala Kaumudy*. Along with the editor's reply came the demand for a study on Malayalam theatre with a focus on the partnership of the Christians, as well as a review of Nikos Kazantzakis's novel *The Last Temptation of Jesus Christ*. While I did the first task, Baburaj wrote a review of the novel. The report, interview, the study and the review were given prominence (as the cover story) by *Kala Kaumudy*. The report problematized the play and triggered a high tide of agitations from both sides. And I can claim with absolute confidence that the struggles that emerged later were crucial in bringing about the great victory for the Left Democratic Front in the elections the following year, 1987.

It was the Jaathi Viruddha Mathetharavedi that initiated in Kottayam district, SEEDIAN playing a major role, the discussions and struggles for the freedom of expression that were taking place within the state and outside. Rajagopal Vakathanam, the leader of the Jaathi Viruddha Mathetharavedi, convened a meeting at Paikadas College with the aim of expanding the protest against the call and action for banning the play. The majority of those who participated in it were activists of SEEDIAN and the Kerala Rationalists' Association. The number of CPI(M-L) members was marginal. At the meeting presided over by Dr K.K. Manmathan it was decided that a procession should be taken around the city. As slogans against the church authorities and the government resounded, the police stopped the procession at the Central Junction. In protest, we squatted on the road. We were arrested by the police and presented in front of the magistrate at 7.30 in the evening. The complaints registered by the police included attempt to create religious hatred and provoke rebellion against the government. We were lodged in the Kottayam sub-jail until remand, but since the arrest took place on a Friday, and the following days, the second Saturday of the month and Sunday, were holidays, the application for bail could be submitted only on Monday. Dr Manmathan was the first accused, and I, the second. Others who had participated in the protest—P.O. John, K.O. Raju, K.K.S. Das, M.D. Thomas and Rajagopal Vakathanam—were also among the accused. The jail stay went off uneventfully. We got bail on Monday. It was the CPI(M-L) activists who completed all the formalities. After four years of litigation, everybody was acquitted.

Although the struggle for freedom of expression took place all over the state, it was at its strongest in Thrissur district. It was the participation of the Janakeeya Saamskaarika Vedi (People's Cultural Forum) activists, and theatre personalities like Jose Chirammal that made the scene vibrant at Thrissur. Many individuals and institutions who had no connection with the Naxalite movement—either in terms of ideology or membership in the organization—formed the vanguard of the struggle. But K.N. Ramachandran, who led it, was backed by the Naxalites. He conducted everything in a totally undemocratic and dictatorial manner, refusing to hold consultations with SEEDIAN and KRA even once, as a result of which every individual and organization that had aligned themselves with the struggle was compelled to take orders from the CPI(M-L). It was on the basis of his successful conduct of the Vypin struggle that the state level convention for the current struggle had decided on

Ramachandran at Thrissur. Despite the fact that neither Dr K.K. Manmathan nor K.K.S. Das had been kept in the loop, SEEDIAN had participated in the convention, and following the decision taken there, its activists were brought in from various places to participate in the struggle. It was for the first time that women took part in a big way at a function associated with the CPI(M-L).

Those who addressed the thousands of people who assembled at the Thekkindkadu Maidan in Thrissur were Thoppil Bhasi,[73] D. Surendranath, Pavanan[74] and K.N. Ramachandran. Not a single representative of the Jaathi Viruddha Mathetharavedi or SEEDIAN had a place on the dais. People like Dr K.K. Manmathan became mere spectators. The discontent among SEEDIAN activists was therefore palpable on the way back after the district convention. Most of them were of the opinion that the link with the Jaathi Viruddha Mathetharavedi ought to be snapped and co-operation with the Naxalites brought to an end. The leaders tried to calm them down, but they eventually gave in to the majority opinion. It was with such behaviour that the Naxalites brought about their own downfall, despite having turned away from the policy of elimination and adopted the path of democracy. In protest, against such hacking measures that were initiated by K.N. Ramachandran, V.C. Rajappan resigned from the CPI(M-L).

Later the High Court removed my name from the list of adjudicators of the play (the 15-member panel constituted in 1987 comprising prominent cultural leaders and litterateurs to watch and examine the play for offensive content, and decide whether a ban was necessary).

---

35. Realizations

Although it's not possible to give a clear picture of the influence that the Jaathi Viruddha Mathetharavedi wielded throughout the state, I can say from personal experience that it succeeded in creating a strong foundation for the CPI(M-L) in several parts of Kottayam district. Hordes of Dalits shifted loyalties from CPI(M) to CPI(M-L) in places like Vaikom, Thalayazham, Maravanthuruthu, Arpukkara, Kallara, Kaippuzha and so on. It became possible to publish the *Comrade* weekly and many books of the Janakeeya Prasidheekarana Kendram from Arpukkara. Once, the top leaders of the CPI(M-L) participated in a two-day meeting at Manjadikkara near Arpukkara. This Kuttanad island, overcrowded with Dalits and Dalit Christians, was inaccessible except through boats. The venue was chosen not merely for its geographical peculiarity but also for the staunch support that was guaranteed by the island residents.

The sudden growth of the CPI(M-L) bothered the CPI(M). In order to overcome the crisis caused both by erosion in numbers and by harsh criticism, it chose the path of violence. A number of CPI(M)–CPI(M-L) clashes followed at places like Arpukkara, Maravanthuruthu and Chembu.

M.K. Dileep had led the consolidation of the CPI(M-L) at Arpukkara, and M. Pavithran at Vaikom, Thalayazham, Chembu and Maravanthuruthu. Pavithran, a Dalit himself, had faced all manner of discrimination as a child. It is what gave him the courage to fight inequality. He had been drawn, like many other students, towards the ideology of the Left and he became an active SFI member in college. As an employee in the Road Transport Department, he joined the NGO Union led by the CPI(M). It was after the Emergency that he joined the CPI(M-L) and was made to pay for it. Implicated in a case on false charges, he was suspended from service. And even when he was subsequently acquitted, his superior officers were unwilling to have him back in the department. Pavithran had to wage a one-man war against this injustice. His suspension was revoked only after he created headlines in the newspapers—by talking about the series of unjust measures meted out to him in front of passengers inside buses and at bus stations, in market places and basically any place where people assembled. When the party became weak at his workplace, he joined hands with the Dalit-Adivasi activist and writer Salimkumar and launched the Adhasthitha Navothana Munnani (Forum for the Uplift of the Downtrodden). Later, he became a member of the state executive committee of the Dalit Aikya Samithi (Dalit Unity Committee). He committed suicide on 27 October 2001 by jumping in front of a moving train.

The Jaathi Viruddha Mathetharavedi celebrated its first state-level meeting at Thalayolapparambu. A decision was taken to publish a bulletin including details of the papers that would be presented at the meeting. The reservation issue created differences of opinion at the state committee meeting convened as a prelude to it. As discussions were going on about the resolutions that should be introduced at the meeting, P. Parameswaran, a member of the committee and president of the Ernakulam district unit of the KRA, argued that the existing reservation system only served to reinforce casteism and therefore needed to be replaced by economic reservation. K.N. Ramachandran, who presided over the meeting, maintained silence. But there was a huge uproar when Dr K.K. Manmathan, K.K.S. Das and I opposed his idea vehemently. Ramachandran brought the committee meeting to an end and instructed that it reconvene the next day. The three of us went to S. Rajappan's house at Kaduthuruthi in the evening and discussed the issue in detail. We decided that there could be no compromise on our views on the reservation policy and also that the idea of economic reservation should be opposed tooth and nail. In addition to that, we jointly agreed that there should be a special session on reservation at the meeting and Dr Manmathan should formally introduce the subject. We also threatened to keep away from the meeting and resign from the organization if these arguments were not accepted at the committee meeting. The members, including K.N. Ramachandran, accepted our arguments the next day.

The meeting at Thalayolapparambu took place on 13 and 14 October 1985. It was the first people's meeting that witnessed the participation of the CPI(M-L) and its being acknowledged in central Travancore. With representatives from various districts—including Ernakulam, Idukki, Thrissur and Thiruvananthapuram, besides Kottayam—attending the meeting, the Government High School Hall was filled to overflowing. The message the meeting conveyed was: with casteist and religious powers strengthening their hold in the social and cultural spheres as in the political, the caste structure had to be eliminated and secularism upheld for the sake of protecting democracy.

The speech made by Kuttikrishnan, the CPI(M-L) leader, however, was unsettling. Quoting D.D. Kosambi, he stated that the Dalits, even in the present day, had not internalized the right historical consciousness and were backward from the ideological point of view. I spoke to Dr Manmathan and K.K.S. Das about it outside the hall. Manmathan shared the sentiment. Both of them agreed that a publication was necessary if this problem had to be confronted and our social consciousness advanced. This was how I became an indispensable part of SEEDIAN.

---

36. Uniform Civil Code

What next? I had considered the activities of the Jaathi Viruddha Mathetharavedi as political work. It was when the organization was euthanized by the Naxalites that I began to re-read Marxism. As far as I was concerned, by refusing to oppose casteist and religious hegemony in the present, the Communists were effectively supporting it. When this realization dawned on me, I began to look at the Marxist ideology, which the Communist parties and Naxalites upheld as their commandment, with suspicion. I began to understand that this ideology did not do justice to people at the grassroots, that the leadership at the top retained the ability to control the organization to suit their interests. Even at this point, I was unable to adopt another method of explanation. I could not completely assimilate the spirit of the SEEDIAN either. At this critical juncture, the person who led me out of the impasse was Civic Chandran.

Following the closure of the magazine *Prerana*, brought out by the Janakeeya Saamskaarika Vedi, Chandran had started another magazine called *Vak* from the Vanchi Lodge in Thrissur. On my way to Bathery and back, the magazine office was my resting place. There I could read many magazines that were unavailable at the regular newsstands. A decision was taken to hold a symposium at Manjeri on the Uniform Civil Code (UCC) under the aegis of the *Vak* magazine.

Civic Chandran asked me to present a paper at the symposium. I was flummoxed at first because I knew nothing about Muslim politics, the Shariat or personal laws. At Wayanad, the only Muslim politics I knew about had been that of the Muslim League. And as the leadership of that organization was in the hands of the rich among the Muslim community, I saw it as another version of the Congress. But I could not wriggle out of the job assigned to me.

Much controversy surrounded the issues of the Shariat and the Uniform Civil Code. The event that triggered it was the Supreme Court directive for the implementation of a Uniform Civil Code while giving the final verdict on the Shah Bano case on 23 April 1985. According to section 125 of the Code of Criminal Procedure (CrPC), a Muslim woman granted divorce had the right to demand alimony from her former husband. The inevitability of a Uniform Civil Code had been pointed out by the Supreme Court while considering the final appeal on the verdict of the lower courts regarding the Ahmed Khan–Shah Bano case of Madhya Pradesh.

The demand for a Uniform Civil Code contained in the 44th Amendment of the Indian Constitution was what caused the institutionalization of concepts such as 'One India, One People' and 'United Bharat'. I felt that steps taken to reform personal laws like the Shariat were an infringement on the rights of the Muslims. The person who separated the Supreme Court's directive from the UCC, the thrust area of the seminar, and made the Shariat controversial was the historian Dr Irfan Habib during a speech delivered at a DYFI (Democratic Youth Federation of India) state meeting at Kozhikode. Politicizing this speech, EMS made the Shariat the main issue, and used it as a weapon to attack the Muslim League. Turning a blind eye to the political implications of a UCC, and ignoring the element of faith in the Shariat, EMS present Shariat to mean 'four weddings'. Arguing thus, he established that the Muslims were an uncultured community who refused to accept such social reforms and stated that only a working-class party like the CPI(M) could discharge that responsibility. When such controversies began to swirl around the Shariat, the Muslim League also entered the fray, rendering the Uniform Civil Code irrelevant. Those who therefore profited the most from the controversy were votaries of the Hindutva ideology. They were able to present Hindu–Muslim enmity as a matter of fact.

I was unwilling to draw my conclusions from newspaper reports. The thrust of the symposium was 'Uniform Civil Code and the Shariat'. I began reading up on the history of our independence struggle for some background on the subject. Besides this, I read a couple of issues of a publication titled *Muslim India* that I picked up from a Muslim establishment at Maravoor Road. It was this reading which helped me realize that the standardization of a people by force of law, rather than a transformation through upliftment and reform, constituted fascism. I arrived at this on the basis of the measures taken during colonial rule.

In 1722, with the appointment of Warren Hastings as the Governor-General of Bengal, British rule became institutionalized through the process of law making, the maintenance of law and order and public administration. The Shariat law was changed when such an administrative reform was made applicable throughout British India. The most important among these reforms was the removal of the criminal laws that were contained in the Shariat. Muslims did not oppose this change because of the pressure exerted by social reform movements as well as the reforms that took shape within the community itself. If the present-day Shariat permitted Muslim men the right to marry four times and denied Muslim women their right to property, they should not be changed through the legal system without the support of reforms within the community—this was the major premise of my paper presented at the symposium.

A majority of those who participated seconded my argument. The only person who opposed me was K.E.N. Kunjahmed, a

CPI(M) loyalist. He focused on the politics of the UCC and argued that in order to put an end to casteist and religious differences in our country, the rights of Muslim women (effected through reform of the Shariat) had be protected. He criticized me for adopting an academic approach and my paper for lacking in facts.

In the speech I made in reply, I pointed out how the Soviet Union, which had been around as a federal state for 60 years, could not be made a military state under the socialist ideology. The United Kingdom, which had witnessed the capitalist revolution, could not, politically speaking, forge a bond between Scotland and England. In contrast to these nations, India was virtually ruled by religious and casteist differences. Attempts to unify it through legal means would therefore be tantamount to fascism. In the article I wrote titled 'Vaividhyangalude Nishedham' ('A Rejection of Diversity'), included in the book *Ekeekritha Civil Code: Akavum Puravum* ('Uniform Civil Code: Inside and Out') (2015), edited by Hamid Chendamangalur and published by DC Books, I included the same arguments, fortified with more studies. The symposium at Manjeri opened pathways unseen by Marxism, and my walk through them was what led me to adopt a different political stand and arrive at a discursive space that could accommodate a confluence of Dalit and Muslim thought.

It was Civic Chandran, as I've mentioned earlier, who paved the way for an exploration of another ideology. Those were the days when the statement 'Indiayude Mochanam Islamiloode' (India's Liberation through Islam) was making waves. The organization named Students' Islamic Movement of India (SIMI) organized a seminar on this slogan at the Town Hall in Kozhikode on 18 January 1986. Civic Chandran asked me to cover the event for *Vak*. I considered this an opportunity to see Islamic politics at close quarters. I had expected to find Islam interpreted as anti-establishment in spirit. That was because I had linked it with Liberation Theology, which had taken shape within the Christian church. I imagined that the seminar would resemble the spirit of the Reformation within the Christian community. However, I was disappointed after carefully reading a few issues of SIMI's *Vivekam*. SIMI was unable to correctly interpret the slogan it had made its own. The pamphlet distributed during the seminar showed the same vagueness and confusion. Nonetheless, I was resolved to do my best to report on the seminar as I had been instructed to. I was given the same treatment as that accorded to mainstream reporters.

Before the seminar began, I went to Hotel Paramount to meet V.T. Rajasekharan, the editor of *Dalit Voice*. He told me that our fight was not against Brahmins but against the value system of Brahminism. This was how, he said, the Brahmins had managed to remain a hegemonic power through several centuries despite being a demographic minority. In numbers, they enjoyed a majority in only a single taluk in Uttar Pradesh. This was a powerful insight. My subsequent reading of Dr B.R. Ambedkar's works was what gave me a sense of direction with regard to the anti-Brahminism struggle.

I sat through the entire seminar and prepared a report titled 'Let God's Slave Nation Live Forever'. In it, I recorded, 'Mohammed Rafath's paper titled "The Liberation of the Oppressed in India" did justice to the thrust of the seminar, "India's Liberation through Islam". His view can be summarized thus: If Gandhiji, Jayaprakash Narayan and the Communists can put forward the idea of India's liberation, why can't Islam? Not only do these movements fail to support 80 per cent of the population who are oppressed, they also align themselves with exploiters who form the rest of the population. Chipko, Sharad Joshi's farmers' organization, the Jharkhand Mukti Morcha, and various Dalit organizations are anti-establishment movements. Such movements came into being with the failure of the previous ideologies to deliver on their promises. If Islam is able to stand with these movements and lead them through a pragmatic path, it will be possible to create an Islamic state. He proved the viability of the idea by pointing to Iran and highlighting the economic and political achievements of that country.'

I had begun my report with the following passage though: 'Instead of the Dalit movements forging a political alliance based on fraternal rapport with a religious community like the Muslims, to argue that the Dalit movements should be led by Islam is to concur with the discursive view of hegemonic ideologies like Gandhism and Marxism. If that happens, it will be a rejection of the culture of administrative partnership brought about through reservation, which was earned as a result of political struggles in the social history of Dalits.' The Dalit representatives who took part in the discussion in the seminar, however, did not interpret the paper from a political point of view.

37. From Mao to Dr B.R. Ambedkar

From the beginning of the 1980s, on the one hand, political party movements including the Communist parties, through the agency of caste organizations, destroyed the independent existence of the Dalits and put them in a state of stupor. On the other, the very same caste organizations attempted to shepherd the Dalits towards Hindutva. It was to resist these two regressive interventions that the politicization of Dalits took place. This happened by simultaneously treading the paths of Mao and Ambedkar. The leadership role played by Dr K.K. Manmathan in this exercise was noteworthy. Although he has been erased from the communitarian and political history of Kerala, he has not been forgotten either by Dalits or votaries of progressive democracy. A native of Changanassery, Manmathan was doing his MBBS course at the Kottayam Medical College when he became attracted to the Naxalite movement. In the initial phase of his organizational activities, he stood shoulder to shoulder with top Naxal leaders, abandoning his studies and choosing instead to be a political activist in Dalit areas, including Kuttanad.

Even as a student, Manmathan was widely read, versed in Marxist works, the history of the Russian and Chinese revolutions and the paths taken by the Indian Communist parties. He was one among the rare Marxists I was acquainted with whose reading was so profound. A compelling orator, Dr Manmathan could present international, national and regional incidents with great clarity. He had an extraordinary insight into things, and his commitment to a people's democratic revolution was utterly selfless. In 1970, he was accused in the Kongad Narayanan Nair murder case, subjected to brutal police torture, and sentenced to two-and-a-half years of rigorous imprisonment in Viyur Central Jail. Following his acquittal by the trial court, he continued to focus his activities in Dalit regions in Travancore. Subsequently, he was arrested as an accused in the Joseph murder,[75] committed in Idukki district under the leadership of Vellathooval Stephen, and once again sentenced to two-and-a-half years in Thiruvananthapuram Central Jail. He was acquitted in this case too but kept in prison as a MISA (Maintenance of Internal Security Act) detainee during the Emergency.

It was at this time that he started thinking of alternate political paths. He struck upon the idea of linking the agricultural revolution with the anti-Brahminist democratic movement. His felt that Dalits, numerically stronger than the Russian population, could be organized ideologically and trained in armed combat in order to empower them for revolution. Further, on the basis of Ambedkar's thought, the struggle could be taken over to other groups of people by means of the democratic movement. During his stay in Thiruvananthapuram jail, he held direct conversations with the Socialist leaders who had been imprisoned and, with the help of the books they supplied, wrote a biography of Jayaprakash Narayan and succeeded in getting it published by Learners' Books in Kottayam. This book, a few articles on the subject of Dalits, and a few speeches published in the SEEDIAN weekly constitute the only tangible legacy of Dr Manmathan. It was when he served as the chairman of SEEDIAN that the Dalit community was drawn from the path of Mao Zedong to that of Dr Ambedkar.

38. To Ayyankali, Respectfully

The internal affairs of India were in turmoil in the 1980s. It was when I recognized the savarna religious and casteist interests as well as the anti-Dalit, anti-Backward Class, and anti-minority sentiment informing the struggles which took shape in the new circumstances that I was compelled to rethink my stand. And only after reading Dr B.R. Ambedkar's works could I see the mutual link between reservations and minority rights.

The rampant mass murder of Dalits and Muslims that took place all over the country not only reinforced my altered stand but also convinced me of the absolute necessity of Dalit–Muslim unity. I saw the Keezhvenmani massacre in Tamil Nadu, the Belchhi and Bhagalpur massacres in Bihar and the Ranvir Sena attacks in Bihar as savarna authorities' acts of suppression. In these circumstances, it was Mahatma Ayyankali's life and struggles that prepared me for public life.

T.H.P. Chentharassery's biography of Ayyankali was brought out by Prabhat Book House in 1979. I could not purchase a copy of this book during my stay at Wayanad. Only when I went back to my village could I read it. Until then I had not viewed Ayyankali as a representative of a community. Due to the absence of recorded history and the attempts by political outfits, including the Communist parties, to erase him, Ayyankali was practically an unknown figure to the Dalits. Besides, when he became a caste symbol, the Dalits were reluctant even to utter his name. Overcoming such problems, even as he continued to discharge his duties as a government servant, Chentharassery retrieved oral accounts and collected memories to write a biography of Ayyankali. It was this book and the Dalit intellectuals' propaganda activities that made Ayyankali a well-known figure in Kerala.

While in Wayanad, since caste never featured in my friendships, I was unaware of even the name of Ayyankali. I happened to read Chentharassery only because I had the habit of reading any book that I got my hands on. I read it in one sitting, going through each and every word and sentence for its import, paying little attention to its language or style of composition. I came to realize that my education, language, sartorial style and right to live were gifts bestowed by Ayyankali. The lesson I learnt from his life—that the community which included me had its own history, valorous heroes and struggles for survival—filled me with tremendous excitement. I had never had such an experience before. If Kumaran Asan's 'Duravastha', Changampuzha's 'Vazhakkula', Thakazhi's 'Randidangazhi' and Kadammanitta's 'Kurathi' conveyed to me the condition of the oppressed classes, through Ayyankali, my caste became central to the awareness of my identity. Earlier, if I was reluctant to describe myself as a Dalit and to admit that I had gained job opportunities through reservation, I did not feel the need to conceal it any more. Ayyankali became the light of my consciousness by showing me that my life in the present times was not a gift of liberal humanism but something that was earned through struggles such as his.

Fundamentally, Ayyankali's life taught me two things: One, unify the Dalits who were scattered, divided into subcastes, weakened by various organizations and totally bereft of original ideas. Two, preserve the rights earned in the past and fight for newer rights. Dalits had to themselves arrive at a conception of their rights, over and above those decided upon by the dominant political groups, including the Communist party. Such rights ought to have a clear-cut social foundation. As Julius Fucik wrote in his *Notes from the Gallows*, it was not easy to lead a community that was fated to live a vegetative life, had no sense of history, nurtured no dreams about the future, and lived only in the present. I now had to wage a war as much against powerful political groups as against Dalit (caste) organizations.

Dalit organizational activities were different from those of other caste organizations. Generally speaking, it was those who were educated and were well read who entered and worked for these organizations. And most of them were employed. In poor households, as labour was the only source of income, the members could not afford to miss a single day's work.

Membership was low in Dalit organizations, contra the caste organizations, since learning and uninterrupted participation were absolutely essential to this work. The employed members of these groups had to endure tremendous hardships. They participated in all the organizational activities and struggles by using up their holidays, taking leave from work, and completing tasks during the night. The tribulations I suffered were no different. I had two children and so had to take care of their daily needs and ensure that their education went well. All I got as my share of family property was a 20-cent plot. Since it was not possible to make ends meet with the income from that piece of land, I could not afford to give up my government job. I also had to take out time for reading and writing, which were an inextricable part of my life, and also essential if I were to sustain the cross-fertilization of organizational activities and the creation of knowledge. But I had to maintain a standard of living that corresponded with my official status, without availing of undue privileges. Surrendering myself to the duty of working towards the advancement of Dalits through an exploration of knowledge, I kept all my personal problems to myself and executed multiple tasks simultaneously in order to remain in the public sphere. That was how I internalized Ayyankali.

---

39. What was Sowed and Reaped

It was the EMS-led Communist ministry, which came into power following the formation of the state of Kerala, that established the Harijan Welfare Department as a special branch on 10 September 1957. The first minister in charge of this department was P.K. Chathan Master, a CPI leader and long-time chairman of the Kerala Pulayar Maha Sabha. All subsequent ministries followed the same pattern of choosing Dalits to head this department. However, the United Democratic Front government that took the oath of office in 1982, with K. Karunakaran as the chief minister, was an exception. Contrary to the prevailing practice, the Chief Minister himself took charge of the department.

Several measures that he took hurt the self-respect of the Dalits and tended to weaken them. The first of these was the declaration that Dalit women who were raped would be paid a compensation amount of Rs 5,000. While political movements and Dalit organizations maintained silence over this step towards the 'uplift of the Dalits', the more enlightened segments among the Dalits, including SEEDIAN, protested. Despite the organization's limitations, a central committee, which included me, discussed the issue and decided to conduct propaganda activities. We subsequently put up posters and organized demonstrations in areas where the organization wielded influence, demanding that the government withdraw the black law foisted on the Dalits.

As a person who took active part in struggles led by SEEDIAN, I constantly discussed this declaration made by K. Karunakaran while I was staying at Harilal's quarters. Harilal shared my opinion, but since he was not a member of any organization, he could not organize a successful protest. However, there existed an active fellowship at Nayarambalam in Vypin which consisted of V.C. Rajappan, C.S. Murali and P.N. Sukumaran. Rajappan was its leader. (He died on 6 December 2009, fighting cancer, at the age of 62.) A unique personality, he had a long history of committed and honest activity in the social and political fields. He was born into a poor family, became a wage labourer as soon as he completed his primary education, and turned an active member in agricultural labourers' struggles as a CPI(M) member. In the early 1970s, he switched loyalties to the CPI(M-L) and was arrested for having given refuge to the accused in the Naxalite-led elimination struggle at Kumbalam during the Emergency period, and subjected to heinous torture. He was one of the frontline warriors in the struggle that followed the Vypin liquor tragedy case. Participation in this protest made him a leader of the masses. His was a vibrant presence as much in the fields of art and culture as of politics. Since Rajappan's wife, Pushpa, joined him in all his activities, their house soon turned into a shelter for Naxalites and cultural activists from all over Kerala. That is the reason Rajappan and his family appear in a scene in John Abraham's film *Amma Ariyaan*.

Although Rajappan was as opposed to the new rule passed by the government as Sukumaran was, as a member of the CPI(M-L), he was helpless. The party was influential throughout Vypin but it remained indifferent to this issue. Rajappan expressed his opposition to fellow activists only in the course of private conversations with them. Sukumaran, despite not being a member of any organization, could empathize with this dilemma of the Dalit Naxalites. So, I invited him to join SEEDIAN. He accepted the invitation and started a unit of SEEDIAN with Nayarambalam as the centre.

This struggle for protecting the self-respect of the Dalits became widespread and attracted everyone's attention during the time of the general elections of 1987. Although the CPI(M-L) did not lend support to the struggle led by SEEDIAN in Narakkal constituency, many Dalits who were members of the party, including Rajappan and Murali, were not against the strike. Gradually, they too joined the propaganda activities, and as a consequence, K.K. Madhavan, the candidate of the Indian Congress (Socialist) (IC[S]), which was part of the Left Democratic Front, declared that if he got elected his first demand in the assembly would be to rescind the law. He won the elections by a margin of 3,968 votes. He kept his promise, and Chief Minister K. Karunakaran withdrew the law. Later, Rajappan and C.S. Murali became activists in SEEDIAN and the Adhasthitha Navothana Munnani. When SEEDIAN gained a stronger presence in Vypin, the CPI(M-L) collapsed like a pack of cards. The Naxalites retaliated by spreading calumnies. SEEDIAN, it was circulated, for example, was involved in causing infighting among the castes, I was an anarchist and so on.

Sometime earlier an anti-reservation revolt had broken out

in Gujarat. In the police shootout that was ordered on 9 March 1985 to suppress it, eight people were killed. On 21 April, three others were shot dead by the police. Later, when things got out of hand in Ahmedabad, the army was ordered to restore law and order in the city. Only then did the anti-reservation rebellion subside. It was as part of this struggle that an agitation for economic reservation began in Kerala. K. Karunakaran was the man who directed it from behind the curtains. He took the initiative to iron out the differences that had arisen in the NDP (the political party created by the NSS), as a result of which, on 25 October 1985, a demonstration and dharna organized by the party took place in Thiruvananthapuram. Lending support to the dharna, the Chief Minister came up with a new interpretation of economic reservation with the infamous statement: 'Poverty has no caste'. While it was acceptable to all political groups, including the Communist parties, the SNDP and Dalit organizations remained silent. Taking advantage of such a favourable situation, in order to bring back the NDP, which had earlier left the UDF, Karunakaran gave his word that the new government that came to power after the assembly elections would grant 15 per cent reservation to those below the poverty line. This took place on 17 April 1987. But as it was the LDF that came to power in the 1987 elections, that hope didn't materialize.

Only SEEDIAN came forward against the idea of economic reservation. It conducted a convention at Kottayam involving its own members and those of other organizations as well as supporters. Among other things, we demanded that caste reservation be protected and its scope widened. 'Poverty has no caste,' said Dr K.K. Manmathan in his inaugural speech, replying to K. Karunakaran, 'but reservation has caste.' The convention was followed by a demonstration and a public meeting.

The decision taken at the convention was that we had to

organize propaganda and struggles against economic reservation. Accordingly, we succeeded in arousing public sentiment in Kottayam, Ernakulam, Pathanamthitta and Idukki districts. I consider this a huge achievement.

Karunakaran had also recommended to the central government the inclusion of Dalit Christians as well as communities in the OBC list—Dheevara, Kudumbi and Vishwakarma, which constituted nearly half of the Hindu community—in the list of Scheduled Castes. This was a move to limit the Dalits' reservation rights and to eventually quash them altogether. The Dalits managed to oppose and defeat it, but it is a fact that certain factional struggles, conducted by a few Dalit organizations, with the support of the Bharatiya Janata Party and the Sangh Parivar, did play a crucial role in driving a wedge between Dalits and Dalit Christians.

40. My First Hunger Strike

Although in the logbook of my life there are numerous entries of the struggles that I either led or participated in, the one that remains evergreen in my memory is the 72-hour-long hunger strike that I undertook at the Gandhi Square in Kottayam. It was the first time in my life that I led such a strike. What made that struggle unique was the significance of the demands that were put forward.

The demand for the return of Adivasi land that had been unlawfully taken away from them was a matter of national concern in our reckoning. It was not a mere issue of asserting an economic right but of achieving a national political right. These were the views I sought to highlight through the fast.

Article 46 of our Constitution provides for the liberation of Adivasis—a people who are demographically a minority, follow customs and rituals that are different from those of the mainstream society, and have a glittering tradition of struggle—against exploitation and for the making and execution of laws that will ensure their progress. Prime Minister Jawaharlal Nehru, who understood its spirit, emphasized in his preface to Verrier Elwin's book *A Philosophy for NEFA*, that the Adivasis' right to their own land and forests must be respected. It was in accordance with the interest taken by the national leadership that the report submitted by U.N. Dhebar, the all-India president of the Indian National Congress, recommended the return of lands confiscated after 26 January 1950 to the Adivasis. Subsequently, the central government convened a meeting of the state chief ministers on 1 April 1975 and instructed all states to create laws to fulfil these demands. A two-year deadline was set to complete the task. In the light of this decision, the Kerala Legislative Assembly passed the Kerala Scheduled Tribes (Restriction on Transfer of Lands and Restoration of Alienated Lands) Act in 1975. It was included in the 9th Schedule of the Constitution, considering its social and political relevance.

The struggle for reservations which became prominent from the mid-1980s onwards made it possible for SEEDIAN to undertake a reading of the Adivasi laws. The protection accorded by Article 21 of the Constitution, including the provision for reservation, was already under the purview of law, and hence it became a national right guaranteed by the Constitution. Therefore, non-enforcement of the law was tantamount to violation of Constitutional rights. Thus, it was not limited land ownership, ensured through the enforcement of law, which was to be the yardstick. Rather, it was the acknowledgement of the Constitutional rights of the Adivasis.

What the SEEDIAN chiefly pointed out was the opposition

between the Adivasis, on the one hand, and the land grabbers and the political movements, including the Communist parties, that were offering them support, on the other. The aim was to convert the Adivasis into a national group by organizing their resistance against land grabbers and political parties. SEEDIAN activists had the foundational theoretical hypotheses and experiences for it. That was why they raised demands like the enforcement of the law of 1975, which assured the return of confiscated lands to the Adivasis, the creation of Scheduled Areas as per Schedule 5 of the Constitution as well as the setting up of Adivasi Self-Governing Councils as per Schedule 6 of the Constitution, and so on. In a bid to forge Dalit–Adivasi unity and fraternity, SEEDIAN decided to bring together Dalit and Adivasi organizations.

Seminars and study classes were subsequently organized to raise awareness among the members about the problems of the Adivasis. It was also decided that statements pointing to the social and legal aspects of confiscated lands be published, and propaganda work, demonstrations and public meetings under the auspices of district and lower committees conducted. It was on the basis of these activities that discussions were held with Kallara Sukumaran and Paul Chirakarrode, top leaders of the Indian Dalit Federation, the biggest Dalit organization in those days.

Along with K.K. Kumaran, I took charge of contacting the Adivasi organizations of Attappadi. First, we spoke to Sreedharan of the Girijan Seva Samithi (Hill Tribes Welfare Committee). From Attappadi I proceeded to Wayanad. There I stayed with G. Harilal. I held discussions with K.K. Surendran, a SEEDIAN activist, and decided to meet leaders of other Adivasi organizations. The first leader I spoke to was Poothadi Balan, head of the Adivasi Federation. I requested him to participate in a convention organized by the Adivasi Samskarika Kendram (Adivasi Cultural Centre), of which his organization was a part, to discuss this issue. The convention held at Meenangadi was inaugurated by Alanthatta Prabhakaran who had led a strike at St Mary's College earlier. I took part in and spoke at the convention along with one of the founder-members of Adivasi Swayam Sevak Sangh, C.M. Yogi, as well as Valsarajan, Poothadi Balan, Raghavan and others.

Amidst all this, I decided to publish a pamphlet titled 'The Problems of and Approaches to the Confiscated Land of the Adivasis'. It was in connection with all these propaganda and protest activities organized by SEEDIAN that I decided to sit on the 72-hour hunger strike at Gandhi Square in Kottayam. The central and state committees of SEEDIAN unanimously agreed to the idea, and commissioned the state secretary, P.A.G. Das, as well as the state committee member P.O. John to help execute the plan.

As I began to prepare myself mentally for my first hunger strike, I was troubled by a serious domestic problem. One acre of land that belonged to my family had been divided into three parts. Two parts were owned by Chaachan and Amma. The middle section had been registered in the name of Chaachan's elder brother's son. Such an arrangement had been made in order to avail of a bank loan. Amma's portion had been mortgaged to a co-operative bank in return for a loan. Chaachan's portion, which contained the house, had no liabilities. But Baburaj had taken a loan of Rs 10,000 under the Self-Employment Project Scheme of the SBT against the guarantee of a government employee (as he is dead, I shall not disclose his name) for the sake of launching November Books. As long as the business made a profit, repayment amounts were duly remitted in the bank, but when financial troubles mounted, that came to a halt. The guarantor came home and created a ruckus. Consequently, Chaachan entered into a written agreement with him, according to which 32 cents of land (that formed the middle segment of the plot) would be leased out to the guarantor. Chaachan received a huge sum from him as advance. The deal would come through on receipt of the remaining amount, a meagre sum. Since the agreement had been registered, if the conditions were not obeyed, we would be legally obliged to give the guarantor the middle segment of our plot.

The condition at home was miserable. We led a hand-to-mouth existence, I was on unauthorized leave, and Baburaj was jobless. We were hardly making anything from November Books. And even before the stipulated period was over, unwilling to agree to any compromise, the man began to pressure us to give the land away. As I sat on hunger strike in the pavilion at Gandhi Square, he showed up there and threatened me to my face in front of the SEEDIAN activists.

Although it sounds simple, a hunger strike demands sacrifice. Absolute confidence in the goal and political support are what give you strength. It was during those days that I fully realized the possibilities of this mode of struggle that Gandhi made universal by staking his life. Another revelation was this: hunger is the direst of human experiences. The only thing that can conquer it is food. Therefore, all activities against starvation ought to be legitimized. The duty of society is to ensure that it does not lead anyone down a dark path.

Hunger gnawed at me, but I paid it no attention, thinking instead about the duty I had undertaken to discharge and the commitment of my colleagues. At night, I got salted water to drink. The first sip tasted very sweet but with each subsequent gulp, it became less appealing. On the third day, after noon, it was impossible to drink water. My three-day hunger strike came to an end with K.K.S. Das giving me a glass of lime juice.

The struggles conducted by SEEDIAN—including my hunger strike—converted the 1975 Act from a mere issue of poverty to one with ideological dimensions. They also helped convey the message of the necessity of Dalit–Adivasi unity.

41. Equality Among Communities

It was not the SEEDIAN activists' dreams of liberation alone that helped convert the organization into a small yet noteworthy one. Their understanding of the political circumstances of the time played a major role in this regard. It was in the mid-1980s that a different political atmosphere began to take shape in Kerala. In 1987, even before the assembly elections, the LDF, led by the CPI(M), severed links with the All India Muslim League and the Kerala Congress for the sake of forging a unity among secular democratic movements and fighting communalism. With this, the LDF, which was characterized as a secular front, became a representative of the Hindu castes. The truth is that an anti-Muslim sentiment had already been created within the Hindu community.

It was the CPI that played a major role in bringing Hindu representation under the control of the savarna caste. The declaration that the Kerala Pulaya Maha Sabha (KPMS)—which had been the party's feeder organization since its inception in the 1970s—should not have any links with any caste organization served only to clip the wings of Dalit caste leaders including P.K. Raghavan, a CPI and KPMS leader. Such an anti-caste stance, applicable only to the Dalits, helped institutionalize the dominance of savarna castes like the Nairs and the Ezhavas who wielded considerable influence within the Communist parties. The party did not insist that its members should not participate in the activities of the NSS and the SNDP. What happened as a result was that the Dalit issue became an insignificant one in the Communist parties. The UDF of course continued to offer shelter to the savarna castes and religious authorities. With the All India Muslim League and the Kerala Congress coming to the

UDF, after being removed from the LDF, the impression that the UDF was a place of shelter for communal parties gained strength.

With caste becoming more of a political than a social issue, it became difficult to find a platform for Dalit rights struggles in the Communist parties. What served as a signboard for me in regard to this issue was the Ezhavas' *Declaration of Rights* published in 1946 which I read in K.S. Subramaniam's biography of Sahodaran Ayyappan. I got that document republished in the SEEDIAN weekly. Under my editorship, the weekly printed 3,000 copies for the first time. What the document demanded was abolition of the caste system, universal education, industrialization, and participation of all communities in the government. With the dream of equality among communities in mind, Sahodaran Ayyappan wrote, 'In India, the various communities do not engage in social interactions but rather exist at upper and lower levels. As a result, the so-called upper group enjoy freedom and power whereas the so-called lower group suffer unfreedom and weakness. In such a condition, each community needs to have its own political, communitarian and cultural vested interests.' In order to establish that social justice is equivalent to communitarian justice based on political rights, I published Ayyankali's Praja Sabha speeches. Such retrievals from the ignored chapters of history were what formed the foundation stone of equality of opportunity for and struggles of the Dalits.

---

42. Rejection of the Status of Agricultural Labourer

It was my journey through Sree Narayana Guru's works that helped me let go of my Marxist principles. My connection with Dr Manmathan at the personal and organizational levels made this possible. Dr Manmathan had great respect for Sree Narayana Guru. The latter had formally initiated Dr Manmathan's father into learning. Growing up, Dr Manmathan would hear a lot about Sree Narayana Guru. It was from Dr Manmathan himself that I first heard about another renaissance hero, Poykayil Appachan. Although Dr Manmathan could not talk about the philosophy of these luminaries in study classes on Marxism, he shared a lot of knowledge about it in his private conversations and committee meetings of SEEDIAN.

What Sree Narayana Guru installed at Aruvipuram, Mr Manmathan told us, was not the idol of Ezhava Shiva[76] but a symbol of the enlightened self. During the Guru's time, Lord Shiva had been Brahminized with the help of superstitions and evil customs. It was therefore impossible to reinstall a tribal god like Shiva in order to lead a community towards sophistication and progress. With this observation serving as a signpost, I attempted to read Sree Narayana Guru from the social and political perspectives.

Having succeeded in bringing the caste problem centrestage, I was inclined to see human relations in term of interdependence and fraternity. The basis of this were the Guru's maxims—'Remember this: we are spirit-siblings' and 'He who knows his self knows, all on earth is One primeval Self—through which I was retrieving an awareness of my own self.

On the basis of this discovery, I wrote thus in an article

titled 'Recapture the Fatherland': 'Dr Palpu gave shape to the SNDP movement by yoking Sree Narayana Guru's teachings with Swami Vivekananda's renewal of the Hindu religion. With this, the prosperous Ezhavas entered the movement and became the steersmen of the Ezhava community. That was why social reform got limited to this group. But the Guru overcame the restrictions of the SNDP by embracing all members of the avarna classes though the establishment of the Sharada temple[77] ("Progress through Education") and consecration of a mirror[78] ("Realize Yourself"). In short, Sree Narayana Guru ought to be assessed not as a god of the Ezhavas but rather as a latter-day founder of ancient India's materialist philosophy.' It was on this philosophical platform that I realized the life conditions of the Dalits, which included myself, and gave shape to an epistemological sphere in order to transform it.

The idea I conceived was that the Dalits of Kerala and India should transcend the divisions of castes, subcastes and their organizations, and become an asset-owning community. It was a view that had come to me through continuous discussions about social experiences. Ownership of assets meant authority, status, wealth and culture. I could arrive at such a concept only because I had succeeded in letting go of the status of 'agricultural labourer' foisted on us by political party organizations, including the Communist parties. Today, such a standpoint has earned general acceptance but SEEDIAN played a major role in the crystallization of it.

I was also involved in SNDP Yogam activities, and therefore read the history of that organization. The book *SNDP Yogacharithram* ('The History of SNDP Yogam') by Prof P.S. Velayudhan included a note on the aims of the organization: establish industries; form companies in order to create capital; make co-operative societies; use new methods for farming; process raw materials locally; and gain enlightenment through education. My interpretation of this was that in attempting to organize the Ezhavas through such a virtuous path, the higher aim was to transform them into an asset-owning community. The message that E.M.S. Namboodiripad conveyed at the Yoga Kshema Sabha meeting to the Namboodiri community at Ongalloor was no different: Namboodiris should manage industries, commerce and large-scale farming in order to maintain the high position that landlords used to have in the past, and thus control the economic structure. Such ideas that contained a modernized version of traditional wealth ownership could not be applied to the lives of Dalits. That was because the Dalit community had been denied ownership of assets by the caste-based division of society. And so, the viability of the above-mentioned hypothesis had not been tried beyond its capacity to effect a consolidation of ideas. Such being the case, it was first necessary to identify a separate set of economic rights that would protect the interests of the Dalits. This project constituted the rejection of the rights framed by the Communist parties and also the label of 'agricultural labourer' the Dalits were stamped with. It served to view Dalit agricultural labourers, Dalit officers, Dalit artisans, Dalit small-scale traders and so on as constituting the larger unit of 'community'.

---

43. The Attappadi March

If SEEDIAN could succeed in organizing struggles, locally and otherwise, to win the economic and social rights of different communities of people in various parts of Kerala, it was because of the organization's unique structure. Although it was smaller than other Dalit organizations, the activists had gained social and political education through reading and participation in symposiums, seminars and study classes. They were individually capable of understanding social problems and organizing struggles. What the committee discussions did was to officially sanction such initiatives and give them ideological as well as organizational guidelines. Consequently, wherever there were SEEDIAN activists, there were organized struggles too. And with growing public trust, the organization had a steady stream of new members.

An exemplary model of a mass struggle took shape at Vypin. When V.C. Rajappan, along with P.N. Sukumaran, became a SEEDIAN activist, a huge contingent of Naxalites joined the organization with him. This helped strengthen the foundation of SEEDIAN. During this time, I read reports in newspapers about certain developments in Attappadi, Palakkad district. These revolved around the plans of the government to start an agricultural farm in order to give employment opportunities to Adivasis. The administrative committee of the farm, which had nearly 400 workers, had mortgaged the firm at the co-operative bank at Perunthalmanna for a loan of Rs 6 crores. Non-repayment of dues had resulted in the accumulation of arrears. The net payable amount had risen to Rs 14 crores. The bank had thus begun to take steps to attach the property, and put it up for auction. A prominent industrialist and owner of Mayil Vahanam at Shornur came forward to make his bid.

Although SEEDIAN had no organizational links there, Rajappan and Sukumaran decided to go to Attappadi on a fact-finding mission. They did this without informing the organization. There they lived with Dineshan, an employee of the co-operative bank, and proceeded to the farm. By then the situation there had become worse. With the auction imminent, not only the Adivasis but members of the local social organizations too were worried. The situation demanded an immediate remedy. So, the two of them stayed at Attappadi for three days, listened to the Adivasis, prepared a memorandum on their behalf, and submitted it to the authorities concerned. The request it contained was that the auction should not be conducted, and also that the ownership of the farm should be transferred to the Adivasis. Only after getting the Adivasis and activists of various social organizations to participate in a demonstration and a public meeting did the two return from Attappadi.

On P.N. Sukumaran's demand, a joint meeting of the state and central committees of the SEEDIAN was convened immediately and it was decided that we should give lead to a struggle. The common consensus was that SEEDIAN activists should carry out a march at Attappadi, and that a dharna should be staged by them as well as members of Adivasi organizations in front of the office of the Palakkad district collector. Further, it was decided that a propaganda vehicle rally should start from Nayarambalam in Vypin and conclude at the Palakkad Collectorate where they would be joined by a similar vehicle rally of the Adivasis from Attappadi. I was entrusted with the responsibility of going to Attappadi before the vehicle rally began, in order to meet with the Adivasi organizations. With that aim in mind, I contacted K.K. Kumaran who worked at the Indian Institute of Telephones at Kanjikode.

The two of us reached Attappadi in the evening hours one day. Kumaran had been to Attappadi several times before but this was my first visit. It was late by the time we reached Agaly, and took up lodgings for the night. In the morning, we met Sreedharan, an employee of the Tribal Co-operative Society and secretary of Girijan Sevak Samithi, and discussed matters with him. By evening, Sreedharan invited some people over—Nanchan Master, Ramaswamy and others. Together, we gave final shape to the vehicle rally from Attappadi. We returned after attending a festival at the Adivasis' Malleshwaram temple.

The participants of the Attappadi march had reached Nayarambalam the previous day itself. An inaugural meeting for the rally was conducted in the evening. C.S. Murali and Mandalam Mohammed, besides a few SEEDIAN activists, had also came here to offer felicitations at the meeting. The rally began the next morning, stopping at various points along the Kodungalloor–Guruvayoor route, conducting meetings to explain our purpose and to collect donations. It was evening by the time we reached Palakkad. We rented rooms and spent the night there. By 11 the next morning, the vehicle rally led by Sreedharan and Ramaswamy reached the venue too. The dharna at the Collectorate was inaugurated by me.

Even as the dharna took place, the memorandum signed by the SEEDIAN and Adivasi leaders was handed over to the collector, Mr Jiji Thomson. He read it and gave the assurance that he would bring the issue to the notice of the government and help find a solution. Later, on the basis of the report submitted by him, the government paid the whole amount to the Perunthalmanna Co-operative Bank and averted the auction proceedings. In the get-together at the lodge that evening we suggested that the word 'Girijan' (hill people) be replaced by the term 'Adivasi'.

SEEDIAN had been taking an interest in the problems of the Adivasis for some time now. Their weekly serialized M.J. Prasad's article 'Through the Girijan Centres' as far back as in 1974. Besides, many agitations had been organized at various points of time to protest against the poverty and neglect they suffered. While in Wayanad, where I had also been involved as an activist in the Adivasi Swayam Sevak Sangh, I could not see the problems plaguing the ancient hill tribes as any different from those that the Dalits in general endured. The articles written and the studies done by V.R. Raghavaiah, L. Natarajan and K. Panoor had served as signposts. In fact, V.R. Raghavaiah's study that had been included in Dr A.R. Desai's edited work, *Peasant Struggles in India*, had been translated into Malayalam and published in four instalments in the SEEDIAN weekly under the title 'The Political Background of Rebellions by the Tribal Classes in India'. According to the study, almost 72 rebellions by the tribal classes had taken place in British India, and thousands of Adivasi lives had been sacrificed in the process. The most powerful and widespread among these had been the Kamma Reddy rebellion.

The rebellion began under the leadership of an Adivasi boy merely 22 years old, aimed at protesting against confiscation of Adivasi land in the name of development; compulsory labour without wages enforced by the government; and implementation of laws restricting the use of forest resources. The Adivasis believed that their leader, Rajaram, had supernatural powers and was invincible. When the rebellion took on shades of guerrilla warfare and began to spread, the British government deployed the Malabar Special Police to suppress it and shoot Rajaram. Raghavaiah wrote that Gandhiji had wept on hearing the news of Rajaram's death. A significant observation made by Raghavaiah was that non-Adivasi individuals working among the Adivasis tended to withdraw themselves when the rebellion took the path of violence, leaving the Adivasis to confront their fate of death and misery by themselves. Nonetheless, it was after the aforementioned rebellion took place that the British government was compelled to acknowledge the Adivasis' rights and implement the Tribal Settlement Act [*sic*] that clamped restrictions on the hegemony over their ecosystem.

The other notable article in the book was L. Natarajan's, which was about the Santhal rebellion that took place in Bengal in 1855. Here too the issues were eviction following unlawful confiscation of land and compulsory labour without wages. The protest led by two Adivasi brothers named Kanu and Siddhu erupted into a violent rebellion. The British government had to call in the army to suppress the rebellion that spread throughout the Santhal region. As in Andhra, here too the rebels adopted guerrilla tactics to confront the army. The fighting stretched on for months. Several hundred lives were lost. Finally, although the rebellion was suppressed, the British government saw it as a warning signal and took measures to control trespass into Santhal regions, grant land ownership, and bring compulsory-labour-without-wages to an end. Hundreds of Adivasis had to sacrifice their lives but, as Natarajan noted, an important achievement of the rebellion was that the British government acknowledged the Santhals as a national minority by granting them a district named 24 Parganas.

In 1975, the chief reason behind the All India Congress Committee and the central government's instruction to all states to create laws for returning confiscated lands to the Adivasis was that the unrest in the Adivasi regions had spread all over the country. The fundamental aim behind the Kerala Scheduled Tribes (Restriction on Transfer of Lands and Restoration of Alienated Lands) Act, 1975 was to safeguard national interests by bringing back the Adivasis, who were becoming increasingly alienated from the democratic system thanks to the rebellions, into the mainstream, and giving them their constitutional rights. There was a sense of urgency in all of it because of the violent rebellion of Adivasis in Tripura. The Marxist party, however, spread stories that totally contradicted the actual facts about what precipitated the rebellion, and seemed fuelled by feelings of enmity. The rebellion was portrayed as an instance of separatism and an attack against the Bengalis.

K. Panoor (d. 2018) wrote an article which made an objective assessment of the circumstances prevailing in Tripura. These were the points he made: In Tripura, ownership of 90 per cent of the land vested in the Adivasis. Besides, Scheduled regions and self-governing councils too existed there. But the Bengalis who settled in Tripura grabbed land indiscriminately and put the Scheduled regions and self-governing councils in disarray. It was when peaceful protests against such encroachments failed to yield results that the Adivasis launched a rebellion, sharing greetings of 'Bloody days'. After years of violence, the Adivasis brought their rebellion to a halt through a decision taken by a three-party committee that included the Adivasis, the state and the central governments. I published Panoor's article in the SEEDIAN weekly with the title 'Tripura: Marxist Party Utters Lies'.

I criticized some of the Adivasi struggles that took place in Kerala because of their rejection of the Constitutional rights which the Adivasis had earned through long and bloody agitations, and for their attempts at erasing the struggles for the implementation of the Act of 1975, in which I too had participated.

44. Struggles That Do Not Feature in History

Certain struggles find an abiding place in history. The struggles initiated by V.C. Rajappan in Vypin are not among those extensively written about even though they later became models worth emulating. After giving up his house in the Laksham Veedu colony near the village of Nayarambalam, Rajappan built a small house in the Four-Cent Colony with the aid of a loan of Rs 5,000 advanced by the GCDA (Greater Cochin Development Authority), and stayed there with his wife Pushpa and four children (three girls and one boy). The wages that the couple earned as labourers in the paddy fields were their only source of income. Since he had been a wage labourer from very early childhood, his expertise in farming was formidable.

During days when work was not available, he cast his fishing net in the canals at high tide and sold the catch at the Nayarambalam market the next day. On days when I stayed with him, I would accompany him and be by his side from 10 in the night to 2 in the morning while he caught fish. Although he could just about keep the wolf from the door because of his hardworking nature, he also shouldered the problems of people at the lowest rungs of society as a matter of duty. Among the actions he got involved in, the most important was the struggle against the practice of leaving the Pokkali[79] fields fallow and permitting shrimp farming there.

Farming activities on the Pokkali fields were the means of livelihood for wage labourers, including Dalits, living in this small island (which was part of the group of Vypin islands), and necessary for the protection of the environmental health of the land. Until then, the usual practice had been to have six months of Pokkali cultivation and six months of shrimp farming. As the market for shrimp grew overseas, it was decided that Pokkali cultivation should give way to shrimp farming. The reason cited to justify the decision was that paddy cultivation was no longer commercially viable. Subsequently, the Pokkali fields were left fallow to aid shrimp cultivation. This adversely affected the lives of hundreds of wage labourers and, following discussions with P.N. Sukumaran and C.S. Murali, V.C. Rajappan began the struggle.

It began with a poster campaign demanding continuation of Pokkali cultivation and an end to shrimp farming. This was followed by demonstrations everywhere, including on the ridges of the paddy fields. As it did not have the support of an established political party or class-dominated organizations, including agricultural labourers' unions, the landowners of the

Pokkali fields did not take the agitation seriously. At the same time, they could not completely ignore the uncompromising stand Rajappan had taken during the anti-spurious liquor struggle. With no resolution to the problem being found, Rajappan declared his resolve to go on an indefinite hunger strike until Pokkali cultivation was resumed. He made this declaration at a meeting convened at the Nayarambalam market. After a few more days of campaigning and other activities, he began his hunger strike in front of the Vypin Block Office on 17 June 1988. He had the support of agricultural labourers, Dalits and public activists as well.

It was on the second day of his hunger strike that I visited the pavilion he was occupying at Pallathankulangara. In a private conversation I had with P.N. Sukumaran, I pointed out certain defects in the conduct of the struggle. Maximum publicity ought to have been given to the news that a leader like V.C. Rajappan was on an indefinite hunger strike. Besides, the activists of the organization too should have been brought to the pavilion along with the local activists. I left after two days. Later, K. Sunilkumar arrived from Mulanthuruthy. He spoke at the public meetings in the evenings. Reji Mathew stationed himself at the pavilion till the very end.

The presence of SEEDIAN activists changed the hunger strike in tone and tenor. Until then, it had the support of local activists only. Now the struggle became a people's affair, and demanded strong interventions. Wide publicity was given to the threat that if the hunger strike was not resolved through a compromise the Pokkali fields would be taken over and farming activities started. This threatened to intensify the conflict. Consequently, a compromise was arrived at, following joint discussions between the revenue division officer, the agricultural labourers' union representatives and the leaders of the strike committee. V.C.

Rajappan brought his nine-day hunger strike to a close. Later, when the owners of the paddy fields tried to defy the agreement, many organizations stepped in, and the Kerala Karshaka Thozhilali Union (KKTU) (Kerala Agricultural Labourers' Union) as well as the feeder organizations of the CPI(M-L) conducted a strike that lasted three years. The leaders of the strike—P.S. Rajiv, Sajeevan and N.K. Jane—had to suffer imprisonment too.

What V.C. Rajappan had led was a people's struggle that included all sections of society. However, when T.C. Subramanian of *Madhyamam* described Vypin island as a venue of Naxalite struggle in 2016, he forgot Rajappan, who initiated the struggles in the Pokkali fields. Did the reporter suffer from a savarna bias that made him think Dalits could not be popular leaders? Not long after the struggle against shrimp farming in the Pokkali fields got over, another one, this time against an attachment of property, was started under Rajappan's leadership. Here, too, the most substantial support came from Sukumaran and Murali. V.C. Rajappan and others had only possession certificates of their four-cent plots because of which they could not sell or transfer their property to anyone for a period of 12 years. The GCDA had granted loans for the construction of houses. Although many years had passed, the beneficiaries could not repay their loans due to poverty, their only source of income being the work they did as wage labourers. Nearly all of them were served attachment-of-property notices but their financial constraints did not allow them to complete the repayment of the loan, which caused the authorities to start the dispossession proceedings. They first arrived at the house of Thomas, who worked as a barber at Nayarambalam market. Even as they carried out their work, a crowd of nearly 200 people including women and children gathered there. Rajappan, who was present in the crowd, demanded that the proceedings be stopped. Just then, Reji Mathew lunged at the officials and snatched their documents from them. Unable to carry on in the volatile atmosphere, the officials left.

Later, Rajappan and Sukumaran convened a people's convention at the Nayarambalam Bhagavathy Vilasam High School hall, and put together a strike committee with Mandalam Mohammed as its convenor in order to demand the annulment of the loans. Mandalam Mohammed, a member of the CPI(M-L), was a follower of T.N. Nagi Reddy, who was not very relevant in Kerala. But it was his spotless reputation that made everyone choose him as the convenor. In the demonstration that was organized subsequently, more than a thousand people participated. This was followed by a public meeting in which it was declared that the house construction loans would not be repaid, and that organized opposition would be put up against any measure to attach property.

The struggle against dispossession spread among the people like wild fire. When things appeared to get out of hand, I visited Nayarambalam. The first thing I did was to have a meeting with the SEEDIAN activists including V.C. Rajappan and P.N. Sukumaran at the latter's compound. We analysed the struggle against the attachment of property in great detail. Besides being a question of money, the struggle had great political significance. I spoke at the meeting about how a demand for annulment of loans to farmers had often been part of agricultural struggles throughout the history of our nationalist movement and the Communist party, forcing the government to create agricultural debt relief commissions from time to time. This struggle against attachment of property had to be evaluated, I said to the activists, as a re-establishment of this experiential history of struggle. Therefore, as soon as this struggle was brought to a close, a broader demand for annulment of the debts of the weaker sections of society had to be taken up. And that SEEDIAN had to shoulder the responsibility.

V.C. Rajappan expressed his willingness to start an indefinite hunger strike once again. I was against the idea. But he could not keep away from a struggle that concerned him too. He also suggested that more widespread propaganda work for the forthcoming struggle be undertaken than was done for the previous one. Following demonstrations, public meetings and marches, the hunger strike began. SEEDIAN activists, including myself, participated in all of them. This resulted in significant support from the people. On the eleventh day of the hunger strike, Rajappan was arrested and shifted to a hospital in North Paravur. He decided to continue his hunger strike despite the health issues he was facing. I was with him at the hospital, and I began to get worried. Fortunately, Mandalam Mohammed intervened in the matter, which led to the district collector putting an end to the attachment procedure.

At the central-state committee meeting of SEEDIAN at Kottayam, the struggle was evaluated as a big success, and V.C. Rajappan, P.N. Sukumaran and Mandalam Mohammed were complimented for their role in it. Following his narration of experiences of the struggle, V.C. Rajappan opined that the Vypin struggle should be converted to one that would take into account the interests of all the people at the bottom. It was decided that the slogan of the struggle should be: 'Annul the Debts of the Weaker Sections'. Moreover, the common feeling was that over and above propaganda work to be conducted by SEEDIAN activists, people had to be lined up to prevent the official measures of dispossession too. The state level struggle was scheduled to begin in Ernakulam district.

With Shaji Joseph expressing willingness to go on an indefinite hunger strike, it was decided that the state committee should take all steps to push the struggle forward and also that, as a central committee member, my presence should be ensured throughout.

The statement that was drawn up was distributed not only all over Vypin but in all areas where the organization wielded influence. We also put up posters about the hunger strike, which began on an evening after a meeting inaugurated by Dr Manmathan. V.C. Rajappan garlanded him and several others, including myself, felicitated Shaji Joseph.

The pavilion was put up on the footpath at the KSRTC boat jetty. There was no cot available. All we had were a few mats and a blanket. P.O. John, M.D. Thomas, K.O. Raju, Reji Mathew, Gopi Vallon and I stayed in the pavilion throughout the hunger strike. V.C. Rajappan, P.N. Sukumaran, K. Sunilkumar as well as a few activists from Kuruchi and Piravam were present during the morning hours. They rarely sat up during the night. Sudheeran (a Bank of India officer now) and P.O. Raju, who were students of Maharaja's College then, came to the pavilion along with Baburaj, and contributed substantially to the struggle. We could use Baburaj's New Hostel lodgings for bath and other purposes.

The biggest challenge that the struggle faced was sourcing food for the activists. During the morning hours, they divided themselves into two groups and set out for collecting funds. One group sought financial help from shops and houses. As far as the city-dwellers were concerned, the outside world did not exist. Besides, they were opposed to politics. Everything had to be explained in detail and occasionally a somewhat threatening tone adopted too. After a full day of wandering in this manner, they would have collected only a very meagre amount. One person who made a substantial contribution was Paulman Vettam, my school friend and owner of Paulson Opticals (situated close to the site of the struggle), now the president of the Railway Passengers' Association.

The only journalist who came to the pavilion frequently was an *Indian Express* reporter. He acknowledged that our demands were genuine and prepared a report that was published along with a photograph of Shaji Joseph. On the eighth day of the hunger strike, Shaji's condition deteriorated. He began vomiting. That day, everyone was present in the pavilion. At 10 o' clock, P.N. Sukumaran, P.O. John and Gopi Vallon went to meet the district collector. They told him that the satyagrahi's condition was critical and therefore immediate measures had to be taken. Subsequently, the police arrived in the afternoon, arrested Shaji Joseph and admitted him to the General Hospital. A *Mangalam* reporter who came there along with a photographer published the news. Shaji Joseph could regain his health only after he underwent Ayurvedic therapy at a hospital in Piravam. The day Shaji's hunger strike was brought to an end, M.D. Thomas started his. As a Kerala Stipendiary Students' Association activist, he had undertaken hunger strikes several times before. So, he did not have to suffer as much. The condition of those who kept them both company, however, was pitiable. Constant wandering for raising funds and limited quantities of food began to take their toll on their health. With the mosquito menace adding to their woes, sleep at night became impossible. When the financial crisis peaked, the hunger strike had to be abandoned.

That struggle, which lasted 19 days, did not get much media attention. But the Ernakulam district unit of the Janata Dal expressed solidarity with our cause and passed a resolution to that effect. Another organization that supported us was the Lohia Vichara Vedi. SEEDIAN, however, carried on. A convention was held at the Hindu Matha Padhashala hall in Ettumanoor on 11 February 1990 to co-ordinate the struggles and the activities of anti-dispossession committees that had sprung up in areas like Athirampuzha, Kidangoor, Kaduthuruthi, Kallara, Manjoor and Kuruppanthura in Kottayam district. M.D. Thomas read out the strike announcement notice:

'The weaker sections of society do not repay their loans because of increasing poverty, unemployment and inflation. When such a situation arose during British rule in India, the nationalist movement and the farmers' movement always demanded annulment of loans.'

It was when other political movements aligned themselves with the struggle, which V.C. Rajappan had extrapolated from our historical experience, that our demand became a people's demand. The Janata Dal took the request of the weaker sections for the annulment of loans to the national level. When V.P. Singh of the Janata Dal became the prime minister, the central government cancelled all the loans taken by farmers throughout India.

---

45. Struggle for Equality of Opportunity—Part I

Ever since they gained a distinctive voice from the mid-1980s, Dalit organizations used it to criticize the CPI(M), the main complaint being that the party did not pay attention to the problems that poor and the neglected Dalits faced. The party countered such experiential truths by resorting to propaganda aimed at retaining the loyalty of ordinary Dalits whose faith in the party was almost second nature to them. The chief arguments it used were that through the Land Reform Act, the Communist government had bestowed kudikidappu rights over 10 cents of land and that the subsequent LDF governments had instituted pensions for agricultural labourers.

In private conversations, I had often heard ordinary CPI(M) workers speak appreciatively about the 10 cents of land given by the party. What that clearly conveyed was that the party's propaganda had been successful. The issue of the agricultural labourers' pension was no different. Concealing the fact that it was the tax payers' money being used to give a pension to various sections of people, feudal Communists, like Chief Minister E.K. Nayanar, spoke as though they were distributing their family wealth. Not having received any such 'benefits' from the previous Congress governments, the poor and illiterate Dalits saw their legitimate rights as the result of the magnanimity of the party. The reality, however, was different.

From my experience as a person who conducted organizational activities among people who lived in Harijan Laksham Veedu colonies, and beside roads, canals and wastelands, I knew that barring a small minority who could enjoy a fairly decent life, thanks to the reservation policy, the great majority of Dalits led a miserable existence. The population in the Harijan colonies and the 10-cent plots had exploded, the land having to be partitioned to ever smaller bits. The ambience in them resembled that of slums. This was the situation everywhere—in the Kurichi colony that had been formed in 1936 with its 75-cent land ownership scheme (the colony was the centre of my organizational activities for a long time); the Madhuraveli Harijan colony formed in 1957 with 10-cent land ownership; and colonies that several SEEDIAN activists lived in. It was this first-hand experience that made me recognize that the land issue of the Dalits demanded immediate attention.

The meetings conducted in various parts of the state by the Indian Dalit Federation, with its clarion call 'Sons of the Soil Battle for Land', had to be stopped because of the provocative attitude of the CPI(M). There were attempts at manhandling Kallara Sukumaran in his own native village of Peerumed. Timely intervention by the activists saved him. What this indicated was that any criticism levelled against the land reforms—touted as the most revolutionary achievement of the party—provoked severe intolerance.

With such intolerance towards Dalit voices raging, I undertook an examination of land reforms. My aim was to arrive at the social and political intent behind it. How did the communities above the Ezhavas in the caste hierarchy get land through the land reforms? I asked myself. Why were the Dalits alone denied? Christians and Muslims, strong religious groups in Kerala, did not support the Communists. It was the Dalits and the Ezhavas who constituted the majority of the party. Despite this, why was the land reform not favourable to the Dalits? Such questions led me to an exploration of the 'class-foundation' of the party. The American social scientist Kathleen Gough's study was what gave me a clear orientation in my analysis. It pointed to the fact that the foundation of the Communist party in Kerala was built not by agricultural labourers' or workers' movements but the farmers' movement. And these farmers belonged to Christian and Nair communities. Those who rose to the top of the party leadership through the farmers' movement saw society in terms of class. This in turn created land relations like the *pattakkar*, *varakkar*, *kanakkar* and so on, that is, those (cultivators) who paid taxes in kind—like *pattam*, *varam*, *kanam*—to the landowner. They were the middle section that came between the landowners and the labouring classes that had no land-owning rights. While Muslims and Ezhavas, though minimally, were to be found in this group, there were no Dalits at all. Caste realities had not been taken into consideration when the land-to-the-tiller yardstick came to be applied.

As a result, what the Dalits got were the 10-, 5- and 3-cent *kudikidappu* rights. In actuality, this was not land ownership but only the right to occupy the land. Because of certain sections in the Land Reform Act, those who had no *kudikidappu* rights were driven to Laksham Veedu colonies and to the sides of roads, canals as well as wastelands. In 1985, P. Sivanandan wrote this about the social implications of the Land Reforms Act which was lauded by all as revolutionary: 'While the demographic minorities such as Brahmins, Nairs and Syrian Christians with more than five acres lay hold of 30.3 per cent of land, Ezhavas, Muslims, the Scheduled Castes and Scheduled Tribes, that formed the majority, with more than five acres of land owned a mere 12.1 per cent.' By problematizing these issues, what slogans such as 'Kerala Model Land Reform Abandoned', which became popular at the time, sought to achieve was a new kind of land reform that would take the caste system and social development into consideration.

It was after long discussions, which took place under Dr Manmathan's guidance, that we arrived at the following demands to be made during our demonstrations in connection with the Avasara Samatwa Prakshobha Jatha, or, literally, equality of opportunity rally, though better described as a *struggle* or *movement*:

1. Implement a comprehensive and scientifically drawn-up land reform scheme and grant lands to the landless people occupying spaces on the sides of roads and canals and in wastelands;
2. put an end to the Harijan Laksham Veedu project;
3. grant land, house and financial assistance to the newer families in the existing colonies;
4. return confiscated lands to the Adivasis and constitute Scheduled regions as well as self-governing councils;
5. ensure reservation to Dalit Christians in proportion to their population;
6. implement reservation in private, public sectors and co-operative institutions;

7. nationalize large-scale businesses and plantations and bring them under state control; establish small- and medium-scale businesses on the basis of national wealth and labour;
8. make national wealth through central and state budgets as well as five-year programmes available to Dalits and Adivasis in proportion to their population;
9. protect traditional employment and handicraft sectors;
10. implement the Mandal Commission Report;
11. ensure the states respect protection of minority rights;
12. give priority to women in appointments to jobs and implement special recruitment of educated Dalit women;
13. cancel the debts of the weaker sections and put an end to attachment of their property;
14. make education and employment fundamental rights;
15. put an end to the oppression of the Adivasis, Dalits, labourers, farmers and religious minorities;
16. grant representation to Dalits in institutions like the Sahitya Akademi, Sangeet Natak Akademi and so on, that receive government funds.

P.P. Thomas was in charge of propaganda. He owned a printing press at Ranni, and agreed to print notices to be distributed throughout the route of the demonstration. P.N. Sukumaran and V.C. Rajappan were given the responsibility of providing mic sets and two bicycles. I was the convenor of the political affairs committee. It was decided that at the end of the demonstration each day, there should be an evaluation of experiences by participants, and that changes in the political stance should be made on the basis of responses elicited from the masses in each region. At Kurichi, a couple of volunteers armed themselves with swords and knives to protect the participants. In the study classes held to build awareness among the participants, strict instructions were given about maintaining discipline because they would have to camp in houses, schools and rest houses along the route.

The life I led during those days are captured in two lines penned by G. Sankara Kurup: 'When life to me became a stove / I used the light to brighten the world'.

My wife had become estranged, leading to a weakening of my family life. Two of my children were at my ancestral house. Since they were looked after by my mother, my sister Shanta and my sister-in-law Ammini, they fared all right. Sharing my life of half-starvation with them, I struggled to take care of my children's other needs. When I was employed, I could provide good food to my daughter Nayana, but I could not extend the same benefit to my son Jayasurya. But despite the crises in my personal life, I felt I was discharging a great social responsibility and could not withdraw from it. Consequently, I went about doing my duty, burying all my miseries and humiliations inside myself. I would borrow money from anyone I could to satisfy my children's needs. Many people, who understood the state I was in, offered help without my asking. But I never accepted any help from K.K.S. Das, any of my relatives, friends or colleagues at the KSRTC.

I still remember one incident from Nayana's time in high school. She wanted Rs 300 to go on an excursion. I approached Dr Manmathan. He had a dispensary at Shanti Niketan in Kottamuri, near Changanassery. More than anyone else, I knew about the money he made from his private practice. Very few people went to his dispensary, set up in that rural area. Since his political past and caste were objectionable, most of his patients were Dalits. Not only did Dr Manmathan not charge huge consultation fees from them, he even helped many of them financially. But I could not approach anyone else for such a small amount. When I made my request, he had no money on him. He asked me to wait till he got fees from his patients. Since there was no other way out for me, I stayed put—for three days and two nights—like a prisoner, until he obtained that amount.

Another problem I had to face concerned the plot of land I have already written about. As Baburaj had left for Kozhikode, there was no one for me either to discuss the issue with or to seek a loan from. There was no valuable object I could mortgage or sell. The government officer who had stood as a guarantor would harass us routinely. Mani and Amma would confront him but Chaachan was more or less indifferent. In the circumstances, the responsibility of solving the problem fell to me. A plot of land worth nine lakh rupees at that time was about to get transferred into the hands of a stranger for a paltry sum. Protected by law, the guarantor's victory was assured. It was not a problem that could be sorted out either by asking him to take pity or by using force. As it was a case of revenue recovery, I went to the tahsildar office at Vaikom to find out what alternate steps I could take. The officer's advice was that I remit Rs 3,000—this was the lowest possible amount—and get Baburaj to meet the revenue minister and secure an order allowing payment of the rest in instalments.

---

46. Struggle for Equality of Opportunity—Part II

The procession conducted in association with the struggle for equality of opportunity began on 25 September 1988 from Thrissur. It would reach Thiruvananthapuram in 45 days. I feel that it was different from all other processions ever taken out in the state because of the demands put forward by the communitarian and political leaders of a subaltern class. At the same time, it succeeded in bringing to the notice of the common people the experiences of the Renaissance that had been rendered invisible by political parties, including the Communist party, as well as the social and communitarian organizations of the savarnas and the avarnas; the criticisms against savarna hegemony; and the economic and social ideals of Dr B.R. Ambedkar, Ayyankali, Sree Narayana Guru, Sahodaran Ayyappan and others.

The procession passed through Thrissur after conducting public meetings and collecting funds at every spot where there assembled enough people to justify it. It was when a valedictory meeting was taking place at Mulanthuruthy that Baburaj appeared there. The subject that we privately discussed was related to our domestic affairs. If the guarantor went ahead with litigation we stood to lose the plot. If Baburaj could pay Rs 3,000, the land could be transferred to his name. There was no alternative in my mind. Baburaj's reply was that if we approached Dr Leelakrishnan, he would give us that amount. But I did not know the man. Baburaj assured me that Dr Leelakrishnan knew me, and had a lot of respect for me too. As soon as the day's meeting got over, I set out for Malappuram.

By the time I reached Thrissur in a KSRTC bus, it was late night. I managed to spend some hours at the bus stand till dawn. Then I took another bus to Dr Leelakrishnan's home at AR Nagar. It was noon by the time I got there. The meeting was a momentous one. It would prove to be a live-saver, for me personally and for the SEEDIAN weekly too. His untimely death is a sad memory.

I arrived at the hospital in AR Nagar where Dr Leelakrishnan lived with his elder brother, Aravindakshan, and younger brother, J.M. Jayachandran. Neither he nor his wife Rema displayed the awkwardness of a first meeting. In fact, they welcomed me warmly. When I presented my problems to him, he told me that he didn't have any money on him just then. But, he said, if I could come two days before I needed the amount, he would pawn Rema's gold ornaments and raise the money for me. The relief I experienced was indescribable. As the procession was still underway, I went to meet Dr Leelakrishnan after two days. He had set apart Rs 3,000 for me, as promised. After spending a night at home, I headed for the taluk office at Vaikom, paid the amount, transferred the responsibility of loan repayment to Baburaj's name and proceeded to Thiruvananthapuram. I was standing in front of the revenue minister P.J. Joseph's office at the Secretariat when I saw Sanu Master, who was an MLA then. When I explained the purpose of my visit to him, he accompanied me to the Minister's room, and secured the order allowing repayment of the rest of the amount in instalments.

When I returned home, the guarantor, three friends of his and a few relatives of mine had assembled in the compound. The guarantor wanted Chaachan to honour the agreement and register the plot in his name. Amma and Mani were putting up a fierce opposition. It was into this tense situation that I made an entry. 'Your liability has come to an end,' I said, showing him the Minister's order. 'Hereafter, it will be Baburaj's responsibility to repay the loan.' I showed the copy of the order to the rest of the people. He refused to accept it, continuing to insist on his claim, all the local residents including our relatives on his side. Even those who acknowledged the order asked Chaachan to keep his word. In the eyes of our relatives, not only I but my entire family were the offenders.

'Do whatever you want!' I burst out, when the anger boiled over. The din lasted a while before the crowd dispersed.

The next day, I joined the procession at Thiruvalla. The explanatory meetings had thrown up good responses because of which everyone was enthusiastic. The financial troubles were not very serious. But we faced some hostility in the evening at Pandalam where a valedictory meeting was taking place. A group led by Shaji Joseph was collecting funds. A textile shop owner, whose showroom stood opposite the venue of our meeting, organized a few headload workers in order to initiate a fight. But since the workers exercised self-restraint, it was averted.

That was only the beginning of the troubles though. The shop owner was an NSS member and office bearer of a merchant–industrialist co-ordinating committee. He made telephone calls to instruct all shops right up to Thiruvananthapuram to not make any contributions. During the following days, we were in dire straits, a situation that lasted till we reached Thiruvananthapuram. On the final day, nearly 40 people turned up from various places. After a demonstration and a public meeting, a few went back. The rest stayed in the house of a SEEDIAN activist. By afternoon the next day, a small group including K.K.S. Das and myself went to the Secretariat and submitted our memorandum to all the ministers including the Chief Minister. We gave a copy of it to C.T. Sukumaran, IAS, Secretary to the Revenue Minister. 'It is the cabinet that should take a decision regarding these demands,' he said after reading it. What I understood from his words was that Dalits had to earn equality of opportunity for themselves through a political struggle.

I was at home when the guarantor's lawyer's notice reached us. We had not expected such a response because he had been relieved of the liability. Realizing that the issue was serious, I gave all the documents related to the property and a little money to a lawyer in Kottayam. Unfortunately, he did not act upon it. Assuming that the matter would take care of itself, I didn't bother to enquire about the case. But even as the case was in court, the guarantor passed away. Nevertheless, the *ex parte* verdict made by the court went in his favour. Neither his wife nor his relatives took any further steps though. Later, after Baburaj landed a job, he repaid the outstanding loan amount. Subsequently, we entrusted the case to a leading lawyer in Kottayam, Advocate Satyavan Nair. As the guarantor's relatives neither appeared in court nor followed up the litigation, the final verdict was favourable to us.

47. Burning Adi Sankara

The day was 1 September 1989. The Adhasthitha Navothana Munnani burnt copies of *Manusmriti*.[80] I arrived at the venue of the meeting along with P.O. John to offer felicitations. On the dais were K. Venu, A.X. Varghese, K.M. Salimkumar and Dalitbandhu N.K. Jose. Before the meeting began, Jose left the dais, came to me and said, 'There is a possibility of a lathi charge against the participants in the struggle. You must keep away.'

I spoke about this to John. I told him that we too would be put behind bars if a lathi charge and arrests take place. Why should we suffer for this organization? I asked him. Besides, we held different views from the members. Even in prison and during the litigation, we would continue to have differences of opinion. Arguments would be inevitable. With John agreeing with me, I spoke very briefly at the meeting and left the scene. John and I walked towards the KSRTC bus stand. The lathi charge started even before we had got to the stand.

A few who had burnt copies of the *Manusmriti* joined us at the bus stand. But all was quiet here. And so, believing that it was safe, John and I joined the crowd and walked out of the bus stand. Just then, the police arrived and attacked us. One policeman raised his baton against me, but seeing my face, pushed me aside and said, 'Kochetta, won't you go away from here?' He was a native of Appanchira, and a relative of mine, and so, I was spared a beating. When I went back to the bus stand, the lathi charge was still going on.

As I went, I saw a youngster rush a policeman, push him down and stomp him, inviting immediate retaliation by the other policemen. Such scenes were a new experience to me. I felt deep respect for that courageous and committed youngster.

He was John Joseph, state leader of the student wing of the Central Reorganization Committee—Communist Party of India (Marxist-Leninist) (CRCCPI[M-L]). A native of Vaduvukode in Ernakulam district, he was the eldest of three boys of a prosperous family. Later, he not only joined me in social and political activities but also became a pillar of support during times of crises in my personal life. He was a compassionate young man, not only towards Dalits but all downtrodden and poor people. These four lines of poetry written by N.V. Krishna Warrier often come to my mind when I think of John Joseph: 'Wherever man's hands are in chains / There my own hands feel pain / Wherever there is torture / Those beatings my own back endure'. It was my deep sense of indebtedness to him that made me dedicate my book *Idathupaksham Illaatha Kaalam* ('A Time Sans the Left Front'), published by DC Books, to him.

On 2 October 1989, SEEDIAN set fire to Adi Sankara.[81]

The 1200th birth anniversary of Adi Sankara was inaugurated at Kalady by Shankar Dayal Sharma, the President of India, in the presence of the Chief Minister E.K. Nayanar and E.M.S. Namboodiripad. The birth anniversary of Adi Sankara, who fortified Brahminical hegemony over India, institutionalized the caste system, and denied the subaltern as well as women the right to knowledge, citing reasons of defilement, was celebrated not as a religious ritual but a national event. In a bid to yoke this savarna-Brahmin nationalism with Marxism, E.M.S. Namboodiripad wrote in an article that 'Sankara has made loftier contributions than most other Indian philosophers. It is a matter of pride for us that he is a Keralite. His views on Advaita are the most sublime form of Indian thought. In Europe, a high version of philosophy appears in the principles of Hegel who was the mentor of Marx and Engels. There is a resemblance between Hegel and Sankara. The position that Hegel enjoys in

European philosophy corresponds to that of Sankara in Indian philosophy. In his argument that only the Brahman exists, the rest is illusion, wasn't Sankara suggesting that there is no God?' It is blind admiration for EMS's scholarship that has placed him beyond criticism. As a result, no one noticed the Brahminism that was concealed within Marxism.

When the central-state committee meetings of SEEDIAN took place at Indraprastha Tourist Home in Kottayam, P.N. Sukumaran and V.C. Rajappan mooted the idea of burning Adi Sankara. That literally shook up all the committee members. Breaking the silence that hung in the room, I asked, 'Should we burn Sankara?' Sensing that no one had any objections, I continued, 'Sankara is a philosopher. Shouldn't we rather say "burn an effigy of Sankara"?' In reply, Shaji Joseph said firmly that we should 'burn Sankara'. This met with unanimous approval. Later, on the basis of the explanation offered by Dr Manmathan, it was decided that propaganda should be conducted on 'Burning Sankara who created a philosophy for the caste system'.

A member proposed burning Adi Sankara at Kalady. But as we had practically no organizational influence there, the suggestion that the burning be done at Vypin was accepted. A committee with P.N. Sukumaran as convenor was constituted. The first press meet in the history of SEEDIAN was held at the Ernakulam Press Club by P.N. Sukumaran and Gopi Vallon. On hearing the statement and the explanation, the journalists expressed their strong resentment against the idea. When Gopi Vallon gave an aggressive response, all the journalists boycotted the meet, as a result of which not a single line was published about the forthcoming event. Nonetheless, an elaborate plan was chalked out for the propaganda work. It was Dr Manmathan who inaugurated the meeting at Malippuram which made the public announcement. His scintillating speech that was published in the

SEEDIAN weekly was a lesson of sorts as far as I was concerned.

Here are some of the relevant portions of Dr Manmathan's speech:

> Sankara, as far as we are concerned, is not Adi Sankara but *jati* [caste] Sankara. He is a great Brahmin who created a philosophy for the caste system. It was because of his philosophy that we became the polluting caste. We were kept at a distance. We became chandalas. This was achieved by crushing the religions of Jainism and Buddhism that were built on compassion and mutual love. Sankara's lackeys claim that his victory was won through scholarship. But history tells a different story. Intoxicated by Sankara's advice, kings and rulers raised their swords and lances, caused rivers of blood to flow. This was how they established their victory. What does this prove? Sankara was hard-hearted. Blood-thirsty. Precisely for that reason, as far as we are concerned, he is not worthy of our respect. Hindus claim that religious clashes were brought to an end in India. But what are the facts? Sankara made temples for the Hindus. He captured Buddhist and Jain places of worship and converted them into temples. There he instituted puja rituals on the basis of *Manusmriti*, the Vedas and the Ithihasas. He ordered that only Brahmins had the right to conduct pujas. What happened thereafter? The lower castes were driven out of temples… As a result of all this, the caste system got entrenched, and the Hindus got divided into thousands of castes. They observed pollution rituals among themselves, fought one another, converted to other religions including Islam. In short, Sankara who sought to unify India through Hinduism caused fissures in the community. What followed was foreign invasion. It was after Sankara that India succumbed to foreigners, right up to the British. As a result of the disunity that Sankara created among the people, our vast country could be vanquished by even the smallest military force and looted for centuries. This is

> the legacy of Sankara. EMS claims that Sankara is Hegel. Hegel was a philosopher who envisioned the destruction of feudalism and the emergence of a democratic state through a revolution. It was through Hegel's teachings that Marx and Engels discovered the concept of working-class governments and socialist ideas. The aim of this latter-day Sankara behind installing Sankara in the place of Hegel, who led the world into a new era, was to ensure the dominance of Brahmins within the Communist party. Through this, Ezhavas and the depressed classes who shed blood for the sake of the party were made its slaves. On the occasion of Sankara Jayanti, those who presented papers along with the great Brahmin Shankar Dayal Sharma and those who raised a rebellion against it converged at the same point. All of them, without a single exception, pointed out Vivekananda as a model. Vivekananda did not denounce the Vedic principles. He did not argue that castes should be abolished. However, he insisted that the Hindu religion should be reformed. Those who idolized Vivekananda for putting forward such an agenda, however, were dismissive of the Buddha, Phule,[82] Ambedkar, Sree Narayana Guru and others. For the sake of Hindutva and Brahminism, Sankara and Vivekananda were praised. We are burning Sankara in order to counter the politics that seeks to take back the rights that were earned through countless agitations. Through that, we will be erasing even the memory of Sankara from our minds. This is necessary not only for our liberation but for the liberation of our nation as well.

The long speech delivered by Dr Manmathan thrilled the SEEDIAN activists, including myself.

Posters proclaiming 'Burning Adi Sankara who created a philosophy for the caste system' were pasted everywhere from Thrissur to Kottayam by a group led by Shaji Joseph. At Piravam, a few RSS volunteers attempted to stop them and announced that they would not permit the burning of Sankara. Arguments and threats followed, but the RSS activists withdrew without making any further provocation. The propaganda march from Sahodaran Ayyappan's house to the Vypin boat jetty was led by me. At the evaluation meeting conducted at Murukkumpuzha, as I was delivering a speech, a few RSS workers belonging to the Kudumbi community[83] created a ruckus. But when the participants of the march raised objections, they withdrew.

We planned our activities very carefully. Since there had been a lathi charge at the burning of the *Manusmriti* at Vaikom, we expected police intervention. Fearing that the activists would be taken into preventive detention, we held our consultative meeting at night in the coir-spinning sheds near the lakeside. We decided to burn Sankara at three in the afternoon. Prior to that, a seven-member team led by P.N. Sukumaran positioned themselves in different houses at Malippuram. A big posse of police arrived at the scene. GROW[84] Vasu and M.P. Vasu who had come from Piravam to convey their greetings were the first ones to be taken into custody. They were put in the Narakkal police station lock-up. By 3 pm, all those who had arrived in buses from the Vypin jetty and Nayarambalam stood by the roadside in groups. Crowds cheered and shouted slogans as the effigy of Sankara was burnt by the activists. The police went towards them, took everyone into custody, and transferred them to the Narakkal police station. But they were not charged with anything and were let free.

Dr M. Kunjaman wrote an article in *Padhabhedam* criticizing the burning of the *Manusmriti* and Sankara. In the article I wrote in response, I commented, 'Sahodaran Ayyappan burnt a caste-demon at Palluruthi, Dr Ambedkar burnt the *Manusmriti*, Poykayil Appachan burnt a copy of the Bible. These historical experiences were struggles against savarna hegemony.' I think it was in that article that the public in Kerala first saw an open reference to Poykayil Appachan's burning of the Bible.

---

48. Dalit Christian Struggles

The Martha Mariam (St Mary's) Church at Kuravilangad in Kottayam district is considered to be one of the oldest churches in Kerala. Christian historians claim that members of four Brahmin illams (Kalli, Kalikkam, Shankuri and Palamattam), converted to Christianity by St Thomas, came from Palayoor, crossed Ettumanoor, reached Kuravilangad in 307 CE and settled there. This church was built under their initiative in 337 CE and consecrated eight years later by Mar Joseph, the Bishop of Edessa. Other historians who dispute this claim argue that the church was established in the 17th century. Even as such conflicting views co-exist, there is consensus on the fact that the church has been renovated many times. Another version claims that the Christians of Kuravilangad are immigrants who came from Kaduthuruthi. The legend cited to give credence to the version is as follows: The Maharashtrians destroyed churches in Bombay and the neighbouring regions, and threw the holy idols into the sea. One of the idols was that of St Mary. It crossed the waters and reached Kaduthuruthi. Although many Christians were ready to take the idol to their churches, the Mother did not consent to their desire. Finally, she decided to go along with devotees who had come from Kuravilangad.

In subaltern discourse, the Kuravilangad region was once the land where the Kuravas, an Adivasi community, lived in huge numbers. It is believed that the name 'Kuravilangad' owes its origin to this fact. Even today, the Pulayas living in this area are considered low-class Pulayas from the east. The Pulayas from the western parts used to maintain physical distance from them until recently. In any case, it was the savarna Christians of Kuravilangad and neighbouring areas like Vayala, Kadappoor and Kulathoor that worshipped at the principal church at Kaduthuruthi. But by the end of the 19th century or the beginning of the 20th, when the Kunnel church—a Pulaya church—was abandoned, Dalit Christians were permitted entry into the Kuravilangad church. This took place when the Renaissance had progressed considerably.

In 1989, a story came out about the dead body of Chirayil Thomas, a Dalit, which was interred in a grave in the Kuravilangad church cemetery (which is under the Pala diocese), being dug out and buried at a distant spot. It had been placed in a section of the graveyard that had been set apart for savarna Christians. This story came out in the open as a result of infighting among the priests. The vicar of the Kuravilangad church and another priest known locally as Mukkathachan were not on good terms for some reason. The latter leaked this story out to a reporter who worked for the *Indian Express*. As soon as the news came out, SEEDIAN activists led a protest at Kuravilangad. The aim was to conduct a struggle against caste discrimination within the Christian church/community and demand legal action against what the church had done.

As the first step towards this goal, it was decided that a Dalit Christian convention be held at Kuravilangad. It was conducted at the National Hotel on KK Road, in front of the church. As the owner of the hotel harboured feelings of enmity towards the vicar of the church, he gave us the hall for free. A lot of Dalit Christians and many savarna Christians in the area attended it from the beginning to the end. The decision taken at the convention was that propaganda work and public meetings should be held all over Pala diocese.

Even as I took part in the struggle, I strongly argued for legal action. My view was that caste discrimination existed within the Christian church. Therefore we had to approach the High Court for redress. A decision to this effect was arrived at in a meeting I had with Advocate C.V. Antony (who later became a member of the state committee of the Peoples Democratic Party [PDP]) and Advocate Saramma Paul. Advocate Antony promised to offer his professional services free of charge. I suggested strengthening our agitation for reservations for Dalit Christians if we obtained a favourable verdict. Caste distinctions still existed within the Christian church. If, on the other hand, we failed, I said, the publicity we get through the case ought to be used to make the savarna–Dalit Christian conflict more widespread. My opinion was accepted.

But as our Kuravilangad struggle began to be noticed all over Kerala we suffered some unexpected setbacks. Simon John of Backward Peoples' Development Corporation (BPDC) and Yohannan, the leader of Sadhu Jana Paripalana Sangham—neither of whom had shown the slightest interest in our agitation—intervened in the issue, and effected a compromise between the church authorities and Thomas's family, who were assured a permanent grave in the cemetery and a gift of Rs 5,000. One of the members of Thomas's family was promised a job in a school or college run by the church. The litigation took an unfavourable turn too. P.O. John had been entrusted with the responsibility of handing over the documents related to the case to C.V. Antony. John not only did not transfer said documents but also lost them. The Kuravilangad agitation came to an ignominious end.

In the process, however, I had made a serious study of Dalit Christians. The person who helped me in this regard was P.P. Thomas, who asked me to present a paper at a seminar he had organized at Ranni. In preparation, I read a number of books on the Christian community of Kerala. Besides these, I took books from the seminary library at Vadavalloor in Kottayam, taking notes as I went. What caught my special attention was the history of family meetings. There were hundreds of books in that library. All were about the savarna Christian families spread across Kerala, and according to them, all the families—without a single exception—originated from the Brahmin community! The factors that united all of them, besides the figure of Jesus Christ, were educational institutions, persons considered holy, like Chavara Achan[85] and Alphonsa Amma,[86] and the church authorities. It was this discursive domain that helped them wield influence in the fields of politics and administration. Dalit Christians did not have such a tradition.

What is more, I also came to understand that the Christian community, like the Hindu community, had a caste system. The main opposition was between savarna Christians and Dalit Christians. The biography of Pampady John Joseph written by T.H.P. Chentharassery in 1989 only buttressed this conclusion I had arrived at. What specifically guided my interpretation was a memorandum submitted by Pampady John Joseph to the British Parliament on 24 April 1935. A copy of the memorandum was included in the book. The two urgent issues confronting Travancore, according to it, were:

1. granting representation to all communities in public service in proportion to their population, and
2. granting representation, on the basis of the aforementioned principle, to all communities in the Legislative Assembly.

He goes on to say:

> The savarna Christians observe untouchability with respect to us. We are not permitted entry into their houses. In certain places, untouchability is enforced in terms of distance as well. They keep us at a specific distance in order to prevent our presence in public spaces. This attitude maintained by our co-religionists towards us will only serve to reinforce the practice

> among caste-Hindus. By constructing separate churches for the depressed Christians, the Syrian Christians and other savarna Christians are strongly establishing caste inequality. The lower-caste Christians are not buried in their cemeteries. There has been an instance of a corpse being disinterred and exhibited in the church premises.

Let me mention one more point from the memorandum. That detail is heart-rending:

> Although certain churches permit us to participate in the Passover feast, we are made to sit in the farthest pews. We are not permitted, as Syrian Christians are, to pick the host [a portion of bread used for Holy Communion] from the platter or drink wine from the chalice. Rather, the host is thrown into our palms. After everyone else is served, we are served into our palms, using ladles.

The most significant part of the memorandum ran as follows:

> However, of late, the depressed Christians have begun to ask for their rights. If they are not considered as a separate community, Parayas (Sambavas), Kuravas, Pulayas (Cheravas) and others, the lowest classes in the Hindu community that converted to Christianity will never get any benefits.

It was on the basis of this that I argued that Pampady John Joseph ought to be seen as belonging in the same league as Renaissance leaders like Ayyankali and Poykayil Appachan, who exhorted Dalit Christians not to abandon their faith in Jesus Christ but transform themselves into a separate community.

I had been, even before I took on the role of a leader in the Kuravilangad struggle, a critic of the proselytization done by the missionaries. From K.K.N. Kurup's article published in *Vignanakairali*, I had learnt that the aim of the missionaries—right from the time of the first conversions at Mallappally in 1854—

was to supply subaltern labour power to the plantation industry in Ceylon and within India itself. Further, the studies undertaken by people like Father Stephen Fuchs, Dr Robin Jeffrey, N.A. Jose and others proved that Christian converts did not get justice in the church. The missionary activities that aimed at bringing slavery to an end were not based on a sense of justice that was outraged by caste discrimination. Rather, they were fuelled by the aforementioned goal. That was why even when the anti-slavery proclamation of 1855 brought an end to slavery, it contained a clause that ensured the continuance of the caste system among them. While Paul Chirakkarode ignored such historical facts and accepted proselytization as a crusade against the caste system, Dr T.M. Yesudas and Dr P. Sanal Mohan described proselytization as religious upliftment and argued that Dalit Christians did not suffer any kind of discrimination. Indeed, religious upliftment was evaluated as a renaissance. Ayyankali's activities were interpreted as the opening of the doors to Hindutva! The aim of such propaganda can be read as being aimed at a rejection of the Dalit Christians' awareness of their communitarian (Dalit) identity and asking for a surrender to savarna Christians.

The Kuravilangad struggle had suffered a setback but the Dalit Christian problem was not insignificant enough to be ignored. Although most of the SEEDIAN activists were Dalit Christians, the demand put forward by the organization was 'Amend the Constitution to include the depressed Christians in the Scheduled Caste list'. In order to get this demand taken up at the national level, it was imperative to secure the organized strength of Dalit Christians. It was with this aim in mind that a Dalit Christian Conference, organized on 10 March 1990 at the Indraprastha Tourist Home, Kottayam, and inaugurated by K.K.S. Das, gave shape to the Kerala Dalit Christian Federation (KDCF). The most significant decision taken at the conference was to organize a dharna in front of the Head Post Office at Kottayam on 24 April 1991—the 55th anniversary of the submission of the memorandum by Pampady John Joseph in the British Parliament—demanding that a special population list of Dalit Christians be published in the 1991 census. What we hoped to accomplish was a public acknowledgement of Pampady John Joseph apart from making Dalit Christians a separate community, which is a yardstick for reservation. After this struggle, however, the KDCF leadership was unwilling to take organizational activities forward.

In 1989, an agitation led by the Adhasthitha Navothana Munnani took place at the famous pilgrim centre of Travancore—the Mannanam church. The issue was the same—caste discrimination within the church. This area had a concentration of Pulayas as a result of which the church—which was more than one-and-a-half centuries old—was known as a 'Pulaya church'. When a Dalit Christian died, the dead body was not permitted into the church for the last rites. The agitation sought an end to this discrimination and put forth another demand as well—representation for Dalit Christians in appointments to educational institutions like schools and colleges run by the church. At the end of a long struggle, the church authorities finally conceded to the demand for arranging the last rites for Dalit Christians inside the church.

Another notable agitation was the one organized at the Koorappali, a church at Ilanji that was under the Pala diocese. Until a local Christian family named Mechirakkar donated land for the expansion of the church, it was also known as a Pulaya church. Syrian Christians attended the Ilanji church before 1965–70. But as soon as the Koorappali came under the sway of the savarna Christians, caste discrimination reared its head. The front pews were reserved for the savarnas. Even the cemetery was divided into separate sections. Even death did not ensure them a status equal to the savarnas. The anguished Dalit Christians approached the vicar and requested that the discrimination be ended, at least in the cemetery. The response, however, was one of abuse. This was how the problem was brought to the notice of Shaji Joseph. He, along with eight others, went to the church and made the same request. The vicar replied that the matter would be settled after the complainants came to church.

Such an unfavourable response provoked Shaji to draft a mass petition to the Pala bishop demanding an end to the discrimination. All Dalit Christians, except four members of the Harijan Christian Maha Sabha that was under the bishop, and many savarna Christians, signed the petition. On being handed over the petition directly, the bishop read it aloud and asked, 'Why was I not informed of this? A similar problem had occurred at Kuravilangad as well. What the priest did was wrong indeed.' He subsequently appointed an enquiry committee. As the matter drew public attention, the rich and the prominent among the local Christians entered the fray. Their accusation was that believers were being divided. Quarrels and threats followed, inviting police intervention.

With the Koorappali issue taking on a new dimension, a diocesan committee was formed with Shaji Joseph as convenor, Chakkappan as president and Chackochan as secretary. This committee approached the bishop once again and submitted its request. The bishop convened a meeting of savarna and Dalit Christians of the diocese at the parish hall of the Koorappali. His opinion was that Shaji Joseph was trying to create disunity among the believers, and therefore had to show repentance. When it was pointed out that all Dalit Christians and a group of savarna Christians had signed the petition, he brought the meeting to a close with the remark, 'Your internal problems should be solved internally.'

This led the diocesan committee to organize an agitation. At first, a group of 30 individuals conducted a march towards the church. In the public meeting convened the same day at Pinekutti, Joseph Pulikkunel, the editor of the magazine *Oshana*, was the chief speaker. In the days that followed, propaganda activities got the support of Liberation Theologists and indirect encouragement from Sister Alice. The Latin Catholic bishops pledged their support and consequently, Dalit as well as Dalit Christian organizations became participants in the struggle. It was when the people's agitation was going on that the diocesan committee sent a petition to the Pope through its office—the Apostolic Nunciature—in Delhi. They made the following demands: (1) Put an end to caste discrimination in Christian churches; (2) stop addressing Dalit Christians by their caste names; (3) stop calling elderly people by their names; (4) ensure job opportunities in Christian institutions, and representation in the appointment of priests and nuns; (5) end caste discrimination in cemeteries; (6) ensure equality and equality of opportunity in the Christian church; and (7) ensure participation of Dalit Christians in the administration of the dioceses.

On the basis of this petition, the Pope's representative in Delhi, Cardinal Abraham Kattumakkal, held a discussion with the diocesan members at Ernakulam. The Cardinal, who had offered his services as a bishop in the African countries, said, 'This is the first time that we have received such a request from India. We shall send your demands to all churches.' Not only was the Koorappali cemetery issue resolved but the issue of caste discrimination in all churches in Kerala was also settled. The first such burial after the change was implemented was that of the committee president Chakappan's father.

The Mary Roy case (*Mary Roy vs State of Kerala & Ors*, 1986 AIR 1011), which opened a new chapter in India's legal history and paved the way for discussions on Christian personal law, became a people's struggle due to the leadership role played by organizations like SEEDIAN and the Democratic Christian Forum. The involvement of people like Anila George, who has made a name for herself as an advocate and human rights activist, Elizabeth, Dr A.K. Ramakrishnan's wife and public activist, John Joseph and John, Shaji Joseph's relatives, require special mention. The organizer of the agitation was Shaji Joseph.

It was when the Christian MLAs, under the leadership of K.M. Mani, decided to pass a bill in the Assembly in order to destabilize a Supreme Court verdict, which had been favourable to Christian women,[87] that Mary Roy came into the picture. Even today, I remember seeing Mary Roy at the one-day dharna at Gandhi Square in Kottayam with a placard hanging from her neck. It read 'My worth is Rs 5,000'. Many Christian women, including nuns, participated in the agitation from beginning to end. It was because of this agitation and the subsequent ones that K.M. Mani's efforts were foiled.

~

Even as organizational activities and agitations were on in full swing, November Books' publications and the SEEDIAN weekly's issues kept coming. Those who worked for the weekly with me did not enjoy financial stability. The person who supported me and the weekly at this difficult time was Dr Leelakrishnan. I would make weekly visits to his hospital at Kottayi before the matter went to the printing press at Arppukkara. Aware of the purpose behind the visit, he wouldn't hesitate to give me money, both for the weekly and my personal requirements. Rema never opposed this.

In the meantime, November Books published T.M.

Abraham's translation of Albert Camus's play *Caligula*. Later, when Jayachandran, who was a book salesman, approached me regarding the publication of books, the publishing firm was relocated from Kallara to a lodge at Marar Road in Thrissur. On the insistence of Jayachandran, Shaji Joseph, G. Harilal and Baburaj, a collection of my articles was brought out under the title *Kalaapavum Samskaaravum* ('Rebellion and Culture'). It was published in collaboration with Shashikumar's Khani Books at Aluva because of the serious financial difficulties I faced. Before he joined November Books, Jayachandran had been associated with Harinarayanan, who had played a lead role in the film *Amma Ariyaan*, and in the production of a documentary that was never completed. Besides, he had translated Frantz Fanon's *The Wretched of the Earth* and Amos Tutuola's *The Palm-Wine Drinkard*. As crises never loosened their hold on me, I could never publish them, and that thought continues to haunt me even today.

---

49. Eventually, I am Isolated

B.R. Ambedkar once remarked that Dalit Christians continue to suffer the same violence as they had at the hands of the Hindus before conversion. It was the untouchables who did not convert to Christianity that took forward the movement meant to redress historical wrongs. This was an extraordinary thing. He had never seen untouchable Christians coming together in order to find a solution to their social disabilities. And it was an indisputable fact that they had disabilities. It was also well known that there were many educated people among them who could lead their struggle. Yet there was not a single movement to solve their problems.

At a time when memories of the Dalit renaissance in Kerala were not remotely alive, the organizational unification of Dalits took place through the agency of the Indian Dalit Foundation, and its ideological fortification, through SEEDIAN. However, neither of these organizations exist today. They had started crumbling even in the beginning of the 1990s. Many reasons contributed to their implosion but the chief factor was differences between Dalits and Dalit Christians over the issue of reservation.

Although it found a lot of publicity, Advocate K.V. Kumaran's case against the revision of the Scheduled Caste list and the sanction of reservation to Dalit Christians did not garner much support. The reason for this was the weakness of caste organizations including the Kerala Pulaya Maha Sabha. Besides, since these organizations were influenced by the Communist parties, they gave little consideration to the reservation issue to begin with. However, the condition of the Dalit Christians was a different one. In 1957, the Backward Class Christian Federation (BCCF), founded by V.D. John, used the authority of the state government to include Dalit Christians in the OBC List, get a two per cent reservation in government service, which was not in proportion to their population, and secure stipends and lump sum grants for students. However, since it went against the Constitution, the state government could not include Dalit Christians in the Scheduled Caste list. The enmity against the Communist party that this triggered was what made the BCCF a participant in the Liberation Struggle. Although it continued to struggle until 1967, the organization could not enlist the support of Dalits or savarna Christians.

But things did change. The Justice Kumara Pillai Commission constituted by the state government in 1965, and the Nettoor P. Damodaran Commission constituted in 1970 made references to the destitution of Dalit Christians. Neither the Dalit Christian organizations nor the churches took up or sought reservation, however. When, in 1978, O.P. Tyagi presented a bill in the Parliament seeking to prevent forcible religious conversion, the churches conducted an agitation in Thiruvananthapuram. Although the problems of Dalit Christians were mentioned on that occasion, no one asked for the inclusion of Dalit Christians in the Scheduled Caste list. But with the Harijan Christian Maha Sabha—which had sustained grievous damage to its image following the agitations at Kuravilangad, Mannanam and Kooru—changing its name to Dalit Christian Maha Sabha (DCMS), it sought to further safeguard the interests of Dalit Christians. It was when the president of the DCMS, under the complete control and with the full support of the church, conducted a cross-bearing march in 1989 from Malayattoor to Thiruvananthapuram that the demand for inclusion of Dalit Christians in the Scheduled Caste list was raised for the first time. The public rally that was organized at the conclusion of the march in Thiruvananthapuram received massive support. This was followed by a hunger strike in front of the Secretariat.

The same year saw the participation of more than one lakh people belonging to various churches in the rally conducted at the Boat Club Maidan in Delhi, heeding to the call made by Rev Lawrence Mar Aprem, president of the Catholic Bishops Conference of India (CBCI). Following this, a front named SCCI (Small Christian Communities in India), formed under the leadership of various churches, organized an evening dharna in front of the Raj Bhavan on 12 November 1990, with 25,000 people participating in it. Thereafter, the agitation spread to other districts. Tens of thousands of people took part in the rallies and dharnas organized on 11 December 1991 and 2 December 1992. In connection with the 1992 rally, an indefinite hunger strike by the priests of India Evangelical Lutheran Church—Rev Spenser,

Rev Poovamani, Rev Y. Sukumaran, Rev Suraj, Rev Stephanos, Rev Joseph and Rev Selvaraj—was undertaken. A huge rally was organized at Kottayam on 6 September 1993 and a public meeting took place at Thirunakkara maidan.

It was now impossible for the political parties to ignore the struggle organized by the Christian church seeking reservation for Dalit Christians. Both Dalit and savarna Christians had united under the leadership of the church. Thus, the Congress and the Communist parties and the Bahujan Samaj Party not only demanded that Dalit Christians be included in the Scheduled Caste list but included that point in their election manifestos as well. With their sights set on winning over the Christian vote bank, several bills were presented in the Parliament. The most noteworthy aspect of the whole exercise was the absolute silence maintained by the Kerala Congress whose victory had been exclusively guaranteed on the basis of Christian votes. If one examines the history of that party, one will notice that it has not nominated a single Dalit Christian as a candidate for the Assembly elections. In the opinion of Joseph Karaly, general secretary of the SCCI, there are 45,000 to 50,000 Dalit Christian votes spread across 50 constituencies in Kerala. But the neglect shown towards them by the Kerala Congress, which would garner all their votes each time, never once came up for criticism by the churches.

The KPMS came out strongly against the demand for inclusion of Dalit Christians in the Scheduled Caste list. P.K. Raghavan, the patron of that organization, created a Scheduled Caste–Scheduled Tribe joint committee comprising the representatives of the Sambava, Velan, Vettuva and Siddha communities and started an agitation to put forward their demand. Other organizations rallied to support it. This caused the rift between Dalits and Dalit Christians to grow wider. (Now, weddings between members of the two groups have stopped once again.) This had its greatest impact on the Dalit organizations that sought to keep them together.

With activists belonging to both groups quitting the Indian Dalit Federation, the organization grew weak. The strong bond between Kallara Sukumaran and Paul Chirakkarode developed fissures. The meeting that was convened at Thiruvalla to iron out differences between them, with me as the mediator, could not put forward anything constructive. The Dalit–Dalit Christian split impacted SEEDIAN as well. The unity that the two groups had maintained all this while was destroyed and the activities of the organization came to an end. V.C. Rajappan's resignation from the post of vice president was a reflection of the death of the organization in Ernakulam district. The efforts that Lukose K. Neelamperoor and I made to dissuade him met with failure. With the dissolution happening everywhere, the decision about floating a political party became irrelevant, and when the general secretary joined the Dalit Christians in their silence, no further discussion could be had. Yet I took the initiative and arranged a leadership-level meeting with Paul Chirakkarode, K.M. Salimkumar and C.C. Kochukunju at the Indraprastha Tourist Home in Kottayam. Dalit Christian members of SEEDIAN rejected the demand for a separate list of Dalit Christians for the purpose of including them in the Scheduled Caste List. Besides, on securing K.K.S. Das's support for their stand, they branded me an enemy of Dalit Christians.

When the KPMS agitation, conducted without the support of any political party, drove a wedge between Dalits and Dalit Christians, the churches too aligned themselves with Dalit Christians and withdrew from their demand for an amendment of the Scheduled Caste list. The demand which surfaced later was that Dalit Christians be added in the Scheduled Caste list as per the

Presidential Order of 1950. What was quoted as a precedent was the reservation status accorded to the Dalits among Buddhists and Sikhs on the basis of this order. Was it possible? According to the second subsection of Article 25 of the Constitution, Buddhism, Sikhism and Jainism are part of Hinduism. For the presidential order that was applicable to this section to be made applicable to Article 26, a constitutional amendment would be necessary. These being the facts, certain Dalit Christian organizations demanded that a constitutional amendment be effected to make reservation a matter of 'equal rights'. But when the Ranganath Mishra Commission recommended the granting of reservation to Dalit Christians and Dalit Muslims, these aforementioned organizations did not speak up. Sangh Parivar outfits were of course there to oppose it. And so, a section of the KPMS, among others, began to see the Sangh Parivar as their saviour. It was through this path, opened by the Bharath Dharma Jana Sena, that the KPMS, led by T.V. Babu, entered the Sangh Parivar. Assessing that the Mishra Commission report recommendations would make the Dalit, Dalit Christian and Dalit Muslim sectors a turbulent space, the Scheduled Caste–Scheduled Tribe Commission suggested that the Mishra Commission recommendation be amended so that Dalit Christians and Dalit Muslims could be accommodated in separate lists in order to be granted reservation. Dalit Christian organizations in South India had problematized the issue of Dalit Christian reservation as far back as 1929 with their petitions to the Simon Commission. The sad fact is that despite the passage of time, they have not been able to put forward a perspective that reflects a self-identity built on a historical foundation, one that is inclusive of their social experiences.

The idea that the far Left put forward towards the end of the 1980s was a coming together of the anti-caste struggle and class struggle. This has today come to be acceptable even to mainstream Communist parties. It was at this juncture, when the anti-caste struggle was assessed to be a part of the class struggle, that I wrote an article 'Marxism-Leninism, Maoism and Ambedkarite Thought and the Caste, Class and Political Problems of India' as a kind of ideological response. It was translated by Father Abraham Ayirukuzhi for presentation at a seminar on 'All-India Dalit Tribes Minorities' Politics' conducted by SEEDIAN on 15 May 1988. Leaders of Dalit organizations and Naxal leaders from Tamil Nadu, Karnataka and Andhra Pradesh, Bihar, West Bengal, Jharkhand, Delhi and Kerala were invited to it. A lot was expected of the seminar but it turned out to be a disaster. Only 35 people participated in it. More than 250 representatives had participated in the state meeting held on the 13th and 14th. The failure of the seminar and the unfavourable response of SEEDIAN activists to my article compelled me to take a new look at it.

The article had been written at a time when the Ambedkar canon was not easily available everywhere. I had to be content with only a few works by Ambedkar and quotations from some of his other works. I had tried to look at Marxism-Leninism and Maoist thought from the prism of Ambedkarite thought. Although it was clear that such an interpretation was not relevant, I decided to publish it anyway so that it could be a lesson for those who argued for a unification of Dalits and Communists (*Lal Salam–Neel Salam*) and the initiation of a joint struggle.

A way out of the ideological impasse I had confronted in the article was provided by a speech made by Dr B.R. Ambedkar. I saw it in a little magazine in English (published in Maharashtra) when I went to the office of *Padhabhedam* on my way to Kozhikode for some work. The speech had been delivered on 22 April 1932 at the Bombay Legislative Council.[88]

> Many efforts have been made to make us think that the problem of the depressed is only a social one and that its solution is

> extra-political. We very strongly record our opposition to this perspective. We loudly proclaim that until political authority is transferred into the hands of the depressed, their problems will not be solved. I believe that if this is a fact we don't have to think otherwise. The problem of the depressed is a serious political one. Therefore, measures for a political solution are what should come about.

The speech was translated by Baburaj and published as a special editorial in the front page of the SEEDIAN weekly, with the title 'On Political Authority'. It was this speech—repeatedly quoted and republished by Dalit organizations in Kerala—that played a major role in giving a political orientation to the Dalit community. I felt that with the publication of such a speech in 1990, the SEEDIAN weekly had accomplished its duty. It marked the end of my exploration of ideology.

Around this time, November Books closed down and our book publication came to an end. Many complaints had been filed at the police station in Kaduthuruthi stating that the institution was a centre for terrorist activities. Acting on them, the police raided the office of November Books, and took Baburaj into custody.

My personal problems too had become worse. The opposition of our relatives and neighbours was now too much to bear. Besides, we had by now mortgaged many pieces of household furniture and equipment in order to raise money to repay the loan taken from the co-operative bank. The family had begun to slip from half-starvation to total destitution. Occasionally, we collected half-ripe coconuts that fell in our garden plot. But that did not bring us enough money to run the family. The only other source of income was the meagre amount Amma made from spinning coir or by weaving mats. We subsisted on the vegetables she grew in our plot. Deprived of food and medicine, Chaachan's body began to weaken. All his elder brothers had passed on after years of treatment and care. Their children had taken care of all those expenses. Chaachan felt that if he were to require medical care, he would be totally helpless. My children—Nayana and Jayasurya—had attended tuition classes since the third standard. But those classes came to an end since their fees could not be paid. And so, I went back to work, and Baburaj started looking for employment. Since I had been on unauthorized leave for a long period of time, I had to secure the permission of the chief officer to rejoin duty. I made a personal visit to C.K. Guptan, who was then the deputy general manager of the KSRTC. He did not behave like a superior officer but rather as a friend. With his intervention, I managed to join the Manandavady depot.

In 1992, a book edited by J.J. Pallath carried an article of mine where I elaborated on communitarianism. This sparked off an ideological clash with Maoists. Soon there was talk that I had abandoned Marxism and Leninism, and taken up casteism instead. There was even an accusation that this was the reason behind my taking the initiative to form the KDCF. When I supported Shaji Joseph in opposing K.K.S. Das's position that minority rights must be democratized, it was interpreted as a partiality towards Christians and Muslims. It was when the organization was rife with ideological confusion and conflicts that V.P. Singh decided to implement the Mandal Commission report and a nation-wide anti-reservation struggle caught on like wild fire. Subsequently, when SNDP leaders like C.K. Vishwanathan and M.K. Raghavan created the Samvarana Samudaya Munnani (Reservation Community Front) by bringing Dalit, backward and minority groups under the same umbrella, although SEEDIAN was not part of it, I aligned myself with it along with Sunilkumar and Shaji Joseph. I also became a member of its state committee. Raghavan was the person I was closest to in this organization.

When I was in college, the Communists had not presented a flattering portrait of him. He was a leader of the INTUC at the Cochin Port Trust and was described as an anti-Communist and a controversial figure. But I had realized that such a portraiture was far from the truth. Moreover, he had a style of public activism that was worth following. In the Samvarana Samudaya Munnani, greater importance was given to Dalit and minority rights than to the interests of the Backward Classes. When he passed on, I was staying at the office of the *Kerala Padhanangal* magazine, along with Narayanan. As soon as the news of his demise spread, the *Madhyamam* office called me urgently, and requested me to write an obituary. The newspaper carried it in the edit page on the day he was cremated.

When the Babri Masjid was destroyed on 6 December 1992, I was taking part in the Ambedkar memorial meeting led by Murali Kannampally and organized by the Communist party at Alappuzha. We got news of it while the meeting was going on. We immediately ended it and took out a demonstration towards the Medical College junction. Thereafter we conducted a dharna to protest against the incident. As we shouted slogans against the Sangh Parivar, nearly 15 RSS activists were seen leading a joyous procession, shouting provocative slogans back.

I hoped for a unity among Dalits, Backward Classes and minority groups. Kallara Sukumaran thought along the same lines. But SEEDIAN did not. The organization felt that it went against the spirit of class struggle espoused by Marxism. While the Dalits were poor and landless, there were both rich and poor people among the Backward Classes and the minority groups. A section of the Ezhavas was prosperous; the SNDP ran its own schools and colleges; and the Muslims similarly had their organization, the Muslim League, which had rich and powerful members and its own institutions. The Dalits, who were extremely poor and had no institutions to their name, could therefore not hold hands with them. Therefore it was not possible to bring them all under the same roof. Instead, since it was necessary to divide people into the rich and the poor classes, and protect the interests of the poor, a Dalit–Backward Class–minority group unity could not be admitted. This was their argument, which a few Dalit Communist leaders espouse even today. The counter-argument about the need to support an oppositional front in order to fight savarṇa Hindutva hegemony was not acceptable to them. Yet I continue to root for Dalit–Backward Class–minority group unity as a national issue.

Dr K.K. Manmathan's life came to a tragic end when the SEEDIAN was already crumbling under the strain of such ideological clashes. He was one of the many persons who had lit up post-Renaissance Dalit life. I quote here a few words written by Dr O.K. Santhosh in his reminiscences about Dr Manmathan:

> *Enjoy the hospital stay as though you have gone underground. View the period of imprisonment as the most joyful period of life. Interpret the sounds of the hands of the watch as messages from Russia. Listen to the radio transmissions from nations like Jordan, Israel and Syria and dream of a world revolution.* Such were the strange and inexplicable worlds that Dr Manmathan created. I do not include him in the category of geniuses who dream of revolutions and then, when they experience disappointment, take refuge in the world of delusions. He never suffered from lack of belief. But the neural network in his brain led him to an unpredictable world, pushing aside time. That life slipped into complications which hospitals and treatments…could not untangle. And so it went…until 24 December 2004.

His absence made judgements against me very easy to make.

When the V.P. Singh government stepped down and announced the next elections, the fissured and weak SEEDIAN committee met at Kaduthuruthi. The majority of members kept away. The report presented by P.O. John focused mainly on anti-imperialist and anti-social imperialist struggles.

'You should be a member of any one of the Communist parties and then speak about Marxism-Leninism and Maoist thought,' I said, in response to the report. 'Lenin said that without becoming a member of the Communist party no one can claim to be a Communist. You refuse to be a member of the Communist party and endure sacrifices and miseries. What do you do? Without becoming a member of the Communist party, you speak about class struggle and Maoism and pretend to be a revolutionary. If you wish to put an end to this hypocrisy and join Dalit activism and build up a Dalit community, admit the Dalit–Backward Class–minority group unity that has risen as the national politics of democratization. Be part of this communitarian politics and vote for V.P. Singh.'

Without waiting to see what response my words elicited, I walked out of the hall. That committee unanimously threw me out, without issuing even a show cause notice, and announced it at a public meeting organized that evening at Kaduthuruthi. The reason cited for the action was that I was anti-Dalit Christian in my outlook. With a few Naxalite groups parroting it, the label stuck.

Since I was ejected from SEEDIAN for ideological and political reasons, and not personal ones, I did not feel sad. Nor did I have complaints against anyone. I had consciously chosen the forum—the organization as well as its weekly—as part of my exploration to create a Dalit ideology, firm up rights, and arrive at a means of democratization that was different from Marxism. It was not possible to attain these goals through any Communist party. I am not ashamed of my SEEDIAN past just as I am not ashamed of my Naxal past. It was through years of study and struggle that I could make visible and gain social acceptance for epistemological domains and subaltern representations that had been rendered invisible. It was what helped me in my work as much in the realm of public life as in the field of literature.

---

50. C.T. Sukumaran, IAS

The withdrawal from communitarian and political activities paved the way for continuous reading. During this period, the work I read with a lot of enthusiasm was the *Mahabharata*. This had been a desire of mine from the time I read Kuttikrishna Marar's *Bharataparyatanam*[89] but had deferred it because I knew that Kunjikuttan Thampuran's Malayalam translation of the *Mahabharata* was not an easy read. It was when Baburaj brought home a copy of the prose version of the epic written by Vidwan K. Prakash (published by NBS) that my long-cherished desire was fulfilled. What influenced me the most were descriptions of nation-formation in ancient times within the vast country of India, and of villages not recorded in history, as well as the value system he decoded from the Bhishma Parva.[90]

Conditions at home got better when Baburaj was appointed to a gazetted post in the Mahatma Gandhi University. As I had not gone farther than being a lower division clerk, my salary was meagre. I had moved out with my family but my salary served only to meet our domestic requirements. Baburaj managed the repayment of the loans that hung above our heads, take special care of Chaachan and Amma, and bring the family to the middle class. I had maintained my warm relationship with Dr Leelakrishnan's family. Nayana would spend her entire Onam vacation with them. It was when I was thus pinned to the domestic sphere that life took another turn, and I was hurled once again into the domain of communitarian and political activism.

I had been transferred from the Kozhikode depot to Vaikom, where life was confined to the office, home and reading, when a struggle was launched by Dalit organizations all over Kerala, including the district of Ernakulam, demanding a CBI probe into the murder of C.T. Sukumaran, IAS. It lasted from October 1992 to April 1994, and was the longest and most well-organized agitation to take place before the Chengara struggle.[91] Like the latter, this too was conducted not by a single organization but was a decentralized exercise with nearly all organizations participating in almost all the districts of the state. Besides, it saw the participation of Backward Class and minority group organizations, as well as prominent political leaders. But it was undertaken on the initiative of and led by Dalits. That is the reason for this detailed description.

C.T. Sukumaran was the son of M.C. Thevan, from Mulanthuruthy in Ernakulam district, and Thiruvanda. He earned his post-graduate degree from Maharaja's College and began his career at St Albert's College as a teacher. While on the job, he cleared the administrative service examinations. Subsequently, he worked as the sub-collector at Alappuzha and Palakkad districts, the collector at Thrissur and Malappuram districts, the MD of the Kerala Financial Corporation, the State Labour Commissioner, the MD of Titanium Travancore Products, the director of Harijan Welfare, the Revenue Board secretary and so on. After 19 years of service, in 1989, he was appointed chairman of the central government institution, Marine Products Export Development (MPED) Authority. While serving in that capacity, he had gone to the Chennai regional office and stayed there. On 28 September 1992, he was found dead. The next morning, newspapers ran headlines and featured reports about his suicide.

When they heard the news, Sukumaran's father, his wife and K.K. Madhavan Master, his uncle and former MLA, contacted the Tamil Nadu Inspector General of Police and requested that the post-mortem examination be done only after their arrival there. But this wish was not honoured. With no official honours, his dead body was taken by two policemen, loaded into a brake wagon (used to transport fish) of the Madras–Alappuzha Express and brought home. This was the main reason the relatives suspected foul play. When the Ernakulam police surgeon conducted an autopsy, it was discovered that all the internal organs, including the brain, the liver and the intestines, had been removed, and cotton and coir pith stuffed in their place. The body carried 22 injuries. The post-mortem examination had been done in Chennai on the request of a person masquerading as Sukumaran's relative. And when the body was brought to Mulanthuruthy on the insistence of a group of officers, it was cremated in a hurry. Relatives and friends were not permitted to have a last glimpse of Sukumaran.

Sukumaran's administrative style had estranged the marine exporters. When he took charge of the office, it was running at a loss of Rs 37 crores. At the time of his death, it had a turnover of Rs 35 crores. He had brought about this change by putting an end to the exporters' looting, and by rooting out corruption that had spread throughout the system. The Seafood Exporters' Association made it known to all that Sukumaran had come to this sad end because he had wiped out theft, inefficiency and corruption in the fish export sector. M.C. Thevan, Sukumaran's 83-year-old father, and Sarala Sukumaran, his wife, sent complaints to all—from state ministers to the President of India—to find an answer to the mystery of his death.

There was no favourable response from either the state or the central government. So, on 30 September 1992, a group of

Dalit students sparked off an agitation demanding a CBI enquiry into the Sukumaran murder case. The same set of students conducted a dharna in front of the Secretariat on 2 October. Subsequently, Dalit officers of Thrissur and Kozhikode districts, KPMS, Sambava Maha Sabha, Harijan Samrakshana Vedi, Scheduled Caste/Scheduled Tribe Employees' Federation, Indian Dalit Federation, Adhasthitha Navothana Munnani and members of the MPEDA (Marine Products Export Development Authority) employees' organization named Team, came to the fore. An action committee was formed at Sukumaran's native village of Mulanthuruthy on the initiative taken by C.K. Prakashan and Venugopalan (Sukumaran's relatives), a public activist named K. Sunilkumar, John Joseph and Reji Mathew. The committee was led by the panchayat president K.A. Joshi. The police station marches organized by the group as well as the MPEDA were noteworthy. On 23 and 24 February 1993, Sukumaran's father went on a hunger strike in front of the MPEDA office. This was followed by various kinds of agitations all over Ernakulam. But it was the dharna led by V.C. Rajappan and P.N. Sukumaran in front of the Nayarambalam Post Office that underscored the view that the agitation was a communitarian struggle for Dalits' self-respect and the protection of their rights. In light of this, there was even a suggestion that all the organizations that had thrown their weight behind the struggle should unite under a communitarian umbrella.

The CPI(M) had also made a demand for an enquiry into the death of C.T. Sukumaran, and the person who showed the keenest interest was the former minister T.K. Ramakrishnan. He issued a statement and paid a visit to Sukumaran's house. The party's opinion was that this was not a struggle to be conducted by the Dalits alone but by all people. K.M. Salimkumar, who was very active in the struggle, shared that opinion. The action committee had its organizational limitations. There was also a criticism that it would be difficult to accommodate Dalits. But Salimkumar was unfazed. He brought together all the action committees to create a District Action Committee and appointed Sharat Chandran, the Mulavukad panchayat president, as its convenor.

I had not been involved in any of those struggles until then. That was because I did not represent any communitarian organization but was only a private citizen. Neither Salimkumar nor anyone else invited me to join either. The details of the agitation came to me only through newspaper reports. My entry into it was quite accidental. One day, when I was returning from P.N. Sukumaran's house, I happened to see an MPEDA march go past MG Road. It was led by the action committee led by K.M. Salimkumar. Nearly 300 people were part of it. A few participants saw me at the roadside and invited me to join them. I participated in the dharna too that took place in front of the MPEDA office. A few people approached Salimkumar and asked him to invite me to offer felicitations but he did not permit it. However, an MPEDA employee named Achuthan offered me a towel to cover my head with, and gave me a glass of lemon juice too. I was the only person to enjoy that privilege! After the dharna, I went back home.

The District Action Committee led by Salimkumar and Sharat Chandran decided to conduct a convention with the help of Sunilkumar and John Joseph at Yatra Auditorium in Ernakulam. I was not invited to it. But I went there as a member of the audience. Besides Salimkumar and Chandran, the dais consisted of T.K. Ramakrishnan, A.P. Varkey, Justice (Retd) Chandrasekharan Nair, V.K. Babu, MLA, P.N. Sukumaran and V.C. Rajappan. Although Sunilkumar and John Joseph wanted to invite me to the dais, Salimkumar did not allow it. At the end of the convention, a resolution was passed demanding a CBI investigation into the mysterious death of C.T. Sukumaran. When opinions from the audience were solicited regarding the resolution, I stood up and said, 'C.T. Sukumaran's relatives, the community and the media believe it was a murder. Therefore "mysterious death" should be replaced with "murder".' Silence descended on the entire audience. A moment later, there was a raucous response. Everyone stood up and loudly demanded that the resolution be corrected. When there was an attempt to ignore the demand and go forward with the unaltered resolution, P.N. Sukumaran declared, 'I am on the dais and I say that the resolution should be corrected.' Without attempting either to correct the resolution or take the meeting forward, Justice Chandrasekharan Nair, T.K. Ramakrishnan and A.P. Varkey walked off the dais. The resolution could not be passed, but I had now come to the forefront of the agitation.

The action committee bit the dust not merely because it succumbed to its CPI(M) masters and diluted the resolution. It did not have the kind of attitude required to co-ordinate all the different struggles to make non-Dalit groups sympathetic to the cause. It became my responsibility to create an apt organizational structure. I would have been wrong to not take it up in the eyes of the Dalit community. So, once again, I set aside my personal problems and decided to take charge of the struggle. P.N. Sukumaran, V.C. Rajappan, V.C. Radhakrishnan, John Joseph, Sunilkumar, Reji Joseph and others who were in the action committee were on my side. We created a Dalit Co-ordinating Committee with the aim of bringing together Dalit organizations in order to form a unified Dalit body, and decided that P.N. Sukumaran would lead the struggle. Since I did not represent any organization, it was P. Shashikumar, convenor of the Ambedkar Unity Centre, who convened a meeting of the leaders of various organizations. The meeting was conducted at Gopi Vallon's house. Among those who attended it were M. Geethanandan, leader of Dalit Organization Committee, E.P. Kumaradas, parliamentary candidate from the Ottappalam constituency, and P.C. Usha, a college student who would later become the convenor of the Dalit Students' Movement. This meeting selected me as the convenor of the Dalit Co-ordinating Committee.

The Committee's first decision was to conduct a Dalit Defence Convention at the BEM School hall at Ottappalam on 31 July 1993 and organize a train blockade. K.M. Unnikrishnan and M. Geethanandan were elected chairman and convenor, respectively, of the Defence Convention. Such a decision was taken because a by-election in the Ottappalam constituency was about to get underway, and we did not want it to disrupt the functioning of the action committee. At the Convention, I presented a paper titled 'Contemporary Violence Against Dalits and the Immediate Relevance of Unity Among Dalit Communities'. The train blockade in the evening was inaugurated by Sunilkumar.

The meeting of the Dalit Co-ordinating Committee held in Ernakulam entrusted P.N. Sukumaran with the task of creating a state strike committee with the participation of various Dalit organizations and action committees. Thus, on 24 October 1993, at a meeting convened at the Maruti Vilasam Lodge in Ernakulam, a Scheduled Caste–Scheduled Tribe state strike committee was formed in order to put forward the demand for a CBI probe into the murder of C.T. Sukumaran, IAS.

The resolution passed at the meeting stated that:

> Instances of Dalit torture and murder in Kerala have risen like never before. At this stage, the agitation demanding a CBI probe into the murder of C.T. Sukumaran, IAS, and the arrest of the murderers has become a self-respect agitation of the Scheduled Caste-Scheduled Tribe groups. It was with the

> help of the national right of reservation for Scheduled Castes and Scheduled Tribes that Sukumaran pursued education and gained this status. The Dalits earned the right to education, authority and wealth through historic struggles. When people like Sukumaran are murdered, it is this set of rights to education, authority and wealth earned by a community that are being denied. This is the system of justice of the *Manusmriti*.

Advocate K.V. Kumaran, P.J. Sabharaj Thirumeni, V. Kamalan Master, Radhakrishnan Chengad, K. Sunilkumar and John Joseph were elected convenors from among the representatives of various organizations. On 28 November 1993, a state strike committee met at Mahakavi G Auditorium to discuss the expansion of the agitation. Advocate T.A. Paraman, ex-MLA, chaired the session. A decision was taken here to conduct an indefinite relay hunger strike in front of the Ernakulam Telephone Office from the next day onwards.

---

51. Conclusion of a Communitarian (Self-Respect) Agitation

The agitation conducted to demand a CBI probe into the murder of C.T. Sukumaran offered a unique model, never before seen in subaltern struggles. The main reason for its success was that we arrived at a slogan that conveyed our goal and resonated not only with the Dalit communities but with the public at large as well. It was what helped push to the background not only the CPI(M)—which was then the opposition to the K. Karunakaran-led UDF government, but obviously a powerful political force—but also those Dalit organizations and their leaders who represented narrow-mindedness and sectarianism. At the same time, there was no attempt to convert any leader of any established political party. What the Scheduled Caste–Scheduled Tribe strike committee embraced was the wish of C.T. Sukumaran's relatives, including his father, as well as that of people at the grassroots level. What helped maintain this position was the presence of a close-knit but decentralized leadership within the committee.

The indefinite hunger strike began at 11 am on 29 November 1993 (Monday) in front of Ernakulam Telephone Exchange office as decided. All the programmes had been scheduled in such a way as to ensure the participation of various social groups and organizations. This was totally unprecedented in the history of struggles in Kerala. On the first day, it was Sukumaran's family and relatives, led by his ageing father, who undertook the hunger strike. The person who presided over the inaugural meeting was S. Rajappan, divisional secretary of the Scheduled Caste–Scheduled Tribe Employees' Association of Canara Bank. Those who offered felicitations were Radhakrishnan Chengad, convenor of the Dalit Students' Co-ordinating Committee, K.A. Joshy, president of Mulanthuruthy panchayat, T.K. Dasan, president of Yuva Chetana, Rajmohan Thamburan, Dravida Class United Front (DCUF) leader, Advocate C.V. Antony, member of the PDP state committee and Shaji Joseph, convenor of the Democratic Christian Federation. T.K. Ramakrishnan too arrived at the venue of the struggle.

On the second day, members of the Scheduled Caste–Scheduled Tribe state strike committee undertook the hunger strike. It was inaugurated by S. Rajappan. Those who offered felicitations were M.K. Raghavan, president of the Samvarana Samudaya Munnani, Advocate Pookooth, president of Jama'at Council, Rev Fr K.M. George, president of the BCCF, Advocate C.N. Balan, general secretary of SRP, P.P. Rajan, Kanayannoor taluk secretary of the SNDP, N. Balasubramanian, zonal convenor of Shastra Sahitya Parishad and Advocate P. Chellappan, president of the Central Government Scheduled Caste–Scheduled Tribe Employees' Union. On the third day, Dalit students who were not part of any organization came to the pavilion. Among those who offered felicitations, the presence of Abdul Rasheed, leader of the Students' Islamic Organization of India (SIO), was noteworthy. On the fourth day, the hunger strike of the Dalit Co-ordinating Committee was inaugurated by Nalinakshi. Ambili offered felicitations.

A number Dalit workers, artists, litterateurs and central government employees undertook the hunger strike in the subsequent days. The ninth day was inaugurated by V.K. Babu, the MLA from Narakkal. Next was the turn of various organizations—Kerala Harijan Samajam, Vypin Yuva Chetana, Akhila Vypin Pulayodharani Sabha, and the Kerala Padhana Kendram which was associated with the CPI(M-L) and IDF. The strike by the Dravida Varga Aikya Munnani (DCUAF) was inaugurated by Fr P.J. Sabharaj. On the fourteenth day, bank employees sat on strike.

The fifteenth day witnessed a strike by PDP workers. This was preceded by a procession in which more than a thousand PDP workers had participated. More than 100 of them undertook the hunger strike. A meeting presided over by Gilbert Austin, the district president, was inaugurated by Abdul Nazar Madani, chairman of the PDP. Dr Prasad, vice chairman, Pandalam Majeed and S. Suvarnakumar, who were state secretaries, and P.M.A. Kalam, state president of PTUC were also present at the meeting. Another day's hunger strike was undertaken jointly by the Mulanthuruthy SNDP Youth Movement and the Kanayannoor SNDP Union. In the days that followed, the Dalit workers of the naval base and railway employees took part without any backing from their organization leaders. The Dalit Movement from Idukki, the Democratic Christian Forum and Navothana Prasthanam also took part.

After 21 days of the hunger strike, the struggle came to an end on 19 December 1993 with a rally, in which more than 5,000 Dalits from different parts of the state participated, and a public meeting at the Kaloor Bus Stand maidan.

What made the struggle in front of the Ernakulam Telephone Exchange office unique was that an idea that was considered unrealistic—Dalit–Backward Class–minority group unity—was made possible. This idea had been put forward at the Dalit Defence Convention at Ottappalam. We were thus able to not only harness the support of the Samvarana Samudaya Munnani (Reservation Communities' Front), which represented these aforementioned categories, but also bring three other groups—SNDP, Jama'at Council and the Christian Democratic Forum—to the venue of the struggle. While the mainstream political parties—Congress, Communist and BJP—kept their distance, we still managed to get the support of the political parties of the Backward Class and minority groups, SRP and PDP.

There were attempts by the mainstream parties, especially the CPI(M), to torpedo the struggle that proclaimed the new communitarian-political movement. For this, they used V.K. Babu, the Congress (S) leader and MLA as well as the District Action Council which had been created under the initiative of K.M. Salimkumar, and of which Sharat Chandran was the convenor. We knew that V.K. Babu was helpless. He had won the elections with the support of the CPI(M). But what led K.M. Salimkumar—who even while being a part of the struggle led and conducted by a united Dalit community became a CPI(M) fellow-traveller—to do what he did is a mystery to this day. The CPI(M)'s assessment of C.T. Sukumaran was that he was a good officer who stood against corruption. Such an evaluation precluded his caste identity. The strike committee constantly questioned this stance. Salimkumar, by pushing C.S. Murali to the forefront of the struggle, became a symbol of sectarianism and narrow-mindedness.

A day after the strike committee announced its decision to launch a relay hunger strike, the District Action Council announced that it too would conduct an indefinite hunger strike in front of the MPEDA office. No one took it at face value, but V.K. Babu and C.S. Murali announced that they were about to sit on a hunger strike in front of the Ernakulam High Court jetty. Thevan Mash, Sukumaran's father, and the strike committee sent Babu a note expressing their appreciation for his participation in the struggle, but suggested that it would be better if the hunger strike be staged in front of the Secretariat, and sought his co-operation with the state strike committee. C.S. Murali, however, with V.K. Babu's support, continued his hunger strike for 16 days. Thereafter Babu himself went on a hunger strike. O. Rajagopal, the BJP leader, V.S. Achuthanandan and M.M. Lawrence, the CPI(M) leaders, and M.P. Veerendrakumar, the Janata Dal leader, went to their strike pavilion and expressed their support to Babu. Besides, organizations like CPI, AIYF and DYFI too expressed solidarity with him. K.K. Balakrishnan, Congress leader and MLA, who had taken the initiative for arranging for the cremation of Sukumaran at Mulanthuruthy conducted a hunger strike in front of the Secretariat along with a thousand other people. K. Karunakaran, the chief minister, who had completely ignored our strike committee's struggle, assured them that all the required steps would be taken. And so, Babu brought his hunger strike to an end on the sixth day, and dissuaded all other political parties from continuing the struggle.

Assessing the events that had taken place, the state strike committee concluded that political parties that favoured the interests of the savarnas would never be able to accommodate the self-respect of Dalits and that they had adopted a very deceitful attitude towards the struggle of, and led by, the Dalit community.

After the struggle in front of the Ernakulam Telephone Exchange office came to an end, a decision was now taken to further expand the struggle. With it, a call went out for the creation of district committees and for a train blockade on 14 February. Such district committees were formed in Thiruvananthapuram, Kottayam, Alappuzha, Idukki, Thrissur and Ernakulam. I took the initiative to form the committees at Thiruvananthapuram, Alappuzha and Idukki districts, along with P.N. Sukumaran and P. Shashikumar. As a prelude to the strike, the Ernakulam committee took the lead in blockading the MPEDA office. All 300 individuals who participated in it were arrested. At Thiruvananthapuram, an indefinite hunger strike was undertaken in front of the Secretariat from 26 January 1994. Thevan Mash participated in the first day of the hunger strike. An indefinite hunger strike was also organized in front of the post office at Thrissur. Finally, the state strike committee gave a call for train blockades at Alappuzha, Thiruvananthapuram, Thrissur and Ernakulam. In Ernakulam, trains were stopped at the North Railway Station and at Mulanthuruthy. That same day, a rally and public meeting with the participation of more than 500 people took place in Idukki.

Despite the state-wide struggle and the participation of numerous organizations representing the Dalits, Backward Classes, minority groups, progressive democrats and thousands of common people, the state and central governments remained indifferent. So, a decision was taken to stop road transport all along the length and breadth of Kerala on 29 March the same year. A vehicle rally to propagate this was undertaken with M.A. Vasu as the captain. It began from Kasaragod on 16 March. When even this failed to provoke a favourable response, the Thiruvananthapuram district committee led by Pandalam Rajendran, the convenor, decided that Thevan Mash would sit on an indefinite hunger strike in front of the Secretariat from 4 April. With greater coverage by the media, the strike attracted wider public attention as well as the political leadership of the state. The first person to reach the pavilion was V.S. Achuthanandan. He not only voiced his support to the strike but also promised to speak to K. Karunakaran, the chief minster. V.M. Sudheeran, Cherian Philip and other leaders who followed also put pressure on the government.

During the initial days of Thevan Mash's strike, I was at Guruvayoor where by-elections were due. My intention was to canvass votes for G. Krishnamurthy, the candidate put up by the Social Justice Party (SJP) of M.K. Raghavan (who served as its president). I had to take over the entire responsibility of the election campaign. Dalit students from Ernakulam and the Dalit Co-ordinating Committee members of Ilanji were there to help me.

The campaign began with a hunger strike organized at Chavakkad demanding a CBI probe into C.T. Sukumaran's murder. In the days that followed we additionally demanded that the Mandal Commission Report be implemented. In the vehicle propaganda rally, the announcements were made by P.C. Usha and Jayasurya, who was then in the eight standard. It had its greatest impact in the UDF. P.K. Kunjalikutty, the Muslim League leader, repeated the demand for a CBI probe into Sukumaran's murder at various meetings. It became an issue that could no longer be ignored in the Guruvayoor by-election.

As soon as the canvassing work was over, that very evening in fact, I set out for the strike pavilion at Thiruvananthapuram. On the second day, Dr Narayana Kurup Jayaraj of the Kerala Congress (Mani) brought a copy of the order sanctioning a CBI probe into Sukumaran's murder to the venue of the strike, and asked us to conclude it. P.K. Kunjalikutty, the industries minister, was the person who had handed it over to Dr Jayaraj.

'This is a strike that has been going on for two years with the participation of thousands of people,' I said to Dr Jayaraj. 'To this day, there has not been a single complaint against us. None of you have ever participated in the strike. Moreover, we had not sought your help to bring this to a conclusion. And precisely for this reason, the strike will continue until we get this order directly from the government.'

Dr Jayaraj returned without saying anything else. The next day, before noon, Pandalam Sudhakaran, the Scheduled Caste–Scheduled Tribe Development minister, came personally to the strike pavilion and handed over the order. Thereafter, I gave a glass of lime juice to Thevan Mash and the strike came to a close.

We had not thought that an effective probe would take place, or that the murderers of Sukumaran would be brought to justice. Such a feeling was informed by the statement made by Varghese P. Thomas, Dy SP, who had investigated the Abhaya case.[92] When he resigned from the CBI, he had stated at a press meet, 'In the current circumstances, it is not possible to bring out the truth even if the CBI undertakes an investigation. The nation's greatest crime investigation agency is in the grip of corruption. The current situation is such that the rich political leaders and high-level bureaucrats can purchase this institution.' The CBI probe into the C.T. Sukumaran murder case was a farce. The CBI, without undertaking a preliminary investigation, or questioning anyone, came to the conclusion that Sukumaran had committed suicide. With the death of Thevan Mash, it was no longer possible to take forward a struggle against the deceitfulness of the state. The curtains eventually fell on the struggle that had braved on until then.

V.K. Babu, however, became the target of Dalit ire. He stood as an LDF candidate at the Narakkal reserved constituency. Also in the fray was Sarala, Sukumaran's wife. With the independent Dalit candidate winning the elections by a margin of more than 3,000 votes, V.K. Babu not only conceded defeat but retired from political life as well. History contains such lessons too.

---

52. With Dalit Students

It was my style to raise problems in communitarian-political activities only very rarely. So, I kept away from many issues and got plenty of time to read and write. Another practice I followed was not to get involved in a struggle conducted by any organization. However, I was invited to intervene on many an occasion. And whenever I obliged, I tried my best to make my intervention as flawless and exemplary as possible. At the same time, I criticized deviations from certain ideas as well. And sometimes this led to a temporary strain on my friendships. It was when I got involved in such theoretical and practical issues of public interest that my domestic life went horribly out of tune. One such case was that of Dalit students of Maharaja's College who had been roughed up by SFI activists.

I was working at the Vaikom depot then. I was not working full time in any organization at the time, getting involved in activism whenever I had some free time after a 24-hour shift at my workplace. One day, things were going on as usual when I got a call from John Joseph on my office phone. 'Many of our boys have been beaten up by the SFI,' he said. 'Please come immediately.' Without a second thought, I set out for Ernakulam, instead of going home. On reaching Ernakulam, I headed straight for the

Post Matric Hostel where Dalit students were accommodated. In P.P. Ashokan's room, there were U.N. Sudheer, Anilkumar, A.K. Vasu, Radhakrishnan Chengad, Girishkumar and others. John Joseph was with them. The students recounted the events that took place three days back.

It all started with the elections to the mess committee of the MCRV (Maharaja's College Rama Varma) Hostel. The majority of students in the hostel were Dalits. It was practically unliveable, with broken doors and windows, unclean toilets, broken water pipes and so on. Most of the time, the students had to go to the terrace, dip their mugs into the tank in order to collect water to have their bath. Such subhuman conditions were reserved for Dalit students. The SFI did not raise a finger to address this issue. The agitations were largely staged by Dalit students. And so, every such issue came to be viewed from the point of view of caste. Students from prosperous families did not live in hostels. A few who did usually went to hotels to have their food. The food served at the mess was very bad and utterly inadequate. The mess committee was a bunch of crooks whose aim was to pilfer as much money as possible. It was in such circumstances that a handful of Dalit students approached the SFI, which had complete authority over the mess committee, and demanded that elections to the committee be held. The response came in the form of violence unleashed on K.K. Appukuttan, K.K. Jayachandran, U.N. Sudheer and Sunil. The SFI activists then brought some goondas to the hostel to create an atmosphere of terror, and got the *Deshabhimani* to carry reports about a Naxal attack in the hostel.

The violence at the hostel became a topic of discussion in college. Subsequently, A.K. Vasu and Radhakrishnan Chengad took the initiative to bring together all the Dalit students of the college and the Post Matric Hostel. Both these boys had personal experience of caste discrimination in the college. Vasu belonged to a family that was committed to the Communist party, and had taken part in an attack on the Edappally police station. He had been beaten up several times in the past at the Kakkanad MAHS High School and Bharat Mata College—both KSU bastions—but had converted them into SFI strongholds. It was his absolute commitment to the SFI that made him join Maharaja's College. But when he was chosen by fellow students as a representative from the Malayalam department, Vasu's name was rejected. Radhakrishnan Chengad and other friends, to whom it was obvious that he had been discriminated against because of his caste, put up Vasu's name as a rebel candidate. He won by a huge margin.

Subsequently, members of the SFI approached him and requested that he co-operate with them but Vasu turned them down. This made Vasu and Chengad SFI's betes noires. Vasu would be routinely roughed up by SFI activists. There were also many instances of fake allegations being made against him. Once he was pushed to the floor near the Islamic Studies department and beaten with kicks. These things happened with such regularity that he once went to the CPM district committee office—the Lenin Centre—and met A.P. Varkey, the district secretary. 'I told him, "Either you kill me or you allow me to study,"' he recounted to me. 'I myself heard him call up the SFI leaders and say, "Don't beat him up again."' What this proved was that the Dalit students were not beaten up without the party's knowledge.

I told the students at the hostel to file a complaint with the police against the SFI leaders and ask them to register a case under the Scheduled Caste and Scheduled Tribe (Prevention of Atrocities) Act, 1989. If they sought the support of the KSU, all these acts of violence would appear to be KSU–SFI clashes. Therefore, I advised them to seek the support of the Dalit community through Dalit organizations. Staying at the hostel, several of us activists—S. Rajappan (Canara Bank Scheduled Caste and Scheduled Tribe Employees' Association), K.M. Salimkumar (Adhasthitha Navothana Munnani), Advocate G. Suresh Babu (Kerala Scheduled Caste and Scheduled Tribe Employees' Association), Advocate K.V. Kumaran (Kerala Scheduled Caste and Scheduled Tribe Federation), P.N. Sukumaran (Dalit Strike Committee), P.K. Rajappan (Dalit Employees Centre) and I (Dalit Co-ordinating Committee)—called a press meet, and in the note that we distributed, pointed out:

> Opposing the mess committee panel of Maharaja's College hostel was the crime committed by Dalit students. Suppressing healthy competition within a democratic set-up and unleashing casteist violence with a kind of racial vendetta, done in the name of any kind of ideology, is pure fascism. If progressive-minded people, driven by justice and humanism, democrats and members of other communities do not rally behind the Dalits in order to resist and defeat such tendencies or put up a struggle, what we are going to lose are equality, freedom and fraternity, values that are the lifeblood of democracy. We demand that the government register a case against the SFI which launched unprovoked attacks against Dalit students under the Scheduled Caste and Scheduled Tribe (Prevention of Atrocities) Act, and request the Opposition as well as other members of the legislative assembly to raise their voice in protest.

Gopi Vallon and P. Shashikumar were with me at the press meet. Among the journalists present there was Ravi Kuttikkad, *Deshabhimani* reporter and friend from my own Maharaja's College days. His response was that it was not fitting that a person like Adv K.V. Kumaran interfere in matters like student clashes.

But SFI's anger was far from spent. Clashes broke out again.

Among the SFI leaders at the time were Rajiv Ravi, who went on to become a film director of such movies as *Kammattippadam*, as well as Amal Neerad, who also went on to become a film director. They did nothing to stop such fascist, racist attacks. The Dalit students and organizations jointly conducted demonstrations in the city and held a public meeting at the boat jetty. When this issue gained wider public attention, nearly 200 students in the campus conducted a demonstration. In this and subsequent activities, Anglo-Indian students like Pelham Agnes, Isaac Clement and Martin Silva and Christian students like Sunny and members of other communities also took part. Female students like Shiny, Sunandamol Sadanandan, Ambili, Valsamma, Surya Nayana, Bindumol and others were in the vanguard of the demonstrations. Students also boycotted classes for a day demanding the arrest of SFI students who had beaten up Dalits in the campus. This was the first ever boycott of classes organized by any group other than units of mainstream political formations.

I too became a target of the SFI. A group of students tried to rough me up at Rajendra Maidan. It was only because of the timely and diplomatic intervention of Radhakrishnan Chengad that I was spared the violence.

A discussion took place inside the Dalit Co-ordinating Committee in order to ensure that the fellowship of Dalit students formed in the college did not dissipate, and a joint resistance was kept up against SFI attacks. The Dalit student leader M.B. Manoj described the facts thus:

> SFI is the organization that Dalit students end up joining, and there is a huge group of individuals who have suffered for the sake of the party, fallen sick as a result, abandoned their studies, and endured violence at the hands of other organizations. Their lives have been shattered because of the SFI. We know of several others who surrendered themselves to the party but were

> discarded by the wayside. Many SFI activists have later been beaten up and sometimes even killed by their rival gangs outside the campus. All these point to issues that the organization should address on its own. The campus is not merely a space, where one establishes one's authority. Fundamentally, it is a place which creates a knowledge society. But such organizations in our campuses seek to create individuals who surrender themselves totally to their ideas. That is why all these struggles have become so violent.

In light of these problems, the Dalit Co-ordinating Committee convened a meeting at Maruti Vilas Hotel in Ernakulam, and gave shape to a Dalit Students' Co-ordinating Committee with Radhakrishnan Chengad as its convenor.

In the 1995 college union elections, the Dalit Students' Co-ordinating Committee not only fielded candidates for all posts but also conducted campaigns, like any other students' organization. This time, unlike in the previous years, there was neither any attempt, by the bigger organizations, at beating up the candidates who did not belong to their party nor any act of tearing up of others' nomination papers. About that election, M.B. Manoj writes: 'The KSU approached us for talks in order to strike up an alliance but we stood as independents. If we had agreed to an alliance, the SFI would have been defeated.'

But they still had to ensure their safety. It was necessary in light of the aggression against Dalit students that the SFI exhibited. I myself went along with A.K. Vasu and U.N. Sudheer to Mukkada in order to meet a priest named Sabharaj and ask for his help. After listening very carefully to what we had to say about the situation in the college, he said, 'They will not touch even a single kid of yours.' On the day of the elections, he, along with a few activists, came to the college in a jeep. In the bus that followed them were dozens of men and women, dressed in black pants, red shirts and caps, with long sticks and other weapons in their hands. They lined up in front of the college.

Sabharaj then headed directly to the CPI(M) district committee office. He went to see A.P. Varkey, the district secretary, at his office, and said, 'If you as much as touch any one of our kids, we will make mincemeat of all your SFI activists.' Varkey did not utter a single word, but went to the district police office and repeated the priest's words verbatim. Realizing that if the SFI made any provocations, it would spark off a very violent clash, the police arranged for heavy protection in the college premises. Given the circumstances, the election went off peacefully. Although none of the Dalit candidates won, each one of them got between 100 and 200 votes. In the hostel union election that followed soon after, seven out of ten seats were won by Dalit candidates.

The Dalit Students' Co-ordinating Committee had been formed on an experimental basis. Through this group, the students gained exposure to the contributions of Dr B.R. Ambedkar and Renaissance leaders like Ayyankali, Poykayil Appachan, Pampady John Joseph, Sahodaran Ayyappan and others. At the same time, we made continuous pleas to the students to be wary of being turned into pawns in the clashes between student organizations that were controlled by political parties. Simultaneously, we made efforts to improve the messy condition the Post Matric Hostel had fallen into. With senior students taking over mentorship roles and holding tuition classes for the juniors, academic standards improved. If in the earlier period, only 10 per cent of hostel students passed their exams, with these organizational activities, the percentage rose to 80 to 90.

The first strike led by the organization demanded a new Post Matric Hostel for girl students. The existing one was a dilapidated, rented building situated close to a cemetery. Dalit students had been condemned to stay there despite the fact that it was not only inconvenient for the inmates but also insecure. The new Post Matric Hostel, built midway between the District Court and Lord Shiva's temple, is a testament to the sheer grit and leadership of students like Ambili and Shiny. Besides, the members of the Dalit Students' Co-ordinating Committee played a very active role in the C.T. Sukumaran struggle and the campaigns during the Guruvayoor and Ottappalam elections.

Several years later, in 2002, John Joseph, who was a constant companion to the Dalit students, organized a seminar at Maharaja's College. It was titled 'Is the Aryan Invasion a Myth?' Students from other colleges also participated in it. The subject of the seminar was presented by the noted historian N.K. Jose, and the deliberations that followed were chaired by Bharathan, the principal, and myself. A three-day state-level camp was also subsequently organized. The person we intended to invite to inaugurate it was the writer C. Ayyappan who stayed at the NGO Home. Vasu and I went there to invite him, but he turned us down, as a result of which, I did the honours. It was at this camp that I presented the document titled 'Dalit Community Formation: Problems and Approaches'.

It did not go into ideological complexities or profound social criticisms; it argued for the need for Dalits to secure property, higher education and employment. It also stressed the necessity of an exemplary domestic life, the need to stop seeing girl children as second-class citizens, the importance of respecting women's desire to wear ornaments, the significance of wearing good clothes, keeping one's house and premises clean and so on. What I meant to underscore was that by bringing about such positive changes on the personal and domestic fronts, Dalits should transform themselves into a community of refined individuals. With the financial support of Narayanan, who worked for a publication named *Kerala Padhanangal* ('Kerala Studies'), it was published as a pamphlet.

It was at this camp that the Dalit Students' Co-ordinating Committee was disbanded, and the Dalit Students' Movement (DSM) created, with P.C. Usha, of Mar Athanasius College, Kothamangalam, as its convenor.

This was followed by a three-day camp at Mangalya Auditorium, Nayarambalam, Vypin, with the aim of raising communitarian and political awareness among Dalit students. The expenses for the camp were arranged for by students from Idukki under the leadership of Shaji Kathippara. P. Shashikumar, P.N. Sukumaran and V.C. Rajappan, along with their families, and Gopi Vallon as well as John Joseph attended the camp. The main subject of discussion was the Dravidian roots of Dalits, and the contemporary relevance of Ambedkarite thought.

The Dalit students did not take the path paved by the SFI. They ploughed their own furrow. Although the DSM did not grow to its fullest potential, it achieved many goals by maintaining an organic link with the community created by the Dalit Co-ordinating Committee. One of most its significant victories was that it rescued Dalit students from the criminal cases they were framed in by the SFI and its political masters. The cases were traps set by the CPI(M) government to catch and suppress Naxalites. The financially backward 'accused' spent endless years waiting in the corridors of the courts for release, and ended up crushed, financially and emotionally. Numerous Dalit students were thus helped by Dalit lawyers free of charge.

The DSM, under the leadership of M.B. Manoj, A.K. Vasu, Marukaraj, O.K. Santhosh, O.P. Ravindran, Jayasurya, P.A. Shashikumar and others, was able to achieve many things besides this. Its 26-day hunger strike in front of the Secretariat, following the suicide of Rajini S. Anand on 20 July 2004, resulted in the appointment of the Justice Khalid Commission. The Aided Sector Reservation Agitation Council, created by the student leaders, filed a case with the help of Advocate Kaleeshwaram Raj, and demanded that the reservation norms set up by the UGC be followed in appointments in the aided educational sector. This got a favourable verdict from the High Court, although the final verdict, on the appeal filed by the NSS office secretary in this particular case is yet to come.

The greatest achievement of the Dalit Students' Co-ordinating Committee and the DSM, however, was that it was successful in grooming writers as well as communitarian and political activists. A.K. Vasu, who once pleaded for his safety with the CPI(M) district secretary, went on to earn a doctoral degree in Folklore Studies and become a teacher. Besides, he made a mark as a poet and also made contributions to the web magazine *Utharakalam*. Dr M.B. Manoj, Dr Rekha Raj and Dr O.K. Santhosh did the community proud by becoming writers of repute as well as well-known activists. One of the earliest activists of the organization, Radhakrishnan Chengad, became the panchayat president of Malayattoor and people like P.C. Usha, P.P. Ashokan, U.N. Sudheer, V.B. Anilkumar, Reji, Jayakumar, Shaji Kathippara, Ajish Thankappan, Visionlal and others also made creditable achievements in their professional and personal lives.

Had they not been rescued, they would have been fated to a lifetime of pasting posters on walls for the CPI(M), adding numbers to their rallies, and maybe even engaging in thuggery for the party in their respective villages. Dalit members were often used for such things and the trend continues in the present too, unlike the case of the savarna members, for whom the SFI is a stepping stone to occupying positions of authority or achieving fame in the fields of art and literature. Even if the KSU or the ABVP don the role of rescuers of the Dalits, this situation will not change as long as the caste system continues to exist.

---

53. Final Thoughts

I abandoned literary compositions like story-telling, poetry and drama a long while back. Later, though rarely, I dabbled in criticism exclusively. That kind of writing was organically related to my socio-political activities. But at the same time I did not ignore the influence of literature on social life. I believed in the possibility of the transformation of the human condition. It was a line in the Bible that lit the path for me: *Man doth not live by bread only, but by every word that proceedeth out of the mouth of the Lord*. Along with food, clothing and shelter, humans need religion, education and government to regulate their social life. Arts and literature, the very marrow of culture, nourish the self-awareness of the individual and the society. Like philosophy, literature not only transforms the world but inspires humans to be favourably disposed to Nature. That is why I believe it is not possible to have politics without culture or its by-product—literature.

When I turned to Dalit activities, I was drawn towards the works of modern as well as African and Latin American literatures. What helped in this regard was the Left-oriented thinking that had moved away from modernism, particularly, the writings of Neruda, Lorca, David Diop, Nicholas Guoillen, Lu Xun and others. Even the writers who were known to be modernist, like K. Ayyappa Paniker, K. Satchidanandan and so on could not but acknowledge this change. And so, though not through mainstream publishers, many works were translated and published by parallel establishments. I not only read books borrowed from the Eloor Lending Library in Ernakulam, but also participated in night-long discussions with people, learning about different creative worlds. I must acknowledge the role Baburaj played in helping me learn more about literature.

Through these books, I was introduced to Dalit literature written in Marathi at the end the 1960s and the beginning of the 1970s. What inspired the Left to acknowledge Dalit literature was the emergence of African and Latin American literatures. Another reason was the persistent Marxist affiliation of writers like Arun Kamble, Daya Pawar, Narayan Surve, Arjun Dangle, Namdeo Dhasal and others whose works were based on Buddhist-Ambedkarite thought. But they could not develop an ideological sphere and aesthetic that was exclusively Buddhist or Ambedkarite in essence. Their interpretation of the crises faced by the nation and the country avoided established Marxist thought and got transformed into a nationalistic Marxism. This made me think of composing a cultural foreword to Dalit literature.

In Kerala, T.K.C. Vaduthala, T.H.P. Chentharassery, Paul Chirakkarode, D. Rajan, V.K. Narayanan, Kallara Sukumaran and others who were known as Dalit writers were reluctant to internalize the creative spirit of African–Latin American and Dalit literatures. That was because they could not breach the caste collectives. These writers continued to adopt the ideology of realism. But the path they chose in order to indicate their difference was that of airing complaints about the failure of Communism.

In the words of O.K. Santhosh, 'Only those who show the courage to alter, even ever so slightly, the dominant streams of sensibility, can outlive time. It has to be admitted, albeit sadly, that the Dalit interventions of this period could not come close to that reality.' He continues, 'In terms of sensibility, the Dalits of that time found themselves in circumstances where they had to have their feet planted in two boats simultaneously, the Left Front and caste collectives. I do not discount the fact that a weekly like the SEEDIAN, which was built on the foundation of ideological discussions, ploughed a different furrow. This double stand of the Dalits converted them into actors who had pawned their self-awareness. Even their journeys in search of their roots subsided into mere mechanical theoretical exercises. The forward surge of the depressed classes/Dalits, which had risen like a wave throughout India in the 19th and the 20th centuries, was discarded due to the dominance of nationalistic Marxism. That the contributions of Ayyankali, Poykayil Appachan (Kumara Guru), Pampady John Joseph and others and the socio-political thought of Dr B.R. Ambedkar were consigned to the marshlands of history at least for a long period of time was the result of this subjugation. I think many writers became invisible because they could not accept Dalit literature that imbibed only the influences of realism and nationalist Marxism.'

Although we had no clear sense of direction regarding Dalit literature, both the SEEDIAN and I tried to overcome the many crises it faced. It was on the basis of such a resolve that I wrote an article titled 'Bhashayum Janatayum' ('Language and People') and attempted a review of C.V. Sreeraman's story 'Duravastha Veendum Vannappol' ('When Crisis Came Again'). Besides, I criticized the interpretation of Nair women's dressing style as a representation of Malayali culture, and the Left movement's adoption of Hindu religious symbols. Baburaj too published essays dealing with similar themes such as his article 'Bhakshanaprashnam—VKN Novelukalil' ('The Problem of Food in VKN's Novels') and a film review titled '*Vaishali* Madhyavargathinte Swargam' ('*Vaishali*—The Heaven of the Middle Class'). The magazine gave space for the works of both Dalit and non-Dalit writers. In 1986, a get-together of artistes and litterateurs was organized at Kallara to explore the cultural foundation of Dalit literature. The foci of the camp were 'Dravidian Essence and Culture' as well as 'African and Latin American Literatures'. What the deliberations threw up was the belief that the concept of Dravidian community should become the national and cultural foundation of Dalit literature. A state-level camp of Dalit students, which was organized at Vypin later, discussed how a synthesis of the Dravidian essence and Ambedkarite thought could be brought about. In short, we attempted a non-Marxist national identity formation for Dalit literature.

I had read the works of the Dalit writers of Kerala as part of an exploration into Dalit literature. But I refused to accept them as Dalit literature. It was V.M. Unni who came to November Books one day and handed over his friend (both were from Perumbavoor) C. Ayyappan's anthology of short stories titled *Uchcha Urakkathile Swapnangal* ('Dreams during Siesta') published by NBS. Although it was different from other Dalit works in form and sensibility, I found it difficult to accept the work as representing Dalit literature. But considering the uniqueness of the stories, I wrote a 10-page review, which the SEEDIAN weekly announced it would carry. Unfortunately, with the publication of the SEEDIAN grinding to a halt for some time, the paper was lost. Later, in 1998, I wrote this about C. Ayyappan:

> Those writers who composed their literary works according to the established laws of aesthetics did not aim to create Dalit literature. The stories written by C. Ayyappan establish this fact. The stories in his anthology *Uchcha Urakkathile Swapnangal* reveal the depth of the fall as well as the brittleness of the Dalit community… Stories written in accordance with existing rules of aesthetics are a mirror turned towards the Dalit community.

Later, I corrected this tendency of maintaining a singular vision which had resulted in rejecting the diversity of Dalit literature.

Serious explorations into Dalit literature on my part, however, began only with my withdrawal from public life. This was made possible by a fortnightly named *Sameeksha*, edited by

K. Venu, which provided a forum for discussions and controversies regarding Dalit ideas. This publication played a significant role in paving the way for a contemporary Dalit socio-political and cultural surge. The first article about Dalit literature I wrote for this magazine was a review of Sajeev's 'Kochalimuthukkiyude Kochumakan' ('The Grandson of Old Kochali').

By the end of the 1990s, *Bhashaposhini*, *India Today* and *Sahitya Lokam* (published by the Sahitya Akademi) brought out special issues on Dalit literature. *Bhashaposhini*, which had no space for me in its special issue, was dominated by the figure of Sunny M. Kappikkad. In his article titled 'Malayala Sahityathile Dalit Saannidhyam' ('Dalit Presence in Malayalam Literature'), he interpreted Dalit literature as a black presence against a backdrop of white. In it, Dalit aesthetics is black as it constitutes a different take on independence. In my long reply that was published in the next issue of *Bhashaposhini*, I mentioned that Dalit aesthetics is not about a black/white binary but rather about the historical experience that came out of a rejection of the established aesthetic norms. In the special issue of *Sahitya Lokam* on Dalit literature, I explained my perspective through the article 'Dalit Sahityathinte Aadyaksharangal' ('The First Works of Dalit Literature'). But two articles that were published in the same issue—E.V. Ramakrishnan's 'Aadhunkika Maratha Dalit Rachanakalile Samvadatmaka Bhavanakal' ('The Dialogic Imagination of Modern Marathi Dalit Writings') and Pradeepan Pampirikkunnu's 'Anyaadheenapetta Randidangazhi' ('The Loss of Two Measures')—served as signboards to me. I wrote a long letter to Pradeepan Pampirikkunnu about his article and requested him to bring his knowledge and experience to bear upon Dalit communitarianism. Besides, I went to meet him at his house in Tirur, accompanied by V.M. Unni. Our friendship continued until his untimely death.

But it was in my criticism of Thakazhi's short story 'Vellappokkathil' ('In the Flood') that I wrote from a clear Dalit ideological perspective for the first time. I established that the work was an anti-Dalit composition, and I did it by deconstructing the strands of class and community within the story and arguing that it constituted a rejection of the community. This article was as much a personal response as a social one.

The weekly, *Samakalika Keralam*, edited by S. Jayachandran Nair, had devoted an entire issue to Thakazhi. It was largely about the story 'Vellappokkathil' but it also republished Thakazhi's preface to his novel *Randidangazhi* ('Two Measures'). The preface described how a loyal retainer of Thakazhi's family, named Madithara Kunjeppu, full of affection for the little Thakazhi, the *ponnu thampuran* (His Little Lordship), sought to pick him up but froze in the act on hearing a menacing admonishment. Yet Kunjeppu's greatest desire was to see His Little Lordship's house—and not his own—capped with roof tiles.

I argued that if a full-fledged feudal lord reigned in the interior of Thakazhi's mind six decades back, that would be only natural. But in contemporary times, when the Dalit community too was attempting to acquire the same wealth, authority, status and culture as those possessed by the community that Thakazhi belonged to, the republication of the aforementioned preface was indicative of a return of caste hegemony. I wrote this article for *Madhyamam*.

The most relevant of my pieces of literary criticism was the one titled 'Keralam maranna samoohika parishkaranam' ('The Social Reformation that Kerala Forgot'). It was a critique of Potheri Kunjambu's novel *Saraswativijayam* ('The Victory of Learning') and was published in *Sameeksha*. O. Chandu Menon's *Indulekha* has been feted in hundreds of critical pieces and studies as the first novel in Malayalam. But *Saraswativijayam*, written during the same period, constituted an acknowledgement of the existence of the subaltern class in literary representation. V.S. Unni brought this article of mine to the attention of Jayachandran of CICC Books. It was published in the third edition of *Saraswativijayam* that came out in 2001. Later, DC Books brought it out, including Dilip Menon's study of the novel. In course of time, it became a textbook prescribed for study at various universities. Today, *Saraswativijayam* enjoys a canonical status equivalent to that of *Indulekha*.

My article '*Indulekha*—Oru Rashtreeya Punarvayana' ('*Indulekha*—a Political Re-reading') was a study of the ostracized characters in the novel. It was published in *Mathrubhumi*, and for weeks on end it provoked responses—from both those that agreed as well as disagreed with my views. Articles such as these were collected under the title *Vayanayude Dalit Padhom* ('A Dalit Lesson from Reading'). *Idathupaksham Illaatha Kaalam* ('A Time Sans the Left Front') was a compilation of literary essays, a book review of K. Sethuraman, IPS's *Malayalathinte Bhaavi* ('The Future of Malayalam') and three film reviews.

When writing had become a part of my life of activity, V.V. Swami, T.K. Mohandas and Prakash (who is now no more) approached me. They were Prathyaksha Raksha Daiva Sabha (PRDS) cultural forum activists, though not members of the PRDS. They had come to invite me to a seminar at Changanassery. I had not appeared at public forums in a long time but agreed to their request solely because it was concerned with Poykayil Appachan's remembrance. Much later, V.V. Swami and T.K. Mohandas sought me out once again. They wanted me to be the editor of the PRDS cultural forum publication named *Soochakam*, a monthly. Agreeing to it, I insisted that the editing and layout had to be of the best quality. Although the magazine was being brought out on the initiative of Dalits, it must contain material on the progress made by the Backward Classes, minorities, women and other marginalized groups on the international, national, political and cultural fronts. It was not to be assumed that the readership would consist exclusively of Dalits. I wanted the magazine to reach non-Dalits. The aim was to make Dalit writing a subject of discussion among the upper classes as well. The editorial policy of the magazine, moreover, had to be governed by a collective and not the editor's personal agency. It was with these hopes that I began work for the magazine at Kunnamkanam near Changanassery. The team comprised V.V. Swami, K.K. Baburaj, T.K. Mohandas, Ravindranath, Prakash, E.V. Anil, P.B. Suresh and Shashikumar. V.M. Unni provided financial support and set out guidelines.

Besides social, political and cultural subjects, the magazine carried articles on national and international issues, stories, poems, film studies, book reviews and so on—the pages of *Soochakam* presented a rich fare. Dalit as well as non-Dalit writers like V.C. Harris, Ajay Sekhar, O.K. Santhosh, M.B. Manoj, P.J. Binoy, V.V. Swami, P.B. Suresh, Don George and so on contributed articles. Besides, space was set apart for works by famous Black writers like Paul Gilroy, bell hooks, Toni Morrison, Dario Fo and others.

The greatest achievement of *Soochakam* was that it succeeded in establishing Poykayil Appachan as one of the Renaissance heroes. Until then he was a larger-than-life representative of a community of believers. The PRDS cultural forum aimed to take him beyond that narrow circle. At a meeting convened to consider the prospects of publishing a special issue of *Soochakam* on spirituality, I asked, 'What is this issue on spirituality for—to establish Appachan as a god among the believers? Or, to establish him along with Sree Narayana Guru and Ayyankali as a Renaissance hero among the Kerala public?' Breaking the silence by way of responding to my query, Mohandas replied, 'It is enough if you establish him as a Renaissance hero.' It was after the distribution of this issue of *Soochakam*, from Kasaragod to Thiruvananthapuram districts, that Appachan became known as a Renaissance hero among the people of Kerala. Now, more than 40 books have been written and published on Poykayil Appachan. Yet, although we managed to discharge this grave responsibility, *Soochakam* met with the same fate as most subaltern publications—untimely death.

I interacted with PRDS activists during the time I worked at *Soochakam*. I participated in a couple of Poykayil Appachan birth anniversary meetings as well. I discovered that Ayyankali, Poykayil Appachan and John Joseph did not project divergences but rather showed complementarity in their thought. Certain leaders of caste organizations, who were forgetful of this historical fact, criticized me, stating that a Pulaya like me was working for Parayas. Raghavan Atholy's letter published in *Madhyamam*, for example, accused me of working for the Paraya Christians of Kozhenchery. On this occasion, when caste differences among the Dalits came out in the open, I gave a fitting reply in the form of a long letter titled 'Aaraanu nalla Pulayan?' ('Who is a good Pulaya?').

I wrote the book *Kerala Charitravum Samooha Roopikaranavum* ('The History of Kerala and Social Reformation') in 2012 for the Kerala Bhasha Institute as a fact-based study of the genesis of the *chaturvarnya*, the four-fold caste system. (In the event, the chapter on chaturvarnya was not included in this book but found its way into another, *Buddhanilekkulla Dooram* ['The Distance towards the Buddha'], published by DC Books.) The idea for it had begun to take hold in me during my SEEDIAN days. The inspiration behind it were the words of P.C. Joseph of SEEDIAN. Nearly a quarter century back, during the course of a personal conversation, he had said, 'We need a history'.

I had no records or books with me. And I could not travel because I did not have any money. These problems could be solved only in 1998–2000. Financial assistance was given to me, as mentioned earlier, by Mohandas, who worked in the Motor Vehicles Department, and J.M. Jayachandran. I travelled to Coimbatore, Chennai and Bengaluru and bought all the books I required. While settling down to write the book, the big problem I faced was the historical methodology I was to adopt.

Generally speaking, there are two ways of recording history. The first one is based on relations of production. Those who follow this method focus on economic growth and the formation of social classes. People like EMS, Rajan Gurukkal and Raghava Warrier adopt this method. The second is based on relations of social reproduction. The works that adopt this method focus on religion, governmental administration and the formation of faith communities. That history is the complementarity of relations of production and social reproduction was an insight I drew from a letter written by A.K. Ravindran, published in *Mathrubhumi*.

But there were other problems. The main one concerned the representation of the subaltern. I needed to oppose the notion that with the collapse of tribal communities, occupational collectives crystallized into castes/races, a system which remained unchallenged for a long time. It required a different approach, one that would go beyond the hypotheses of traditional historiographies and account for the communitarianism of contemporary times.

A few of the chapters of the book were published in the *Madhyamam* and *Soochakam* weeklies. The reason for this was that I wanted some inputs which I was hoping to get through their readers. After reading these articles, Dr K.S. Madhavan, a professor of history at the University of Calicut, helped by not only lending me several documents as well as books but also sharing useful suggestions. I would not have been able to complete the project without his intervention.

During the days of the composition of the book, I stayed at the house of my wife Usha's nephew (her elder sister's son). I was then working at Vadakkanchery. Although I was a senior assistant, I had to work in the Ticket and Cash section. That gave me plenty of holidays. During the time I lived there, I participated in almost all agitations, except the Plachimada and Endosulfan struggles, along with Sreedharan Therambil, C.A. Ajithan, Joy Kaitharam and T.K. Vasu, not only in Thrissur district but throughout the state.

I was not the main actor in these struggles, only my presence was required. But I was a member of the committee that sought the release of Abdul Nazer Madani who had been arrested and incarcerated in the Coimbatore jail; and the general convenor of the strike committee (the chairperson of which was Sreedharan Therambil) formed to seek justice for a girl named Neethu of Irinjalakkuda who had been murdered. When I participate in people's struggles, I do not worry about ideological or political positions. That is the reason why I am a frequent presence at various forums. I am often troubled by the fact that a consolidation of anti-establishment movements has not taken place.

As I am penning the last chapter of the story of my travels through time and space, I cannot deny that through these journeys—sometimes tiring, sometimes exhilarating—I have confronted violent hatred. But I have experienced boundless affection and respect as well. Nevertheless, I have never harboured any personal animosity towards anyone in the social and political spheres. Like O.K. Santhosh said about Dr K.K. Manmathan, I am an ideological individual. Precisely because of this inclination towards ideology, I can say with absolute confidence that I have not made compromises with any single caste organization or established political party. That is also the reason why I have kept my personal life out of this autobiographical discourse to a considerable extent.

It was Kallen Pookkodan who asked, 'Does a Pulaya have an autobiography?' He, who stood out as a separate chapter in our history, composed two autobiographies. C.K. Janu and Selena Prakanam too. Not only are these incomplete narratives but they were jotted down by others. This work of mine is the first Dalit autobiography in Malayalam. The inspiration behind its composition was a sliver from Brecht's poem titled 'A Worker Reads History':

> Young Alexander conquered India.
> He alone?
> Caesar beat the Gauls.
> Was there not even a cook in his army?

In my analysis of the story 'In the Flood', the reason for sidelining Chennan Parayan and making the dog a Dalit was no different. This autobiography is an elaborate version of that textualization. Mega-narratives are full of kings, castles and battles; there are no servants, no people who are trampled upon, no animals who slump in sheer exhaustion after pulling the vehicles. These people who are ignored and rendered invisible too are creators of history. Microcosms, that are ostracized, too need to get space alongside the macrocosm.

Years back, Taha Madayi and Prakash Marahi interviewed me for a magazine named *Samayam*. Their final question was: 'What is your greatest desire?' The image that immediately appeared in my memory was of Ayyankali. So I said, 'Ten intellectuals should take birth in my community.'

'Why?'

'Only intellectuals will be able to lead the Dalit community—to whom wealth, power, status and culture have been distant dreams and who have forever been soaked in the endless rain of misery—towards hope. When such a responsibility is shouldered, while they work towards their own salvation, they will make it possible for others too. That is because no human is an island. Everyone is a part of the mainland. That is the reason why all are able to stand firmly. Through interdependence—in the community. And through society—in Nature.'

I hope this autobiography contains insights that will help people shoulder such a responsibility.

Notes

1 Considered a backward community, the Ezhavas come under the avarna category in the traditional Hindu caste system.

2 Used in this context as a way of conveying respectful agreement.

3 Socially, Economically and Educationally Depressed Indian Ancient Natives. This Dalit organization was started as a study group, headquartered at Kottayam, during 1969–70 under the leadership of M.J. Prasad, K.K.S. Das, V. Padmanabhan and others. For some time, it brought out a weekly newspaper also named SEEDIAN, which was published by E.M. Koshy from Kottayam. The organization was wound up in 1990.

4 The whole body of canonical and non-canonical Hindu texts.

5 The song that runs to 4,950 lines is about a valiant young man named Edanadan who takes revenge on his father Kaimal's murderers. What makes the song particularly interesting is the vivid picture of Kuttanad it gives—the land, its resources, the different communities of people who lived there, their lifestyles, beliefs, language, values and rituals. 'Edanadan' literally means 'between lands'. The hero was born in a boat as it was crossing a lake between the lands.

6 'Kadu' in Malayalam means 'forest'.

7 Considered to be one of the oldest literary works composed in Malayalam. It is a message-poem, on the lines of Kalidasa's famous *Meghaduta*, with Unnuneeli as the female protagonist. Its literary merit apart, the work is considered valuable for the information it gives about the region of Kerala during that period of time.

8 A writer whose magnum opus—the eight-volume *Aithihyamaala*—captures nearly all the legends about Kerala.

9 The cultural and religious reform movement that spanned across the end of the 19th century and the beginning of the 20th century in Kerala. Its leader was the revered Sree Narayana Guru, who sought to demolish the caste system and the inequality it propagated by spreading the light of spiritual wisdom, advocating ahimsa, and founding schools and temples for the uplift of the avarnas, literally, those without caste. The other leaders were Mannath Padmanabhan, Ayyankali, Chattambi Swami, Vagbhadanandan, V.T. Bhattathiripad and so on.

10 Mahatma Ayyankali (1863–1941), a social reformer of Travancore who founded an organization named Sadhu Jana Paripalana Sangham (SJPS) in 1907 for the uplift of the Dalits.

11 This was uttered using a slang of the Pulayas that was a mixture of Tamil and Malayalam. Here, *amman* means 'father'.

12 Pampady John Joseph (1887–1940), a Dalit activist who considered Pulayas as the first inhabitants of Kerala, and called them Cheramar.

13 This covered today's Tamil Nadu, Kerala, Puducherry, Lakshadweep and southern parts of Andhra Pradesh and Karnataka.

14 Paul Chirakkarode (1938–2008) was a Dalit novelist, thinker, activist, biographer and critic. His novel *Pulayathara* (1962) is considered to be the first Dalit novel in Malayalam (written by a Dalit about a Dalit hero). His other novels are *Mathil* ('Wall'), *Nizhal* ('Shadow'), *Velicham* ('Light'), *Nyaayaasanam* ('Seat of Justice'), *Ekaanthathayude Dweep* ('Island of Loneliness') and so on.

15 The pen name of Kizhakkepainummoodu Easo Mathai (1924–1981), a famous novelist, short story writer and screenplay writer. Of the 20 novels he wrote, *Ara Naazhika Neram* (1967) is considered the best.

16 The house of the Namboodiri. It is described as 'mana' also.

17 In this context, the word implies, 'a fellowship of the Pulayas' that used to exist in olden times.

18 Officially known as Poykayil Sreekumara Gurudevan (1879–1939), he was a Dalit activist, poet and founder of a socio-religious movement called Prathyaksha Raksha Daiva Sabha (PRDS) ('God's Church of Obvious Salvation'). He was also a member of the Dalit advocacy group named Sadhu Jana Paripalana Sangham founded by Ayyankali.

19 T.H.P. Chentharassery (1928–2018) was a historian and biographer whose works include *Ambedkar on Indian History*, *History of the Indigenous Indians*, *Ayyankali: The First Dalit Leader*, *Pampady John Joseph*, *Poykayil Appachan*, and so on.

20 Unstitched, usually white, cloth wrapped around the waist.

21 A kind of stiff hoodie (without the front flap or sleeves) made from woven screw pine leaves. It covers the head and the back so that when the sower bends double to plant saplings during monsoon, she doesn't get wet.

22 Famous for his Kundara Proclamation in which he declared the British as the enemy and called upon the nation to expel them.

23 A kind of solid chutney.

24 Ayyappa Paniker (1930–2006), professor of English, literary critic, editor, translator and famous Malayalam poet who played a crucial role in ushering modernism into Malayalam poetry. His most famous poetic work is *Kurukshetram* (1960).

25 Written in 1974 by M. Mukundan (b. 1942), one of the leading novelists in Malayalam, the novel captures the political and social life of Mahe (known in Malayalam as 'Mayyazhi') that was a French colony until 1954.

26 A reference to his works, *Uchcha Urakkathile Swapnangal* ('Dreams during Siesta'), *Njandukal* ('Crabs').

27 A struggle conducted in Travancore in 1924–25 that aimed at putting an end to caste discrimination and untouchability among the Hindus.

28 Sree Narayana Guru (1856–1928) was a renowned philosopher and social reformer who led a movement to end casteism and spread the message of equality. He propagated the motto One Caste, One Religion, One God for All.

29 Vaikom Muhammed Basheer (1908–1994) was a freedom fighter and famous Malayalam short story writer and novelist. His most notable works are *Balyakaalasakhi*, *Paathummayude Addu*, *Mathilukal*, and *Ntuppuppakkoranendarnu*, among others.

30 A kind of training centre (*kalari*) or rudimentary school where a teacher (*asan*) introduced children to the alphabet, and imparted the basics of arithmetic, astrology and so on. This institution existed till the first half of the 20th century in Kerala.

31 It is commonly believed that St Thomas came to Kerala in the month of Dhanu (December–January) 52 CE. He died in Mylapore in Karikadam in 72 CE.

32 Issued by Maharaja Chithira Tirunal Balarama Varma of Travancore on 12 November 1936, abolishing the ban on avarnas entering temples.

33 Tin which the devotees held a small, flower-decorated wooden tray (*kaavadi*)—fitted with a narrow overarching canopy—on their shoulders, and danced (*aattom*) to the accompaniment of music, as a form of worship. Pots of milk or materials like grains, holy ash, camphor, etc. were placed inside the tray as votive offerings to the God.

34 The ritual where the devotee prayed at the temple from dawn to dusk, and witnessed all the pujas.

35 Harvest festival of Kerala, also commemorating the defeat of King Mahabali by Vamana (the fifth incarnation of Lord Vishnu). Keralites welcome their favourite king with floral carpets laid out in the front yard of their houses for ten days.

36 A solid measure. One para weighed a little below one kilogram.

37 Sweet pudding.

38 'Rama, Rama, protect me / I take refuge at Rama's feet / Mukunda, Rama, protect me'.

39 A.K. Gopalan (1904–1977), one of the founding members of the Communist Party of India.

40 K. Damodaran (1912–1976) was a Marxist theoretician and one of the leading figures of the Communist Party of India.

41 A theatrical movement in Kayamkulam, Kerala, which was formed in the 1950s by a group of individuals who had close ties with Left-wing politics. The club was very influential in popularizing the Communist movement in the state.

42 Ponkunnam Varkey (1910–2004) was a prominent Malayalam writer and one of the pioneers of the progressive writers' forum called Sahithya Pravarthaka Sahakarana Sangham. He published 24 anthologies of short stories and 16 volumes of plays, besides two collections of poems and one collection of essays and an autobiography.

43 This was apparently a paper run by a Left-leaning group within the Nair Service Society.

44 One of the most celebrated works in Malayalam. A pastoral elegy written in 1936 by Changampuzha Krishna Pillai (1911–1948) on the death of his friend Edappally Raghavan Pillai, it revolves around the tragic love between a poor shepherd named Ramanan and a rich girl named Chandrika.

45 An art form in which a raconteur tells a story (usually stories from epics and popular classics) through acting, singing and commentary, to the accompaniment of a couple of instruments.

46 Nair Service Society, founded by Mannath Padmanabhan in 1914, for reforming the Nair community.

47 A social service organization founded in 1903 by Dr P. Palpu and blessed by Sree Narayana Guru, in order to lead the Ezhava community towards religious reform, economic prosperity and better education.

48 Sacred grove.

49 Muttathu Varkey (1913–1989) was a Malayalam novelist, short story writer and poet.

50 Kanam E.J. (1926–82) was a popular Malayalam novelist, short story writer and lyricist.

51 *Ettan* means 'big brother', an appellation applied to any older male in order to show respect and affection.

52 The reference is to the countries in the Persian Gulf, especially

Bahrain, Kuwait, Oman, Qatar, Saudi Arabia and the UAE, where men from Kerala went for employment in the 1970 and '80s.

53 The single largest Scheduled Tribe in Kerala.

54 A hill tribe.

55 The savarna men were addressed as 'Thambran' (Lord) by the Dalits. The Dalits were not served food on banana leaves laid out on the floor as was customary among all in those days, but in pieces of spathe inserted in small pits on the ground.

56 Indian National Trade Union Congress, founded in 1947.

57 Now called Group C, it includes telephone operators, head clerks, police head constables and so on.

58 Headquartered at Kozhikode.

59 Prathyaksha Raksha Daiva Sabha (God's Church of Obvious Salvation), a religious protest movement started by Poykayil Appachan in 1909.

60 Raja Ravi Varma (1848–1906) was one of the most famous Indian painters, who is popular largely for his depiction of characters and scenes from Indian mythology, following the methodology of European academic art.

61 Among the Hindus, it is believed that a few drops of water from the holy river of Ganga will take the soul to Heaven.

62 In Hindu philosophy, spiritual enlightenment is attained through four *yogas* or paths: *jnana* (knowledge), *karma* (action), *raja* (mind control) and *bhakti* (devotion). Here, however, the words are used in a more general, secular sense.

63 An engineering student who was caught for his alleged involvement in Naxalite activities in 1976, and tortured to death by the police during the Emergency period. The charges against him were never proved or his body ever recovered.

64 Kerala Yuktivadi Sangham (KYS) in Malayalam. It was an offshoot of Sahodara Sangham (Fraternity Forum), formed by K. Ayyappan on 29 May 1917 at Cherai, in Ernakulam.

65 Kallara Sukumaran (1939–1996) was a Dalit activist, litterateur, orator and thinker. He was instrumental in popularizing the

Kerala Harijan Federation throughout the state. He has written 17 books of which *Vimochanathinte Arthashastram* ('The Economics of the Liberation Struggle') is considered the most significant.

66 'Lord of Vaikom', i.e. Lord Shiva.

67 The other two were Bahuleyan (an Ezhava) and Govinda Panicker (a Nair). The three men tried to march past the signboards fixed nearly 100 yards from the western entrance of the temple on 30 March 1924 but were arrested.

68 A newspaper started in 1913 by Changaramkumarath Krishnan Vakeel, an advocate, community leader and social reformer, for propagating Sree Narayana Guru's message and uplifting the downtrodden. It continued until Krishnan Vakeel's death in 1938.

69 A literary journal started by Kumaran Asan, the poet, in 1904 to lend voice to the untouchables of Kerala. He was inspired by Swami Vivekananda and Sree Narayana Guru.

70 Ayya Vaikundar (1809?–1851?) was a humanist and thinker. He is remembered as the first social reformer in India, who questioned the caste hierarchy and spoke against untouchability.

71 Parammekkal Thoma Kathanar (1736–1799) was a Syrian Christian priest and one of the earliest proponents of Indian nationalism and civic self-rule. His book *Varthamana Pusthakam* (1790)—which records the experiences during his travel to Rome and back—is considered to be the first travelogue in India. He tried to bring unity in the church of Kerala that had splintered following the Oath of the Slanting Cross (1653).

72 Hermann Gundert (1814–1893) was German missionary who is chiefly remembered today as an Indologist and compiler of the Malayalam-English dictionary.

73 Thoppil Bhasi (1924–1992) was a playwright, screen writer and film director who played a key role in popularizing the Communist movement in the state of Kerala, with his phenomenally successful play *Ningal Enne Communistaaki* ('You Made Me a Communist') (1952).

74 Pen name of Puthan Veetil Narayanan Nair (1925–2006), well-known literary critic, rationalist and Left intellectual.

75 Kallarkutty Joseph, a money lender and estate owner, was killed in Idukki by Naxalites on 21 July 1970. It was subsequently discovered that he was no oppressor of the poor.

76 The famous Aruvipuram Prathishta of 1888. Sree Narayana Guru, social reformer and Advaita philosopher, in defiance of prevailing caste laws (that prevented the lower-caste people from entering temples) consecrated a Shiva lingam at Aruvipuram. When questioned by the savarnas about this act, he replied that he had installed an Ezhava Shiva. This incident was one of the first acts meant to bring about social and religious reform in the state.

77 Designed by Sree Narayana Guru himself and dedicated to the goddess of knowledge. Unlike the traditional temple, it has windows. Besides, it does not follow the customary rituals of worship like *nivedyam* (offering food to the deity) or *abhishekam* (oblation of oil or ghee).

78 Installed in 1927 at a place called Kalavangodam, near Cherthala.

79 A variety of rice that is saline, water-tolerant and disease-resistant. It is grown in Vypin island, parts of Thrissur, Malappuram and Kannur.

80 The Laws of Manu which prescribe, among many other things, the duties and obligations of the Hindus according to their stage in life (ashramas—*brahmacharya*, *grihasta*, *vanaprastha* and *sanyasa*) and their social class (varna—*Brahmana*, *Kshatriya*, *Vaishya* and *Shudra*). In modern times, the text has come under heavy fire for the many biases it contains.

81 Sankaracharya (700?–750? CE), one of the foremost exponents of the philosophy of Advaita (non-dualism), was born in Kalady, Kerala.

82 Jyotirao Phule (1827–1890) was a social activist, thinker, anti-caste social reformer and writer who fought for the eradication of untouchability and the caste system.

83 Konkani-speaking farming community.

84 Gwalior Rayons Organization of Workers. GROW Vasu was a trade unionist and Naxalite before becoming a human rights activist.

85 Kuriakose Elias Chavara (1805–1871), a Syro-Malabar Catholic priest, the first Catholic male priest to be canonized.

86 Alphonsa of the Immaculate Conception (1910–1946), the first Indian nun to be canonized. She belonged to the Syro-Malabar church.

87 A reference to the repeal of the Travancore Christian Succession Act of 1916, applicable to Christians residing in the erstwhile Travancore state, according to which, a daughter was entitled to only one-fourth the share of a son in family property or Rs 5,000/-, whichever was less.

88 The following is a translation from the Malayalam and not the original speech.

89 An iconic work in Malayalam literary criticism that gives an insightful analysis of Vyasa's *Mahabharata*.

90 The sixth book of the *Mahabharata* which contains the Bhagavat Gita.

91 Conducted by the Adivasis of Chengara in Pathanamthitta district, for regaining possession of their lands that they alleged had been confiscated by a prominent tea plantation company.

92 The longest murder investigation case in Kerala over the murder of Sister Abhaya, a Knanaya Catholic nun in 1992. It hit many roadblocks but was continually revived with the intervention of human rights activists and the support of people. The case was finally closed by the end of 2020 with the conviction of two individuals who were sentenced to life imprisonment.

ALSO FROM SPEAKING TIGER

BALUTA

Daya Pawar

Translated by Jerry Pinto

> '[An] outstanding example of self-writing... Daya Pawar ought to be seen as the heir to [the] radical intellectual tradition that harks back to Phule and Ambedkar.'—*Biblio*

First published in Marathi in 1978, *Baluta* caused a storm-not just with its unvarnished depiction of the pervasive cruelty of the caste system, but also the extraordinary candour with which Daya Pawar wrote about himself and his family, his community, and Dalit politics of his time. Set in rural Maharashtra—in the Maharwada, the area designated in each village for the Mahars so that they would not 'pollute' the other residents—and in Mumbai of the 1940s and '50s—its chawls, slums, brothels and gambling dens, where the poor and the outcast found ways to make a life—*Baluta* is a triumph of storytelling, social commentary and self-reflection.

Jerry Pinto's brilliant translation brings this classic of Indian literature to English-language readers for the first time.

ALSO FROM SPEAKING TIGER

THE YELLOW SPARROW

Memoir of a Transgender

Santa Khurai

Santa Khurai was seventeen when she decided to start dressing like a woman. Born male, she had always believed herself to be female, and she claimed her feminine identity fiercely and openly. Her bold act of wearing dresses and make-up in public brought down upon her the wrath of her father, insults and ridicule wherever she went, and, frequently, beatings at the hands of the armed forces who are a constant presence in her native Manipur. The humiliation and physical attacks did not deter her. In her words, 'My desire to be a woman, a beautiful, fashionable woman, was so strong that I was not afraid of challenging anything that came in the way… I felt that I could bear anything but I could not live like a man.'

The price she has had to pay is high. Knocking on doors for a job, she found that most times, no one would employ her because of the way she looked. When she eventually found success as a make-up artist, with her own beauty parlour, the stress of her struggles sent her spiralling into drug abuse and penury.

Fighting her way through these troubles, she became involved with the transgender movement, and in 2010, she was appointed Secretary of the All Manipur Nupi Maanbi Association (AMaNA). Since then, she has worked closely with AMaNA and its sister organization, Solidarity and Action Against The HIV Infection in India (SAATHII). Today, she is at the forefront of the LGBTQ movement in Manipur, travelling the world to speak for her community.

Santa Khurai has known the heartbreak of an abusive marriage with a heterosexual man, and the joy of adopting a son; the highs and lows of international recognition and disownment by her own family. Through it all, she has remained true to herself, and refused to be broken. Her story is an inspiration for all humanity.